CAPTAIN
AMERICA

RED MENACE

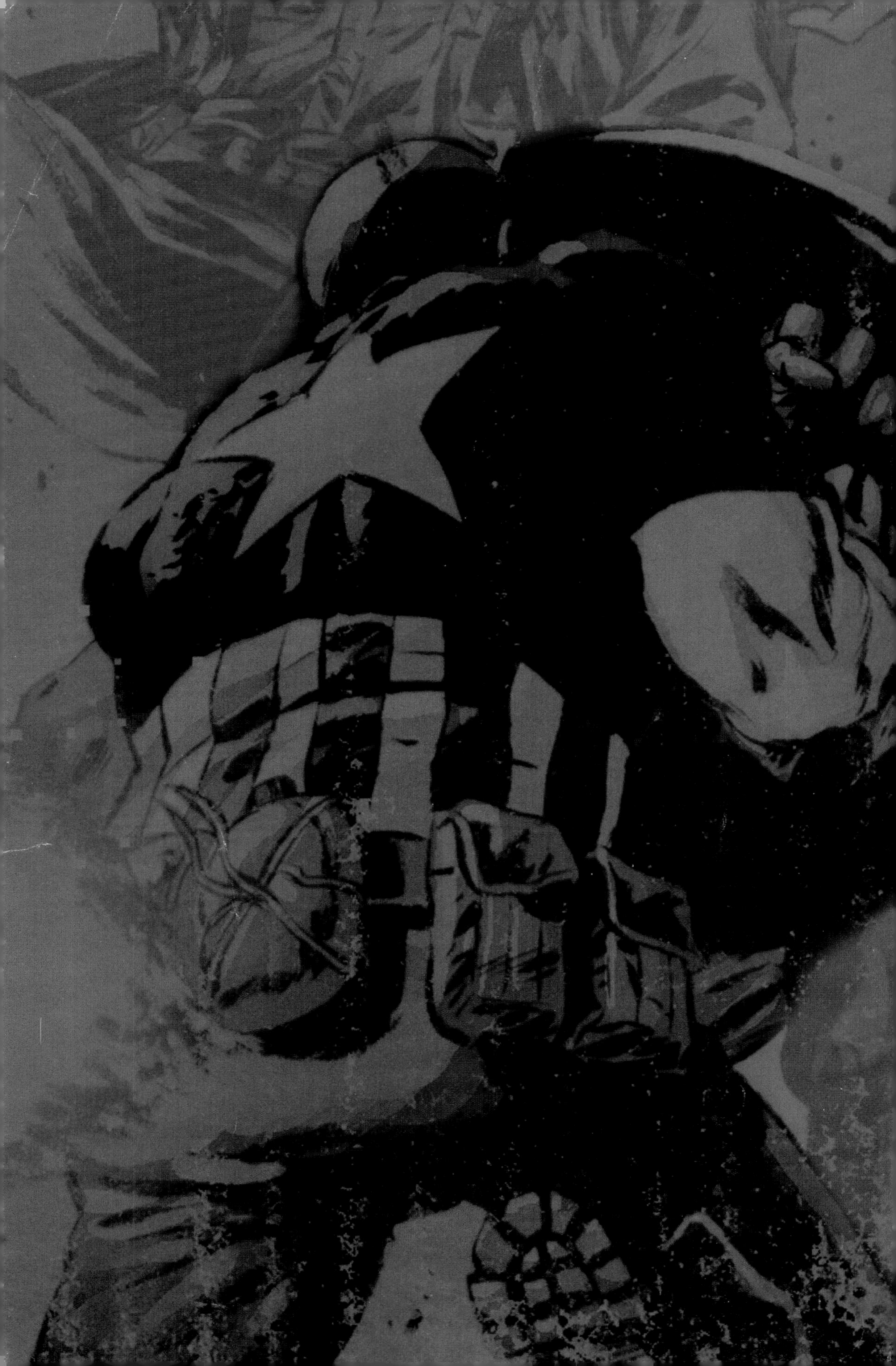

CAPTAIN AMERICA
RED MENACE

WRITER: Ed Brubaker
ART: Mike Perkins
COLOR ART: Frank D'Armata
LETTERER: Virtual Calligraphy's Joe Caramagna
COVER ART: Steve Epting

65TH ANNIVERSARY SPECIAL
ART: Javier Pulido (Chapters 1, 4 & 5) &
Marcos Martin (Chapters 2, 3 & 6)
COLOR ART: Javier Rodriguez
EPILOGUE ART: Mike Perkins & Frank D'Armata
LETTERER: Dave Lanphear
COVER ART: Eric Wight

ASSISTANT EDITORS: Molly Lazer & Aubrey Sitterson
ASSOCIATE EDITOR: Andy Schmidt
EDITOR: Tom Brevoort

Captain America created by
Joe Simon and Jack Kirby

COLLECTION EDITOR: Jennifer Grünwald
ASSISTANT EDITOR: Michael Short
SENIOR EDITOR, SPECIAL PROJECTS: Jeff Youngquist
VICE PRESIDENT OF SALES: David Gabriel
PRODUCTION: Jerry Kalinowski
BOOK DESIGNER: Dayle Chesler
VICE PRESIDENT CREATIVE: Tom Marvelli

EDITOR IN CHIEF: Joe Quesada
PUBLISHER: Dan Buckley

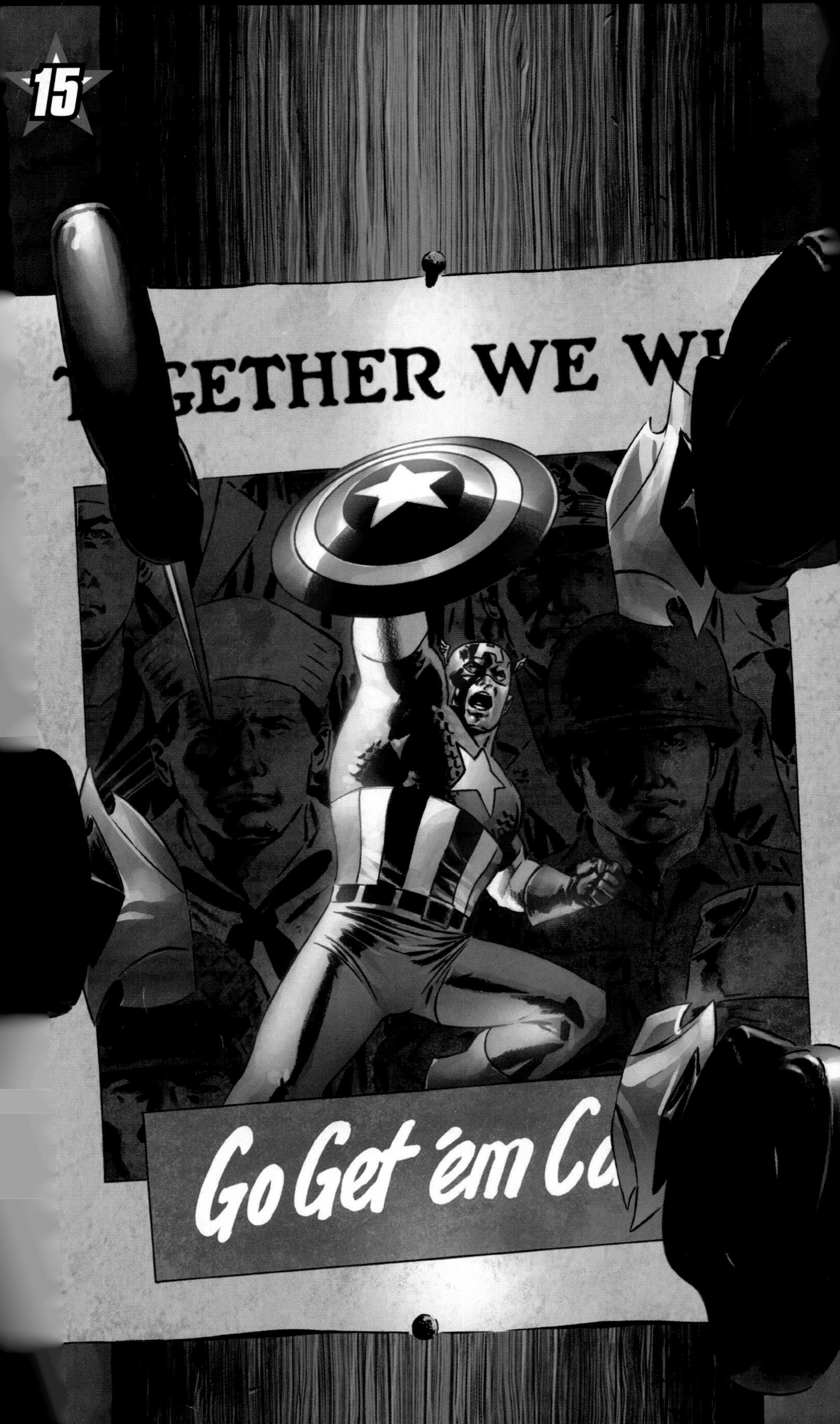
15
GETHER WE W
Go Get 'em Ca

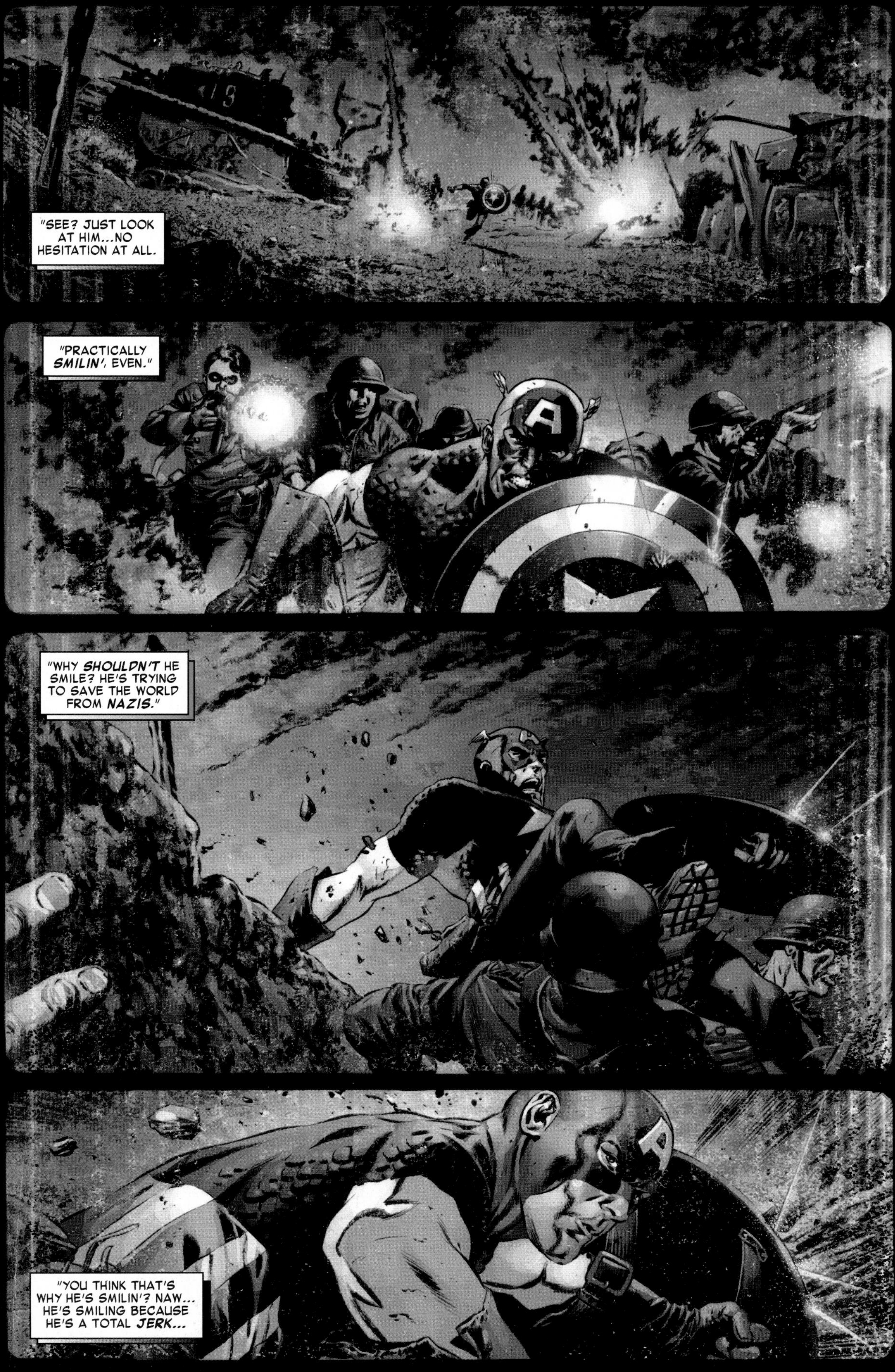
"SEE? JUST LOOK AT HIM...NO HESITATION AT ALL.
"PRACTICALLY *SMILIN'*, EVEN."
"WHY *SHOULDN'T* HE SMILE? HE'S TRYING TO SAVE THE WORLD FROM *NAZIS*."
"YOU THINK THAT'S WHY HE'S SMILIN'? NAW... HE'S SMILING BECAUSE HE'S A TOTAL *JERK*...

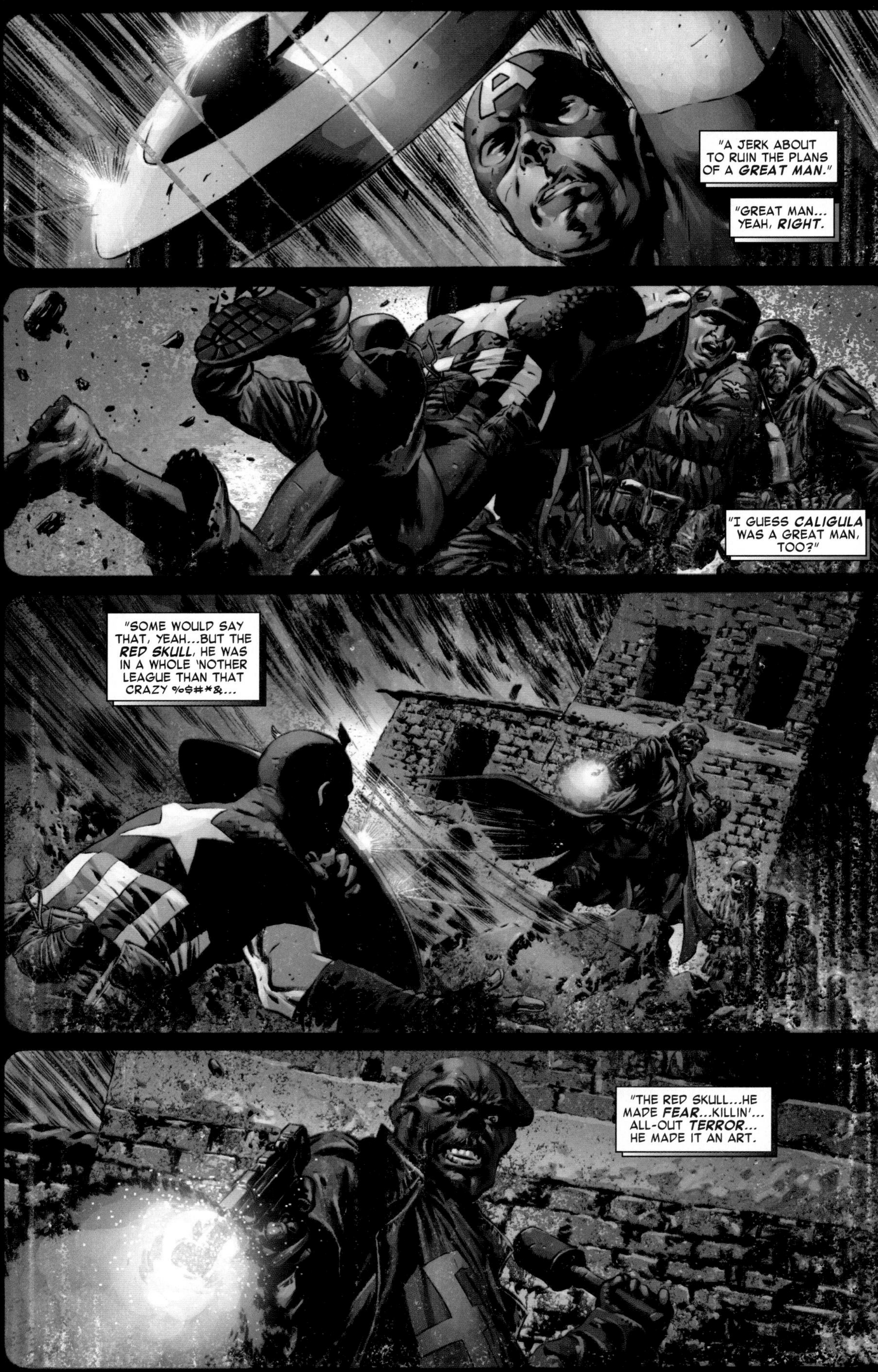
"A JERK ABOUT TO RUIN THE PLANS OF A GREAT MAN."
"GREAT MAN... YEAH, RIGHT.
"I GUESS CALIGULA WAS A GREAT MAN, TOO?"
"SOME WOULD SAY THAT, YEAH...BUT THE RED SKULL, HE WAS IN A WHOLE 'NOTHER LEAGUE THAN THAT CRAZY %$#*&...
"THE RED SKULL...HE MADE FEAR...KILLIN'... ALL-OUT TERROR... HE MADE IT AN ART.

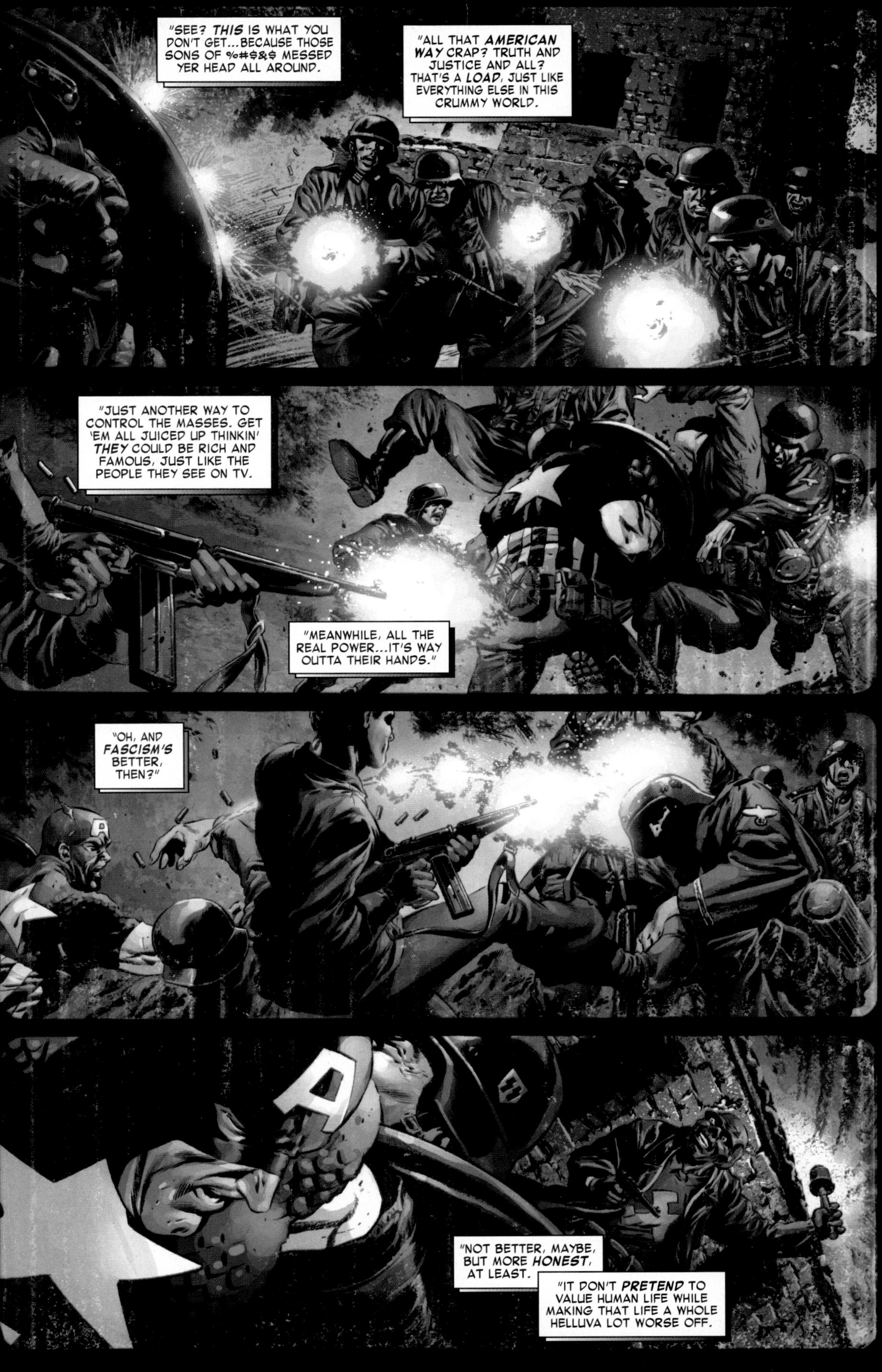
"SEE? THIS IS WHAT YOU DON'T GET...BECAUSE THOSE SONS OF %#$&$ MESSED YER HEAD ALL AROUND.
"ALL THAT AMERICAN WAY CRAP? TRUTH AND JUSTICE AND ALL? THAT'S A LOAD, JUST LIKE EVERYTHING ELSE IN THIS CRUMMY WORLD.
"JUST ANOTHER WAY TO CONTROL THE MASSES. GET 'EM ALL JUICED UP THINKIN' THEY COULD BE RICH AND FAMOUS, JUST LIKE THE PEOPLE THEY SEE ON TV.
"MEANWHILE, ALL THE REAL POWER...IT'S WAY OUTTA THEIR HANDS."
"OH, AND FASCISM'S BETTER, THEN?"
"NOT BETTER, MAYBE, BUT MORE HONEST, AT LEAST.
"IT DON'T PRETEND TO VALUE HUMAN LIFE WHILE MAKING THAT LIFE A WHOLE HELLUVA LOT WORSE OFF.

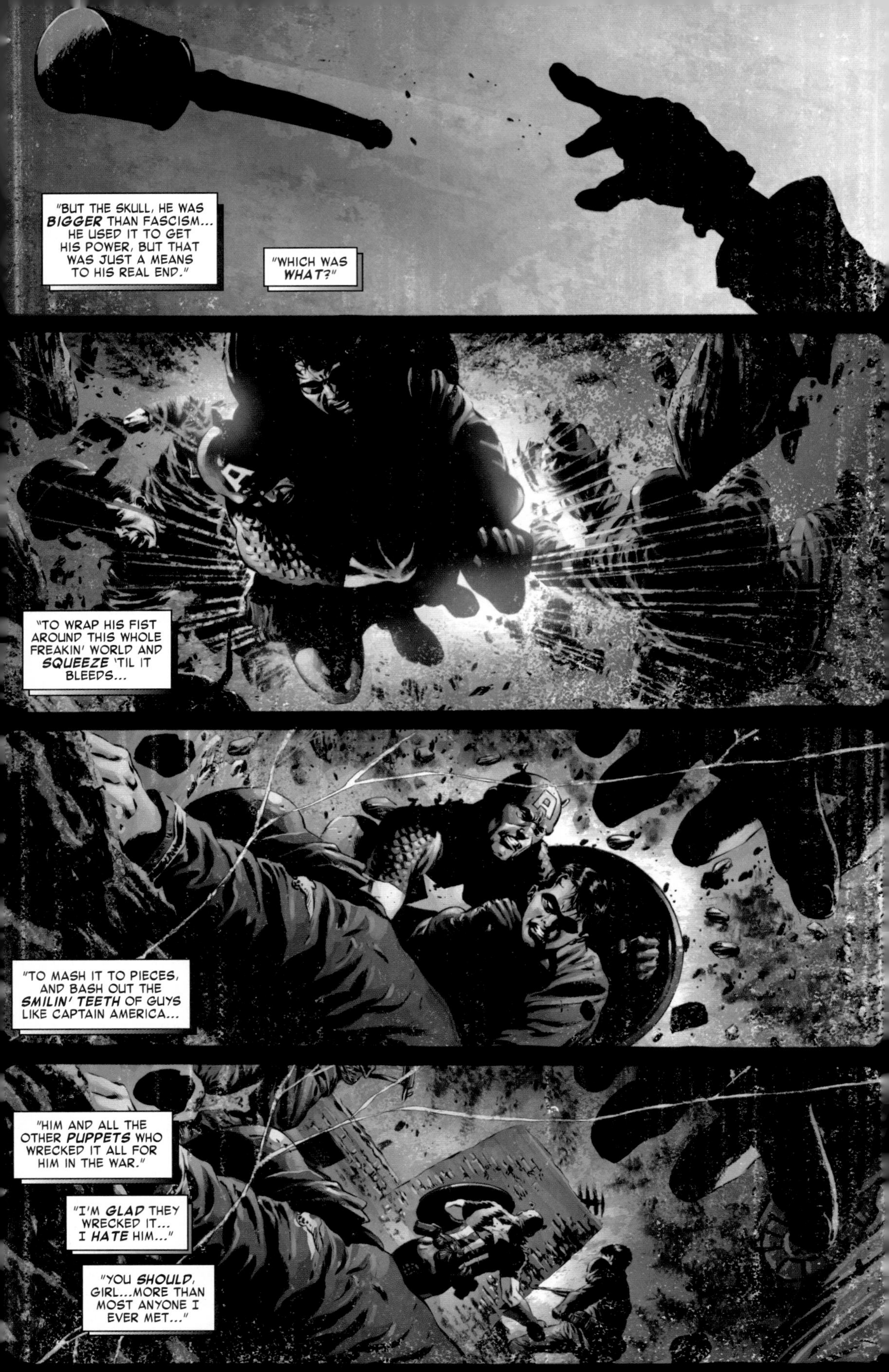
"BUT THE SKULL, HE WAS BIGGER THAN FASCISM... HE USED IT TO GET HIS POWER, BUT THAT WAS JUST A MEANS TO HIS REAL END."
"WHICH WAS WHAT?"
"TO WRAP HIS FIST AROUND THIS WHOLE FREAKIN' WORLD AND SQUEEZE 'TIL IT BLEEDS...
"TO MASH IT TO PIECES, AND BASH OUT THE SMILIN' TEETH OF GUYS LIKE CAPTAIN AMERICA...
"HIM AND ALL THE OTHER PUPPETS WHO WRECKED IT ALL FOR HIM IN THE WAR."
"I'M GLAD THEY WRECKED IT... I HATE HIM..."
"YOU SHOULD, GIRL...MORE THAN MOST ANYONE I EVER MET..."

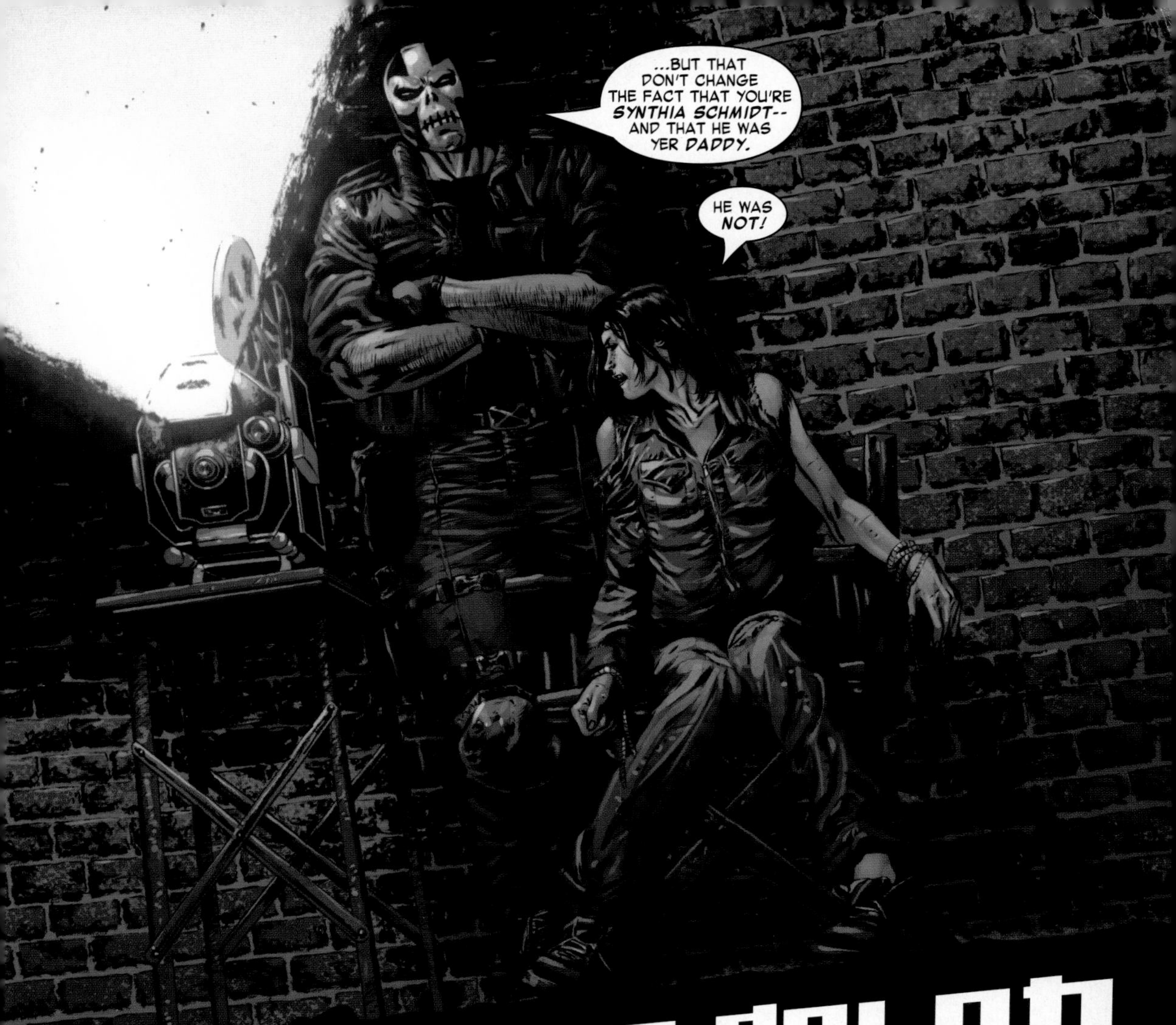
...BUT THAT DON'T CHANGE THE FACT THAT YOU'RE SYNTHIA SCHMIDT-- AND THAT HE WAS YER DADDY.
HE WAS NOT!

RED IS THE DARKEST COLOR

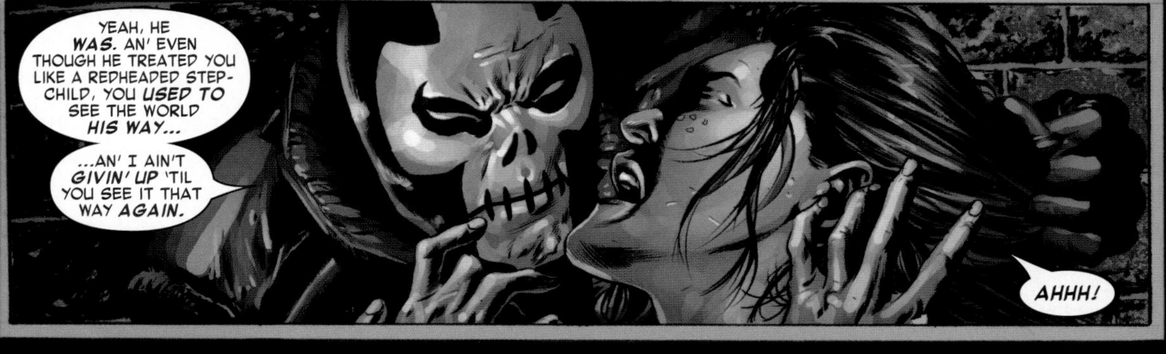
YEAH, HE WAS. AN' EVEN THOUGH HE TREATED YOU LIKE A REDHEADED STEP-CHILD, YOU USED TO SEE THE WORLD HIS WAY...
...AN' I AIN'T GIVIN' UP 'TIL YOU SEE IT THAT WAY AGAIN.
AHHH!

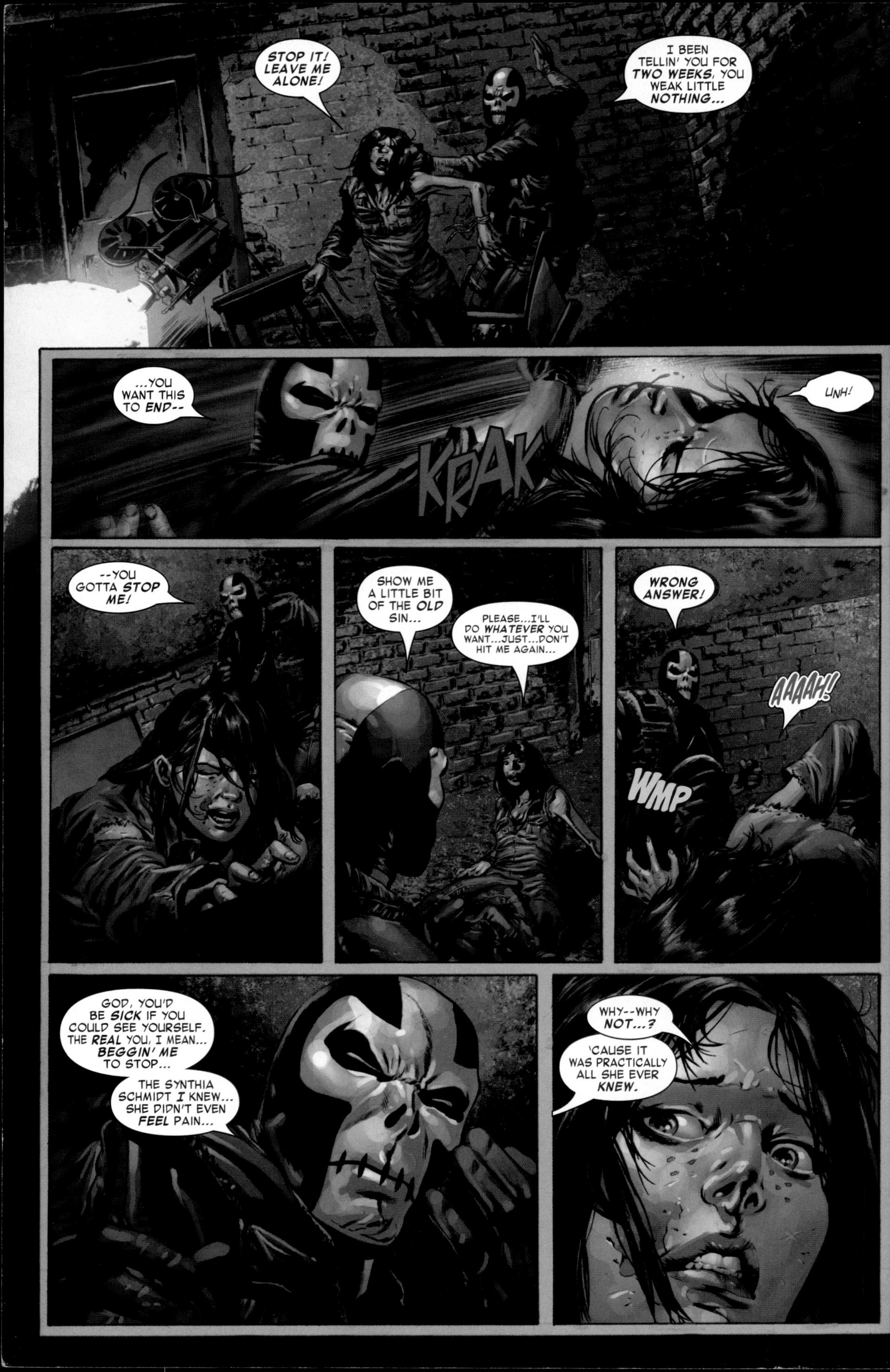
STOP IT! LEAVE ME ALONE!
I BEEN TELLIN' YOU FOR TWO WEEKS, YOU WEAK LITTLE NOTHING...
...YOU WANT THIS TO END--
KRAK
UNH!
--YOU GOTTA STOP ME!
SHOW ME A LITTLE BIT OF THE OLD SIN...
PLEASE...I'LL DO WHATEVER YOU WANT...JUST...DON'T HIT ME AGAIN...
WRONG ANSWER!
WMP
AAAAH!
GOD, YOU'D BE SICK IF YOU COULD SEE YOURSELF. THE REAL YOU, I MEAN... BEGGIN' ME TO STOP...
THE SYNTHIA SCHMIDT I KNEW... SHE DIDN'T EVEN FEEL PAIN...
WHY--WHY NOT...?
'CAUSE IT WAS PRACTICALLY ALL SHE EVER KNEW.

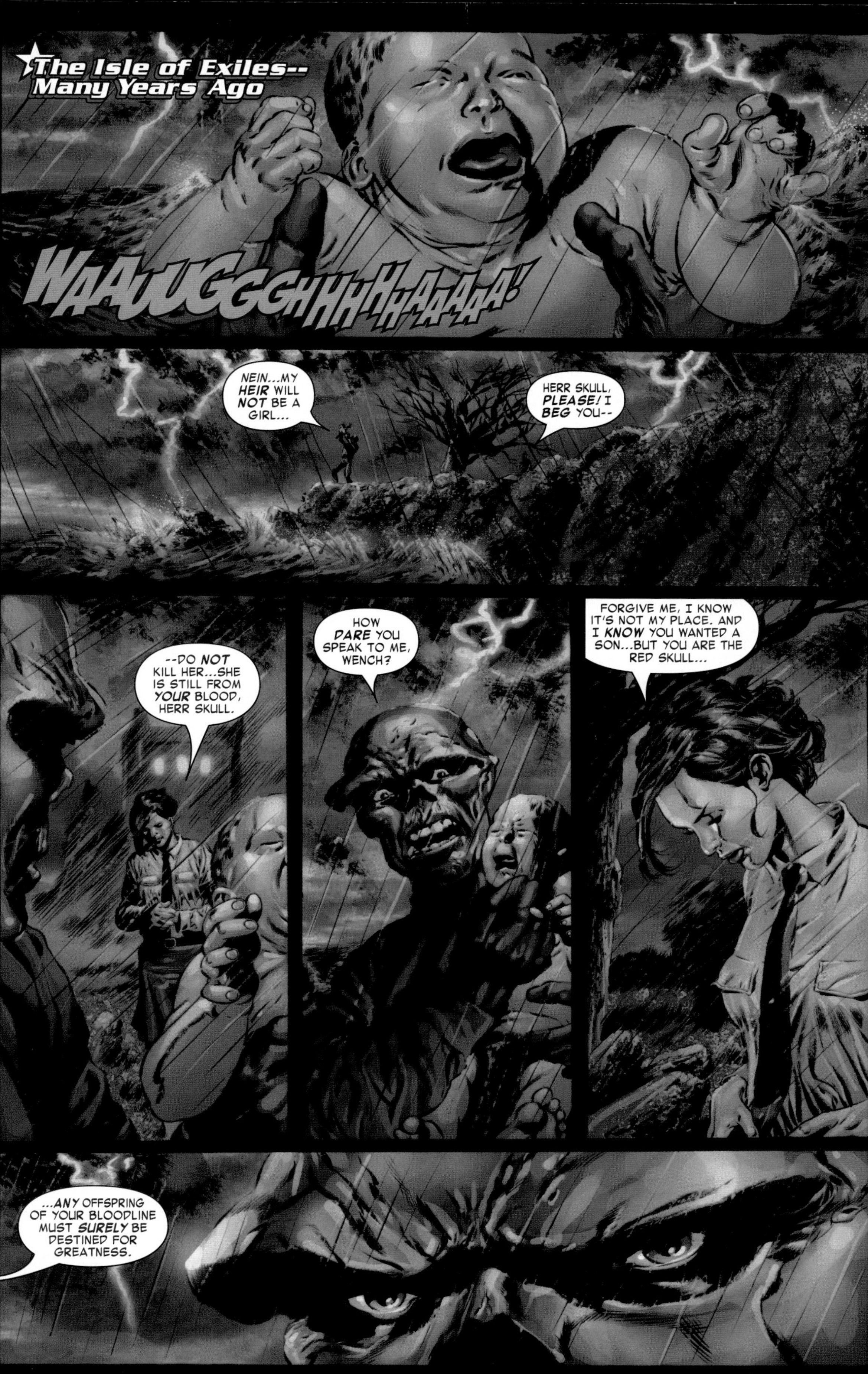
The Isle of Exiles-- Many Years Ago
WAAUUGGGHHHHAAAAA!
NEIN...MY HEIR WILL NOT BE A GIRL...
HERR SKULL, PLEASE! I BEG YOU--
--DO NOT KILL HER...SHE IS STILL FROM YOUR BLOOD, HERR SKULL.
HOW DARE YOU SPEAK TO ME, WENCH?
FORGIVE ME, I KNOW IT'S NOT MY PLACE. AND I KNOW YOU WANTED A SON...BUT YOU ARE THE RED SKULL...
...ANY OFFSPRING OF YOUR BLOODLINE MUST SURELY BE DESTINED FOR GREATNESS.

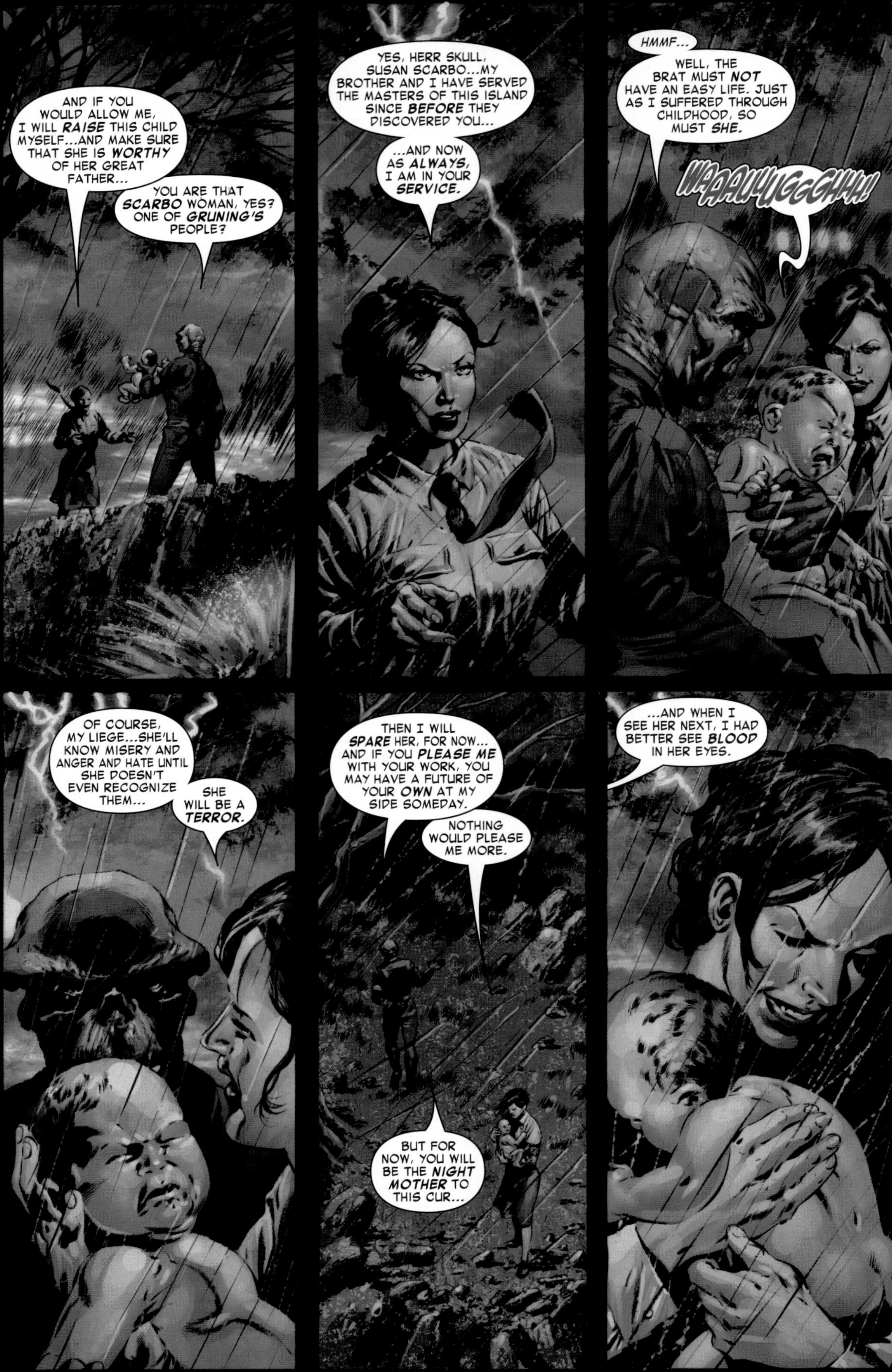
AND IF YOU WOULD ALLOW ME, I WILL RAISE THIS CHILD MYSELF...AND MAKE SURE THAT SHE IS WORTHY OF HER GREAT FATHER...
YOU ARE THAT SCARBO WOMAN, YES? ONE OF GRUNING'S PEOPLE?
YES, HERR SKULL, SUSAN SCARBO...MY BROTHER AND I HAVE SERVED THE MASTERS OF THIS ISLAND SINCE BEFORE THEY DISCOVERED YOU...
...AND NOW AS ALWAYS, I AM IN YOUR SERVICE.
HMMF...
WELL, THE BRAT MUST NOT HAVE AN EASY LIFE. JUST AS I SUFFERED THROUGH CHILDHOOD, SO MUST SHE.
WAAAUUUGGGHHH!
OF COURSE, MY LIEGE...SHE'LL KNOW MISERY AND ANGER AND HATE UNTIL SHE DOESN'T EVEN RECOGNIZE THEM...
SHE WILL BE A TERROR.
THEN I WILL SPARE HER, FOR NOW... AND IF YOU PLEASE ME WITH YOUR WORK, YOU MAY HAVE A FUTURE OF YOUR OWN AT MY SIDE SOMEDAY.
NOTHING WOULD PLEASE ME MORE.
BUT FOR NOW, YOU WILL BE THE NIGHT MOTHER TO THIS CUR...
...AND WHEN I SEE HER NEXT, I HAD BETTER SEE BLOOD IN HER EYES.

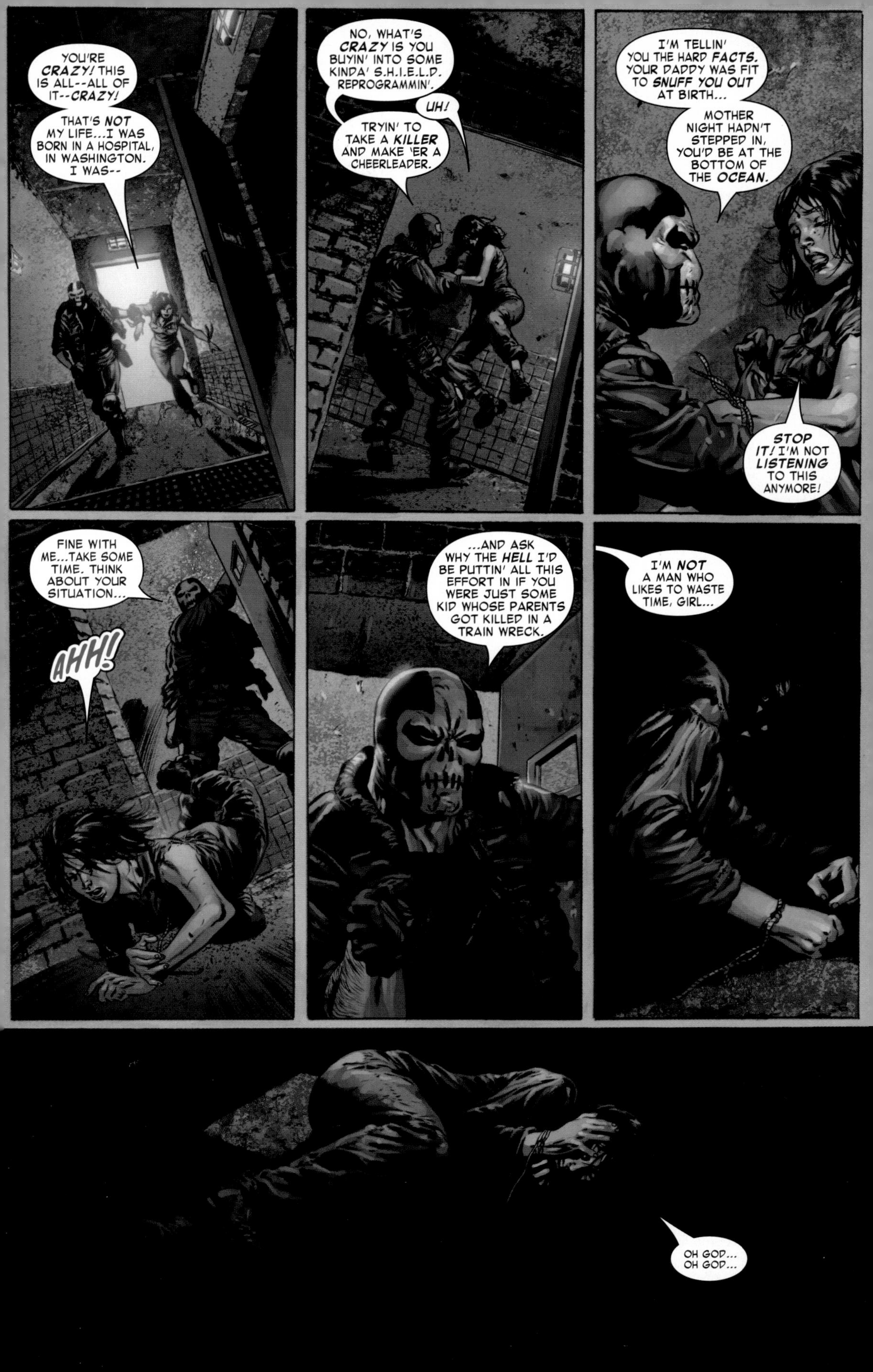
YOU'RE CRAZY! THIS IS ALL--ALL OF IT--CRAZY!
THAT'S NOT MY LIFE...I WAS BORN IN A HOSPITAL, IN WASHINGTON. I WAS--
NO, WHAT'S CRAZY IS YOU BUYIN' INTO SOME KINDA' S.H.I.E.L.D. REPROGRAMMIN'.
UH!
TRYIN' TO TAKE A KILLER AND MAKE 'ER A CHEERLEADER.
I'M TELLIN' YOU THE HARD FACTS. YOUR DADDY WAS FIT TO SNUFF YOU OUT AT BIRTH...
MOTHER NIGHT HADN'T STEPPED IN, YOU'D BE AT THE BOTTOM OF THE OCEAN.
STOP IT! I'M NOT LISTENING TO THIS ANYMORE!
FINE WITH ME...TAKE SOME TIME. THINK ABOUT YOUR SITUATION...
AHH!
...AND ASK WHY THE HELL I'D BE PUTTIN' ALL THIS EFFORT IN IF YOU WERE JUST SOME KID WHOSE PARENTS GOT KILLED IN A TRAIN WRECK.
I'M NOT A MAN WHO LIKES TO WASTE TIME, GIRL...
OH GOD... OH GOD...

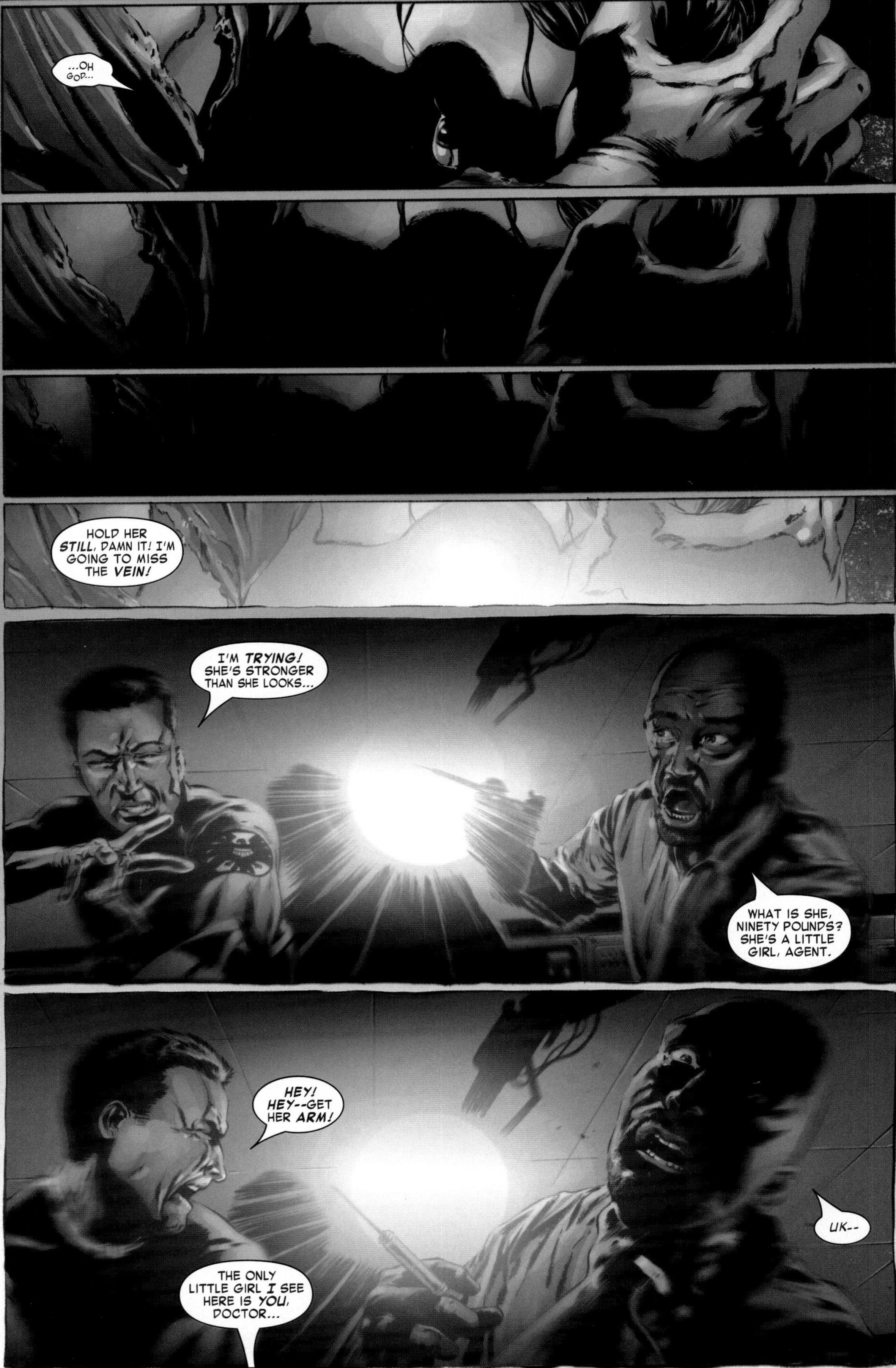
...OH GOD...
HOLD HER STILL, DAMN IT! I'M GOING TO MISS THE VEIN!
I'M TRYING! SHE'S STRONGER THAN SHE LOOKS...
WHAT IS SHE, NINETY POUNDS? SHE'S A LITTLE GIRL, AGENT.
HEY! HEY--GET HER ARM!
UK--
THE ONLY LITTLE GIRL I SEE HERE IS YOU, DOCTOR...

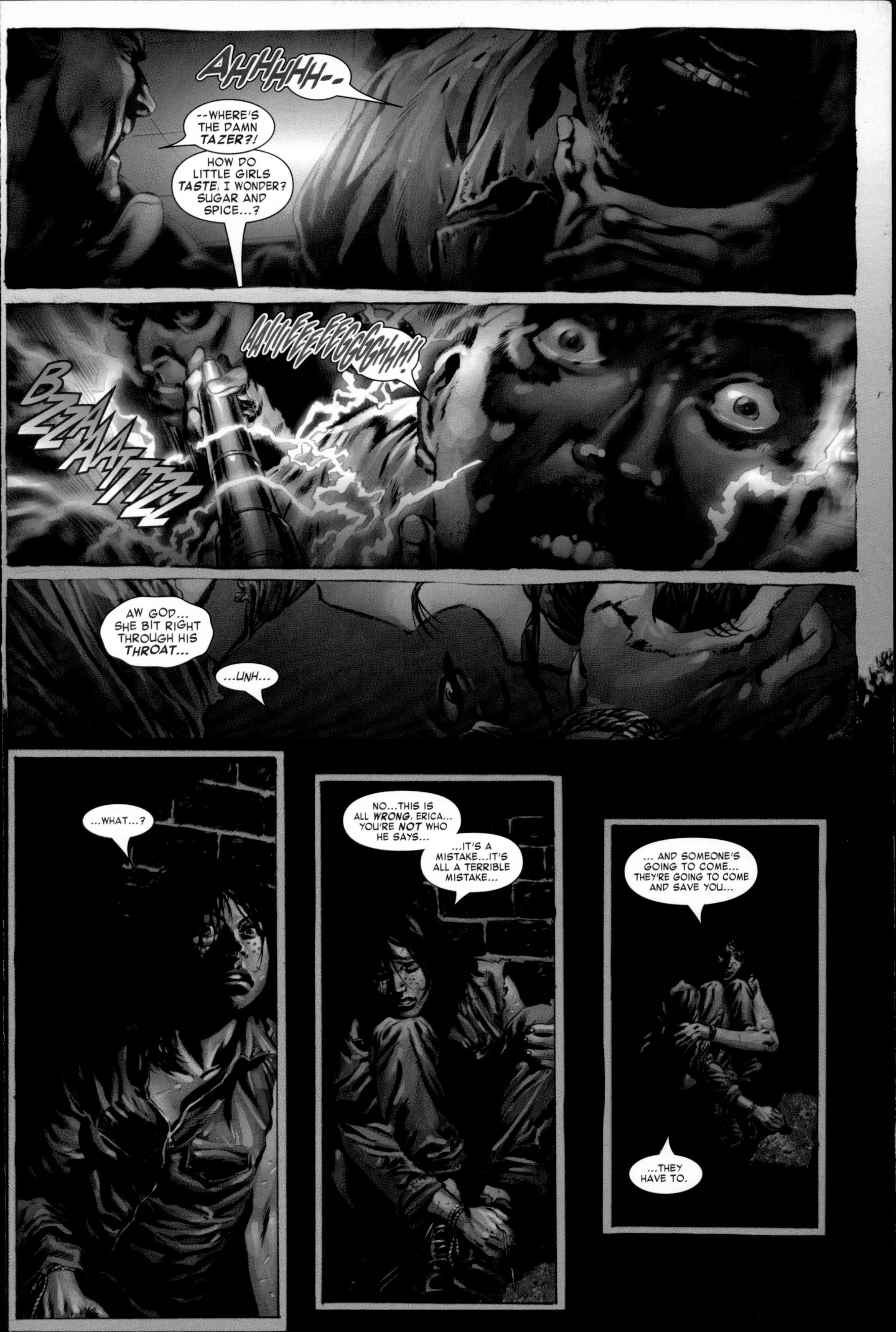

AHHHHH--
--WHERE'S THE DAMN TAZER?!
HOW DO LITTLE GIRLS TASTE, I WONDER? SUGAR AND SPICE...?
BZZAAATTZZ
AAIIIEEEEGGGHHH!
AW GOD... SHE BIT RIGHT THROUGH HIS THROAT...
...UNH...
...WHAT...?
NO...THIS IS ALL WRONG, ERICA... YOU'RE NOT WHO HE SAYS...
...IT'S A MISTAKE...IT'S ALL A TERRIBLE MISTAKE...
... AND SOMEONE'S GOING TO COME... THEY'RE GOING TO COME AND SAVE YOU...
...THEY HAVE TO.

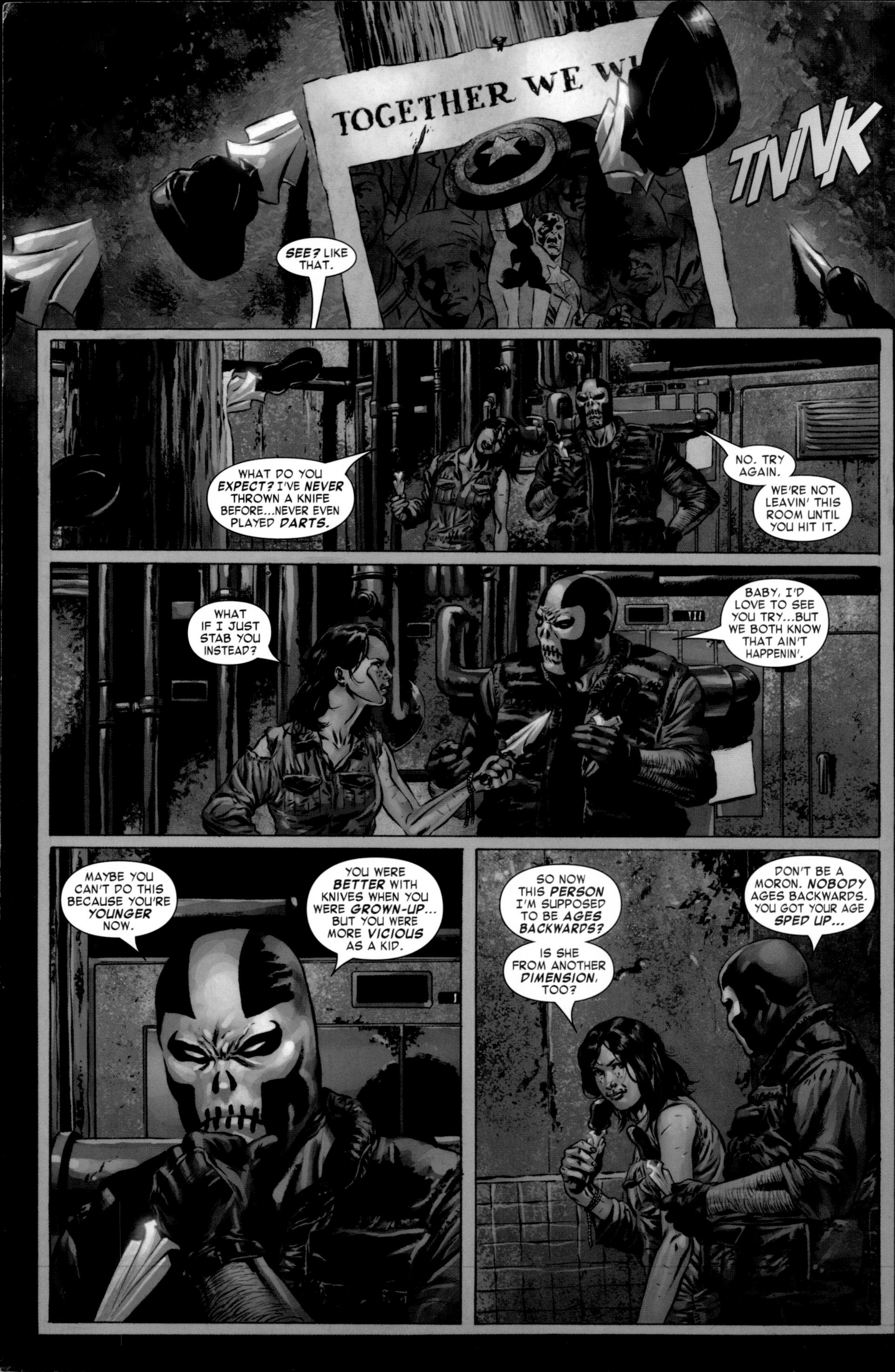
TOGETHER WE W
TNNK
SEE? LIKE THAT.
WHAT DO YOU EXPECT? I'VE NEVER THROWN A KNIFE BEFORE...NEVER EVEN PLAYED DARTS.
NO. TRY AGAIN.
WE'RE NOT LEAVIN' THIS ROOM UNTIL YOU HIT IT.
WHAT IF I JUST STAB YOU INSTEAD?
BABY, I'D LOVE TO SEE YOU TRY...BUT WE BOTH KNOW THAT AIN'T HAPPENIN'.
MAYBE YOU CAN'T DO THIS BECAUSE YOU'RE YOUNGER NOW.
YOU WERE BETTER WITH KNIVES WHEN YOU WERE GROWN-UP... BUT YOU WERE MORE VICIOUS AS A KID.
SO NOW THIS PERSON I'M SUPPOSED TO BE AGES BACKWARDS?
IS SHE FROM ANOTHER DIMENSION, TOO?
DON'T BE A MORON. NOBODY AGES BACKWARDS. YOU GOT YOUR AGE SPED UP...

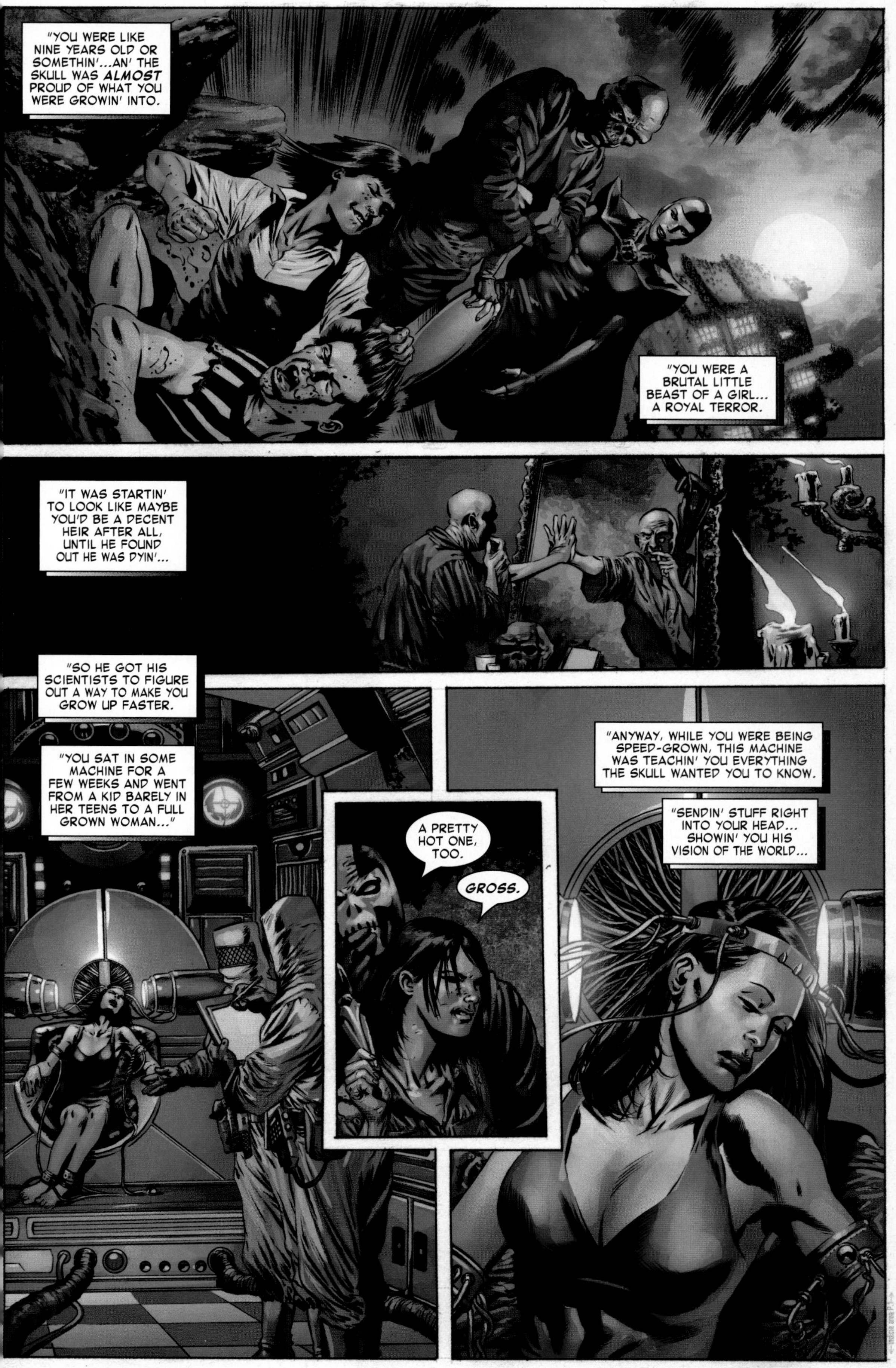
"YOU WERE LIKE NINE YEARS OLD OR SOMETHIN'...AN' THE SKULL WAS ALMOST PROUD OF WHAT YOU WERE GROWIN' INTO.
"YOU WERE A BRUTAL LITTLE BEAST OF A GIRL... A ROYAL TERROR.
"IT WAS STARTIN' TO LOOK LIKE MAYBE YOU'D BE A DECENT HEIR AFTER ALL, UNTIL HE FOUND OUT HE WAS DYIN'...
"SO HE GOT HIS SCIENTISTS TO FIGURE OUT A WAY TO MAKE YOU GROW UP FASTER.
"YOU SAT IN SOME MACHINE FOR A FEW WEEKS AND WENT FROM A KID BARELY IN HER TEENS TO A FULL GROWN WOMAN..."
A PRETTY HOT ONE, TOO.
GROSS.
"ANYWAY, WHILE YOU WERE BEING SPEED-GROWN, THIS MACHINE WAS TEACHIN' YOU EVERYTHING THE SKULL WANTED YOU TO KNOW.
"SENDIN' STUFF RIGHT INTO YOUR HEAD... SHOWIN' YOU HIS VISION OF THE WORLD...

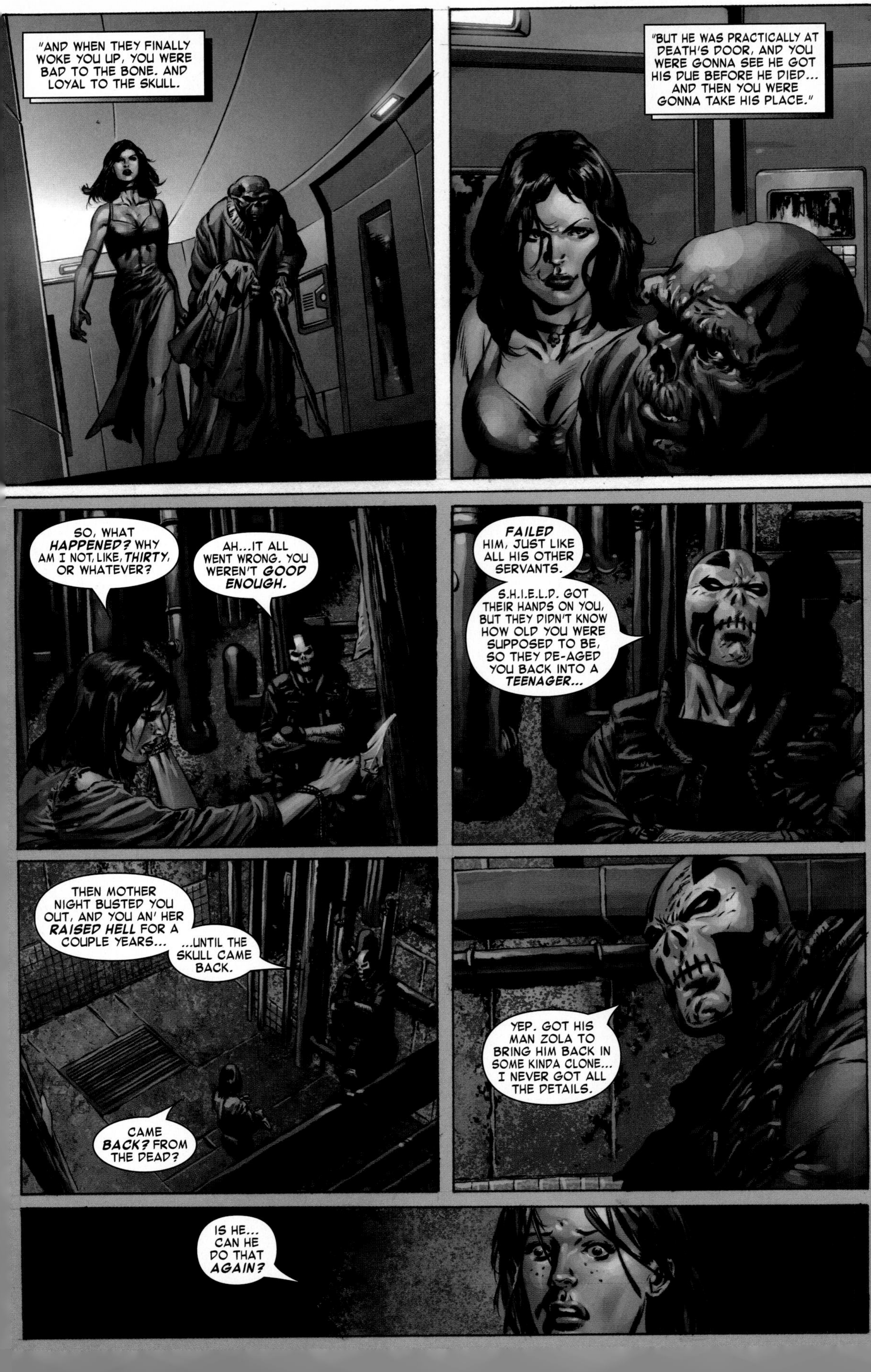
"AND WHEN THEY FINALLY WOKE YOU UP, YOU WERE BAD TO THE BONE. AND LOYAL TO THE SKULL.
"BUT HE WAS PRACTICALLY AT DEATH'S DOOR, AND YOU WERE GONNA SEE HE GOT HIS DUE BEFORE HE DIED... AND THEN YOU WERE GONNA TAKE HIS PLACE."
SO, WHAT HAPPENED? WHY AM I NOT, LIKE, THIRTY, OR WHATEVER?
AH...IT ALL WENT WRONG. YOU WEREN'T GOOD ENOUGH.
FAILED HIM, JUST LIKE ALL HIS OTHER SERVANTS.
S.H.I.E.L.D. GOT THEIR HANDS ON YOU, BUT THEY DIDN'T KNOW HOW OLD YOU WERE SUPPOSED TO BE, SO THEY DE-AGED YOU BACK INTO A TEENAGER...
THEN MOTHER NIGHT BUSTED YOU OUT, AND YOU AN' HER RAISED HELL FOR A COUPLE YEARS...
...UNTIL THE SKULL CAME BACK.
CAME BACK? FROM THE DEAD?
YEP. GOT HIS MAN ZOLA TO BRING HIM BACK IN SOME KINDA CLONE... I NEVER GOT ALL THE DETAILS.
IS HE... CAN HE DO THAT AGAIN?

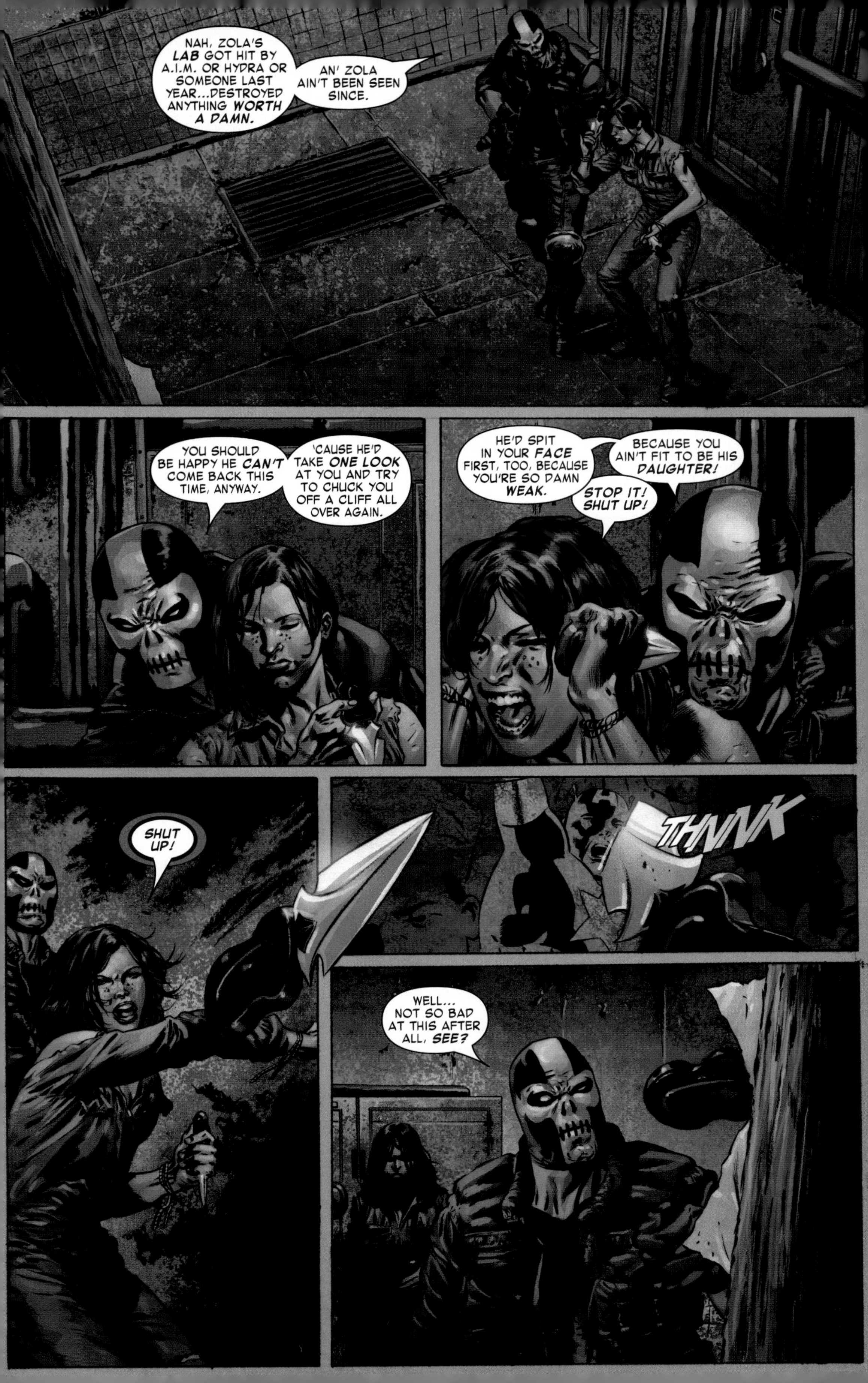
NAH, ZOLA'S LAB GOT HIT BY A.I.M. OR HYDRA OR SOMEONE LAST YEAR...DESTROYED ANYTHING WORTH A DAMN.
AN' ZOLA AIN'T BEEN SEEN SINCE.
YOU SHOULD BE HAPPY HE CAN'T COME BACK THIS TIME, ANYWAY.
'CAUSE HE'D TAKE ONE LOOK AT YOU AND TRY TO CHUCK YOU OFF A CLIFF ALL OVER AGAIN.
HE'D SPIT IN YOUR FACE FIRST, TOO, BECAUSE YOU'RE SO DAMN WEAK.
BECAUSE YOU AIN'T FIT TO BE HIS DAUGHTER!
STOP IT! SHUT UP!
SHUT UP!
THNNK
WELL... NOT SO BAD AT THIS AFTER ALL, SEE?

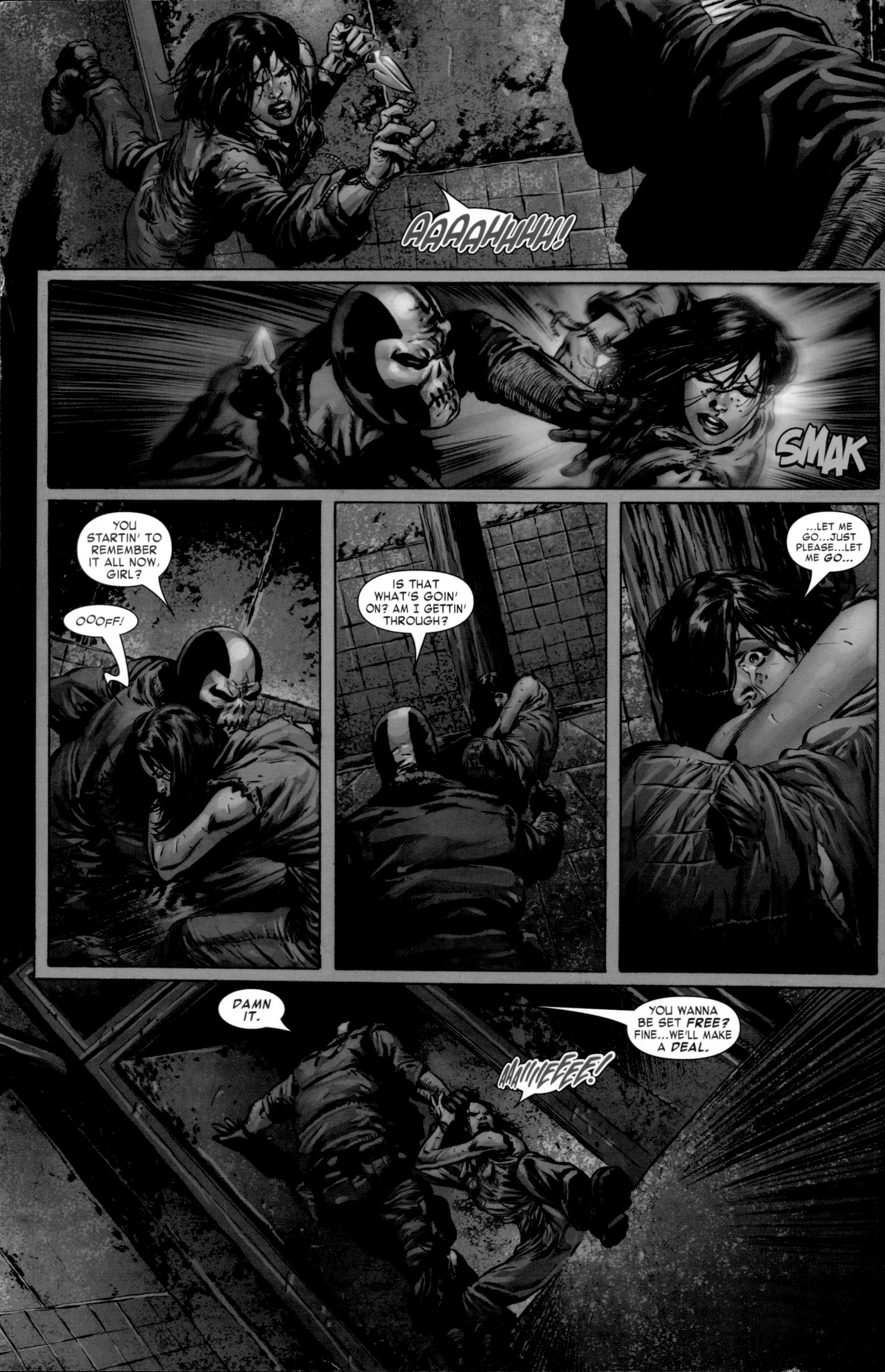
AAAAHHHH!
SMAK
YOU STARTIN' TO REMEMBER IT ALL NOW, GIRL?
OOOFF!
IS THAT WHAT'S GOIN' ON? AM I GETTIN' THROUGH?
...LET ME GO...JUST PLEASE...LET ME GO...
DAMN IT.
YOU WANNA BE SET FREE? FINE...WE'LL MAKE A DEAL.
AAAIIIEEEEE!

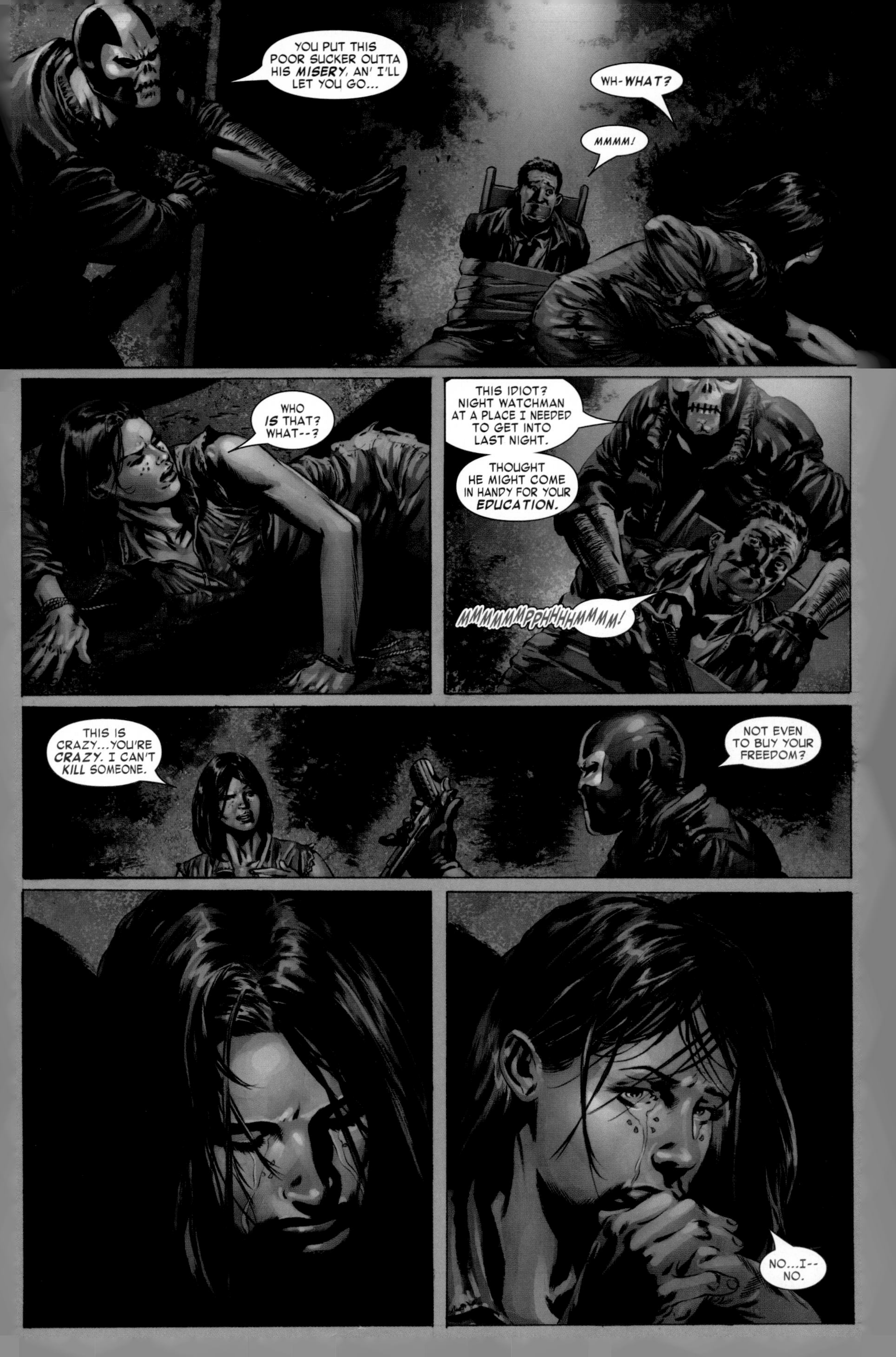
YOU PUT THIS POOR SUCKER OUTTA HIS MISERY, AN' I'LL LET YOU GO...
WH-WHAT?
MMMM!
WHO IS THAT? WHAT--?
THIS IDIOT? NIGHT WATCHMAN AT A PLACE I NEEDED TO GET INTO LAST NIGHT.
THOUGHT HE MIGHT COME IN HANDY FOR YOUR EDUCATION.
MMMMMMPPHHHHMMMM!
THIS IS CRAZY...YOU'RE CRAZY. I CAN'T KILL SOMEONE.
NOT EVEN TO BUY YOUR FREEDOM?
NO...I-- NO.

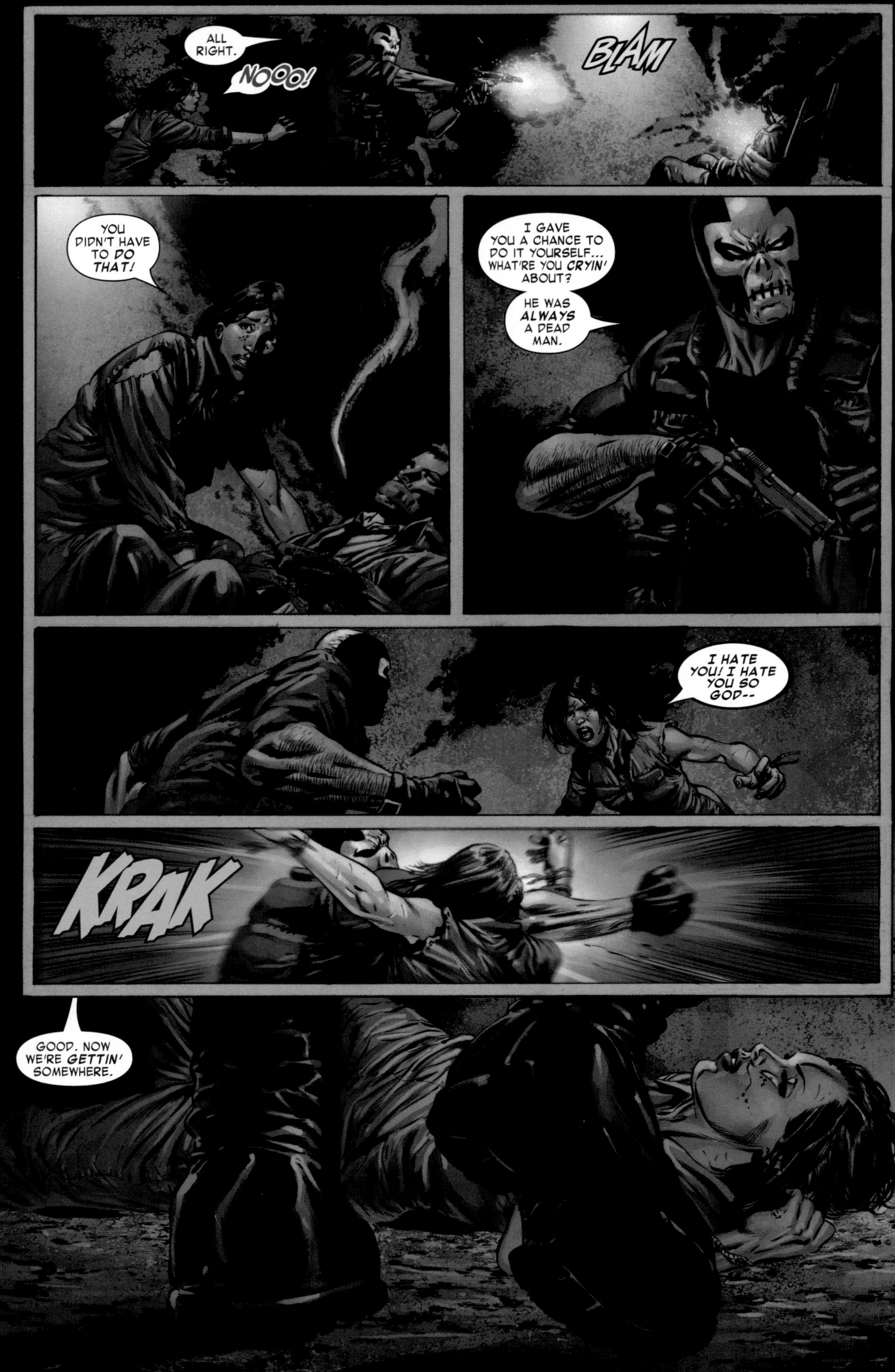
ALL RIGHT.
NOOO!
BLAM
YOU DIDN'T HAVE TO DO THAT!
I GAVE YOU A CHANCE TO DO IT YOURSELF... WHAT'RE YOU CRYIN' ABOUT?
HE WAS ALWAYS A DEAD MAN.
I HATE YOU! I HATE YOU SO GOD--
KRAK
GOOD. NOW WE'RE GETTIN' SOMEWHERE.

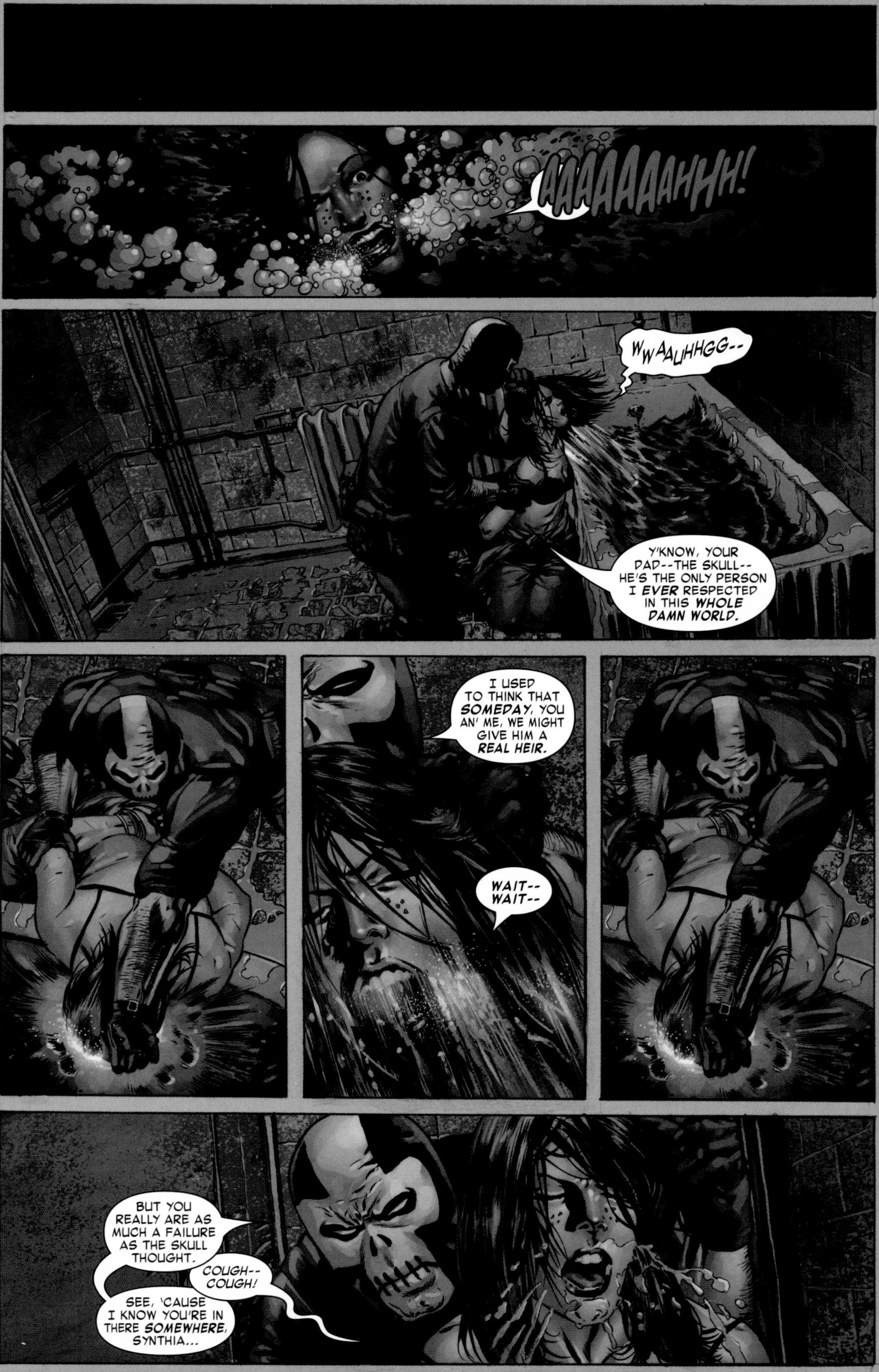
AAAAAAAAHHH!
WWAAUHHGG--
Y'KNOW, YOUR DAD--THE SKULL--HE'S THE ONLY PERSON I EVER RESPECTED IN THIS WHOLE DAMN WORLD.
I USED TO THINK THAT SOMEDAY, YOU AN' ME, WE MIGHT GIVE HIM A REAL HEIR.
WAIT--WAIT--
BUT YOU REALLY ARE AS MUCH A FAILURE AS THE SKULL THOUGHT.
COUGH--COUGH!
SEE, 'CAUSE I KNOW YOU'RE IN THERE SOMEWHERE, SYNTHIA...

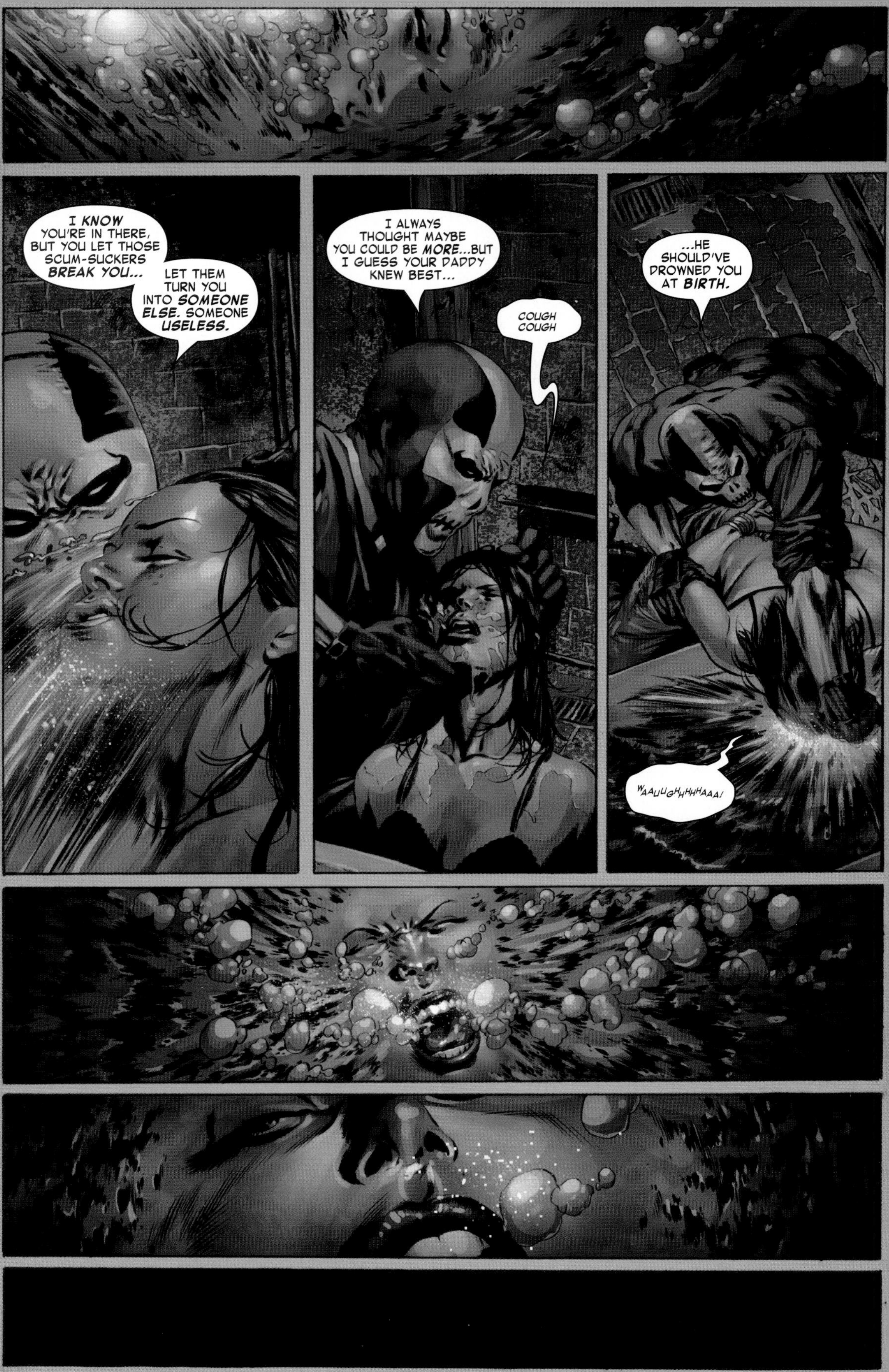
I KNOW YOU'RE IN THERE, BUT YOU LET THOSE SCUM-SUCKERS BREAK YOU...
LET THEM TURN YOU INTO SOMEONE ELSE. SOMEONE USELESS.
I ALWAYS THOUGHT MAYBE YOU COULD BE MORE...BUT I GUESS YOUR DADDY KNEW BEST...
COUGH COUGH
...HE SHOULD'VE DROWNED YOU AT BIRTH.
WAAUUGHHHHAAA!

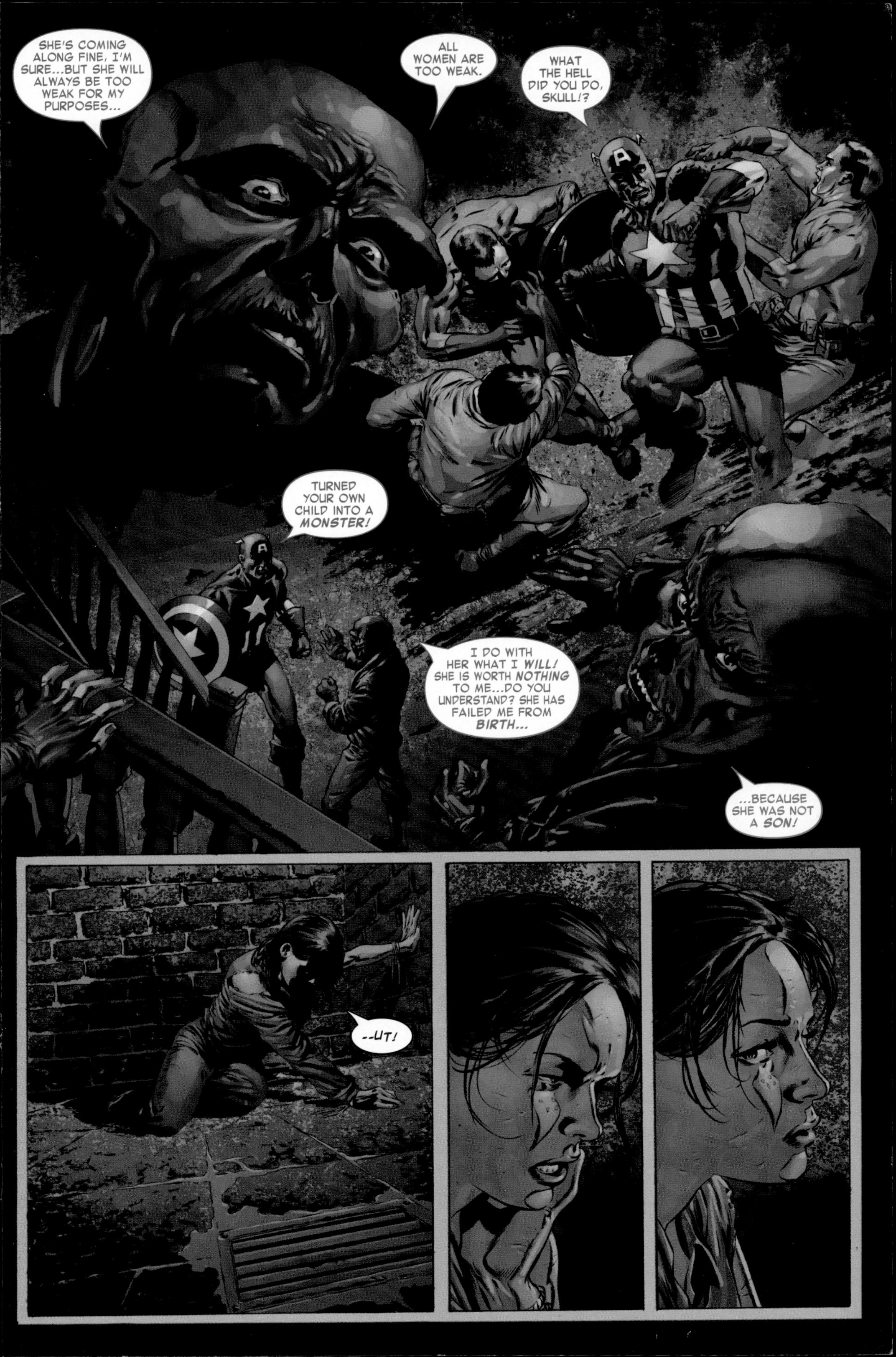
SHE'S COMING ALONG FINE, I'M SURE...BUT SHE WILL ALWAYS BE TOO WEAK FOR MY PURPOSES...
ALL WOMEN ARE TOO WEAK.
WHAT THE HELL DID YOU DO, SKULL!?
TURNED YOUR OWN CHILD INTO A MONSTER!
I DO WITH HER WHAT I WILL! SHE IS WORTH NOTHING TO ME...DO YOU UNDERSTAND? SHE HAS FAILED ME FROM BIRTH...
...BECAUSE SHE WAS NOT A SON!
--UT!

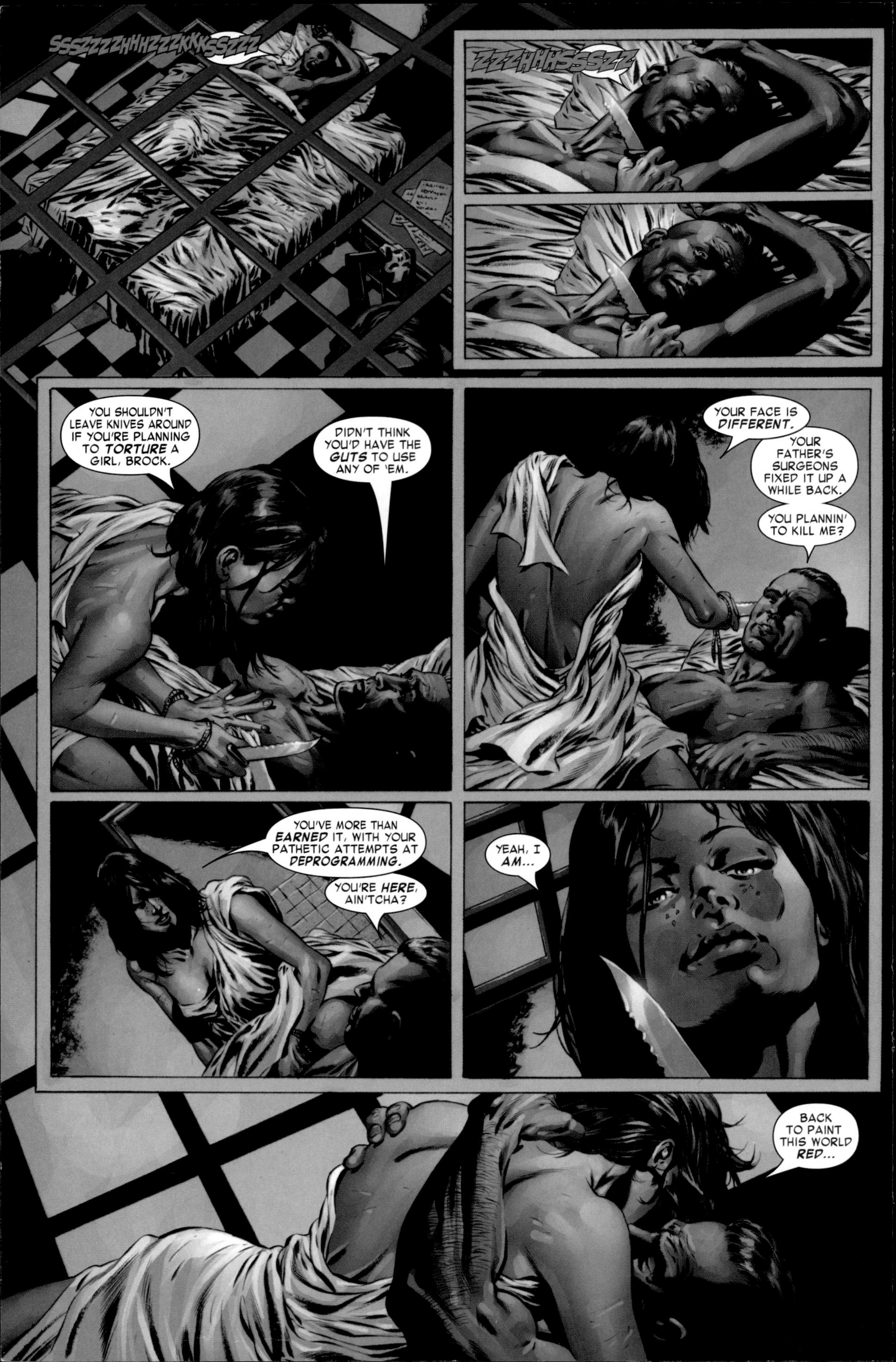
SSSZZZZHHHZZZKKKSSZZZ
ZZZHHHSSSZZ
YOU SHOULDN'T LEAVE KNIVES AROUND IF YOU'RE PLANNING TO TORTURE A GIRL, BROCK.
DIDN'T THINK YOU'D HAVE THE GUTS TO USE ANY OF 'EM.
YOUR FACE IS DIFFERENT.
YOUR FATHER'S SURGEONS FIXED IT UP A WHILE BACK.
YOU PLANNIN' TO KILL ME?
YOU'VE MORE THAN EARNED IT, WITH YOUR PATHETIC ATTEMPTS AT DEPROGRAMMING.
YOU'RE HERE, AIN'TCHA?
YEAH, I AM...
BACK TO PAINT THIS WORLD RED...

16

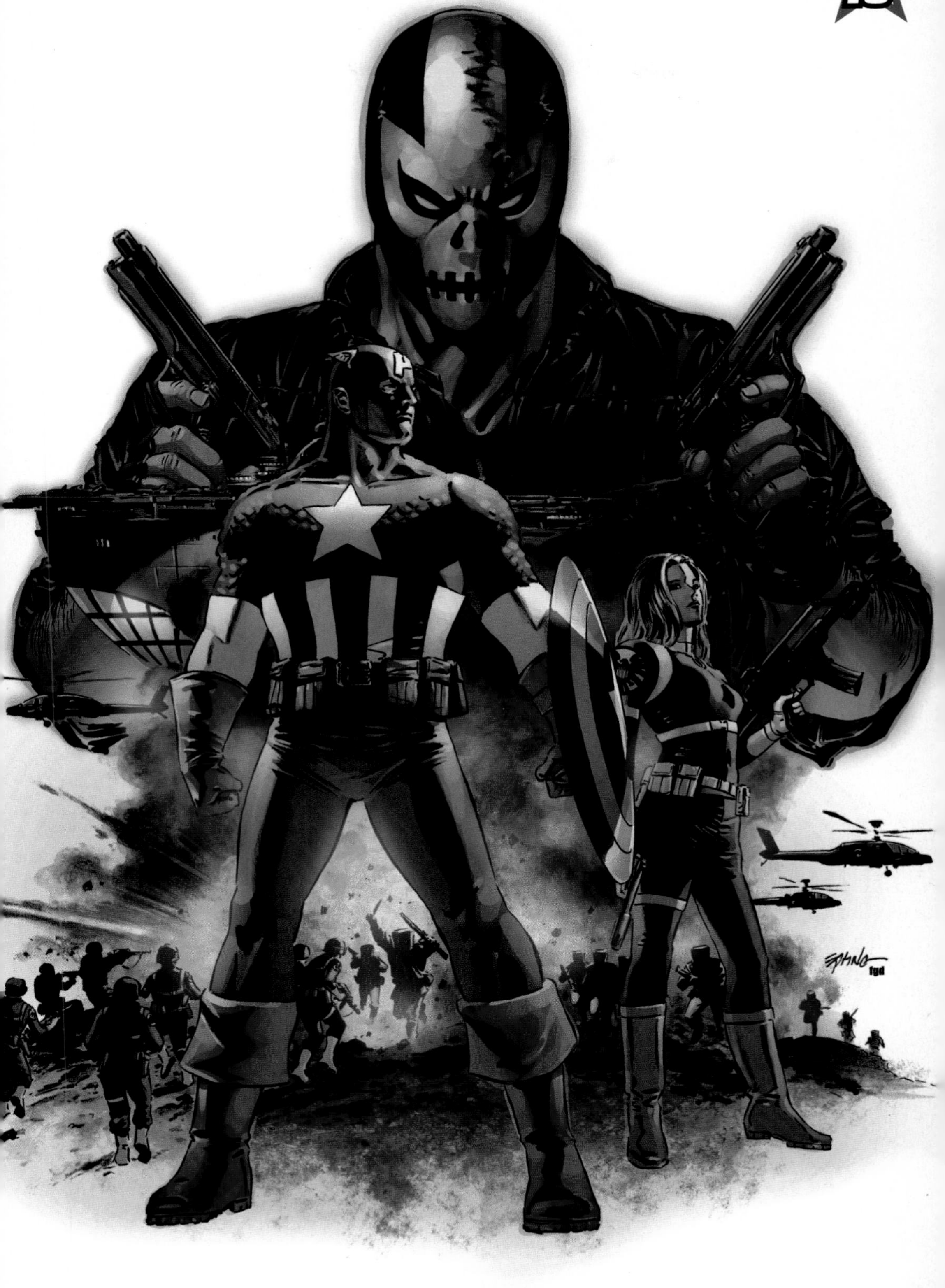

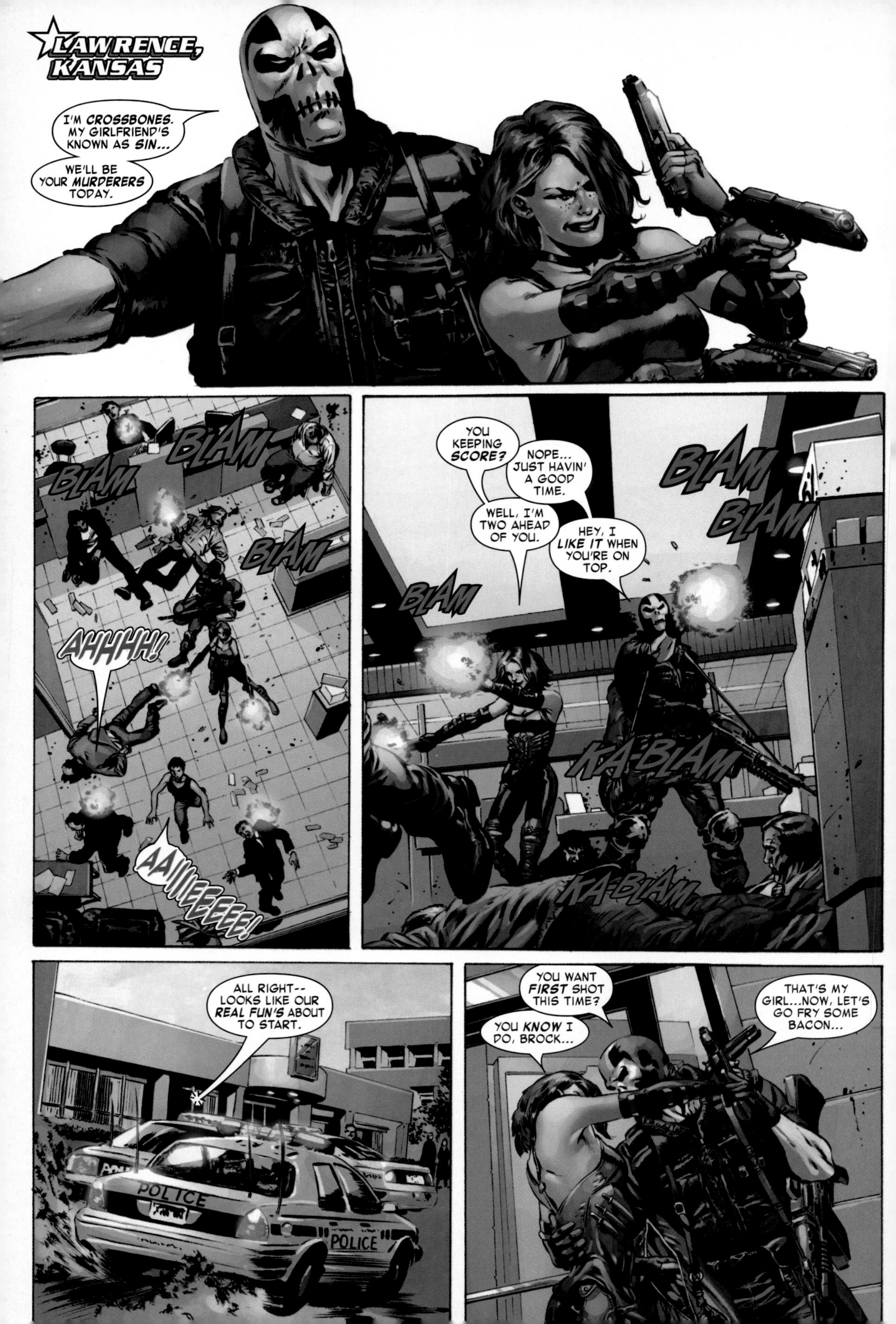
LAWRENCE, KANSAS
I'M CROSSBONES. MY GIRLFRIEND'S KNOWN AS SIN...
WE'LL BE YOUR MURDERERS TODAY.
BLAM
BLAM
BLAM
AHHHH!
AAIIIEEEEEE!
YOU KEEPING SCORE?
NOPE... JUST HAVIN' A GOOD TIME.
WELL, I'M TWO AHEAD OF YOU.
HEY, I LIKE IT WHEN YOU'RE ON TOP.
BLAM
BLAM
BLAM
KA-BLAM
KA-BLAM
ALL RIGHT-- LOOKS LIKE OUR REAL FUN'S ABOUT TO START.
POLICE
POLICE
YOU WANT FIRST SHOT THIS TIME?
YOU KNOW I DO, BROCK...
THAT'S MY GIRL...NOW, LET'S GO FRY SOME BACON...

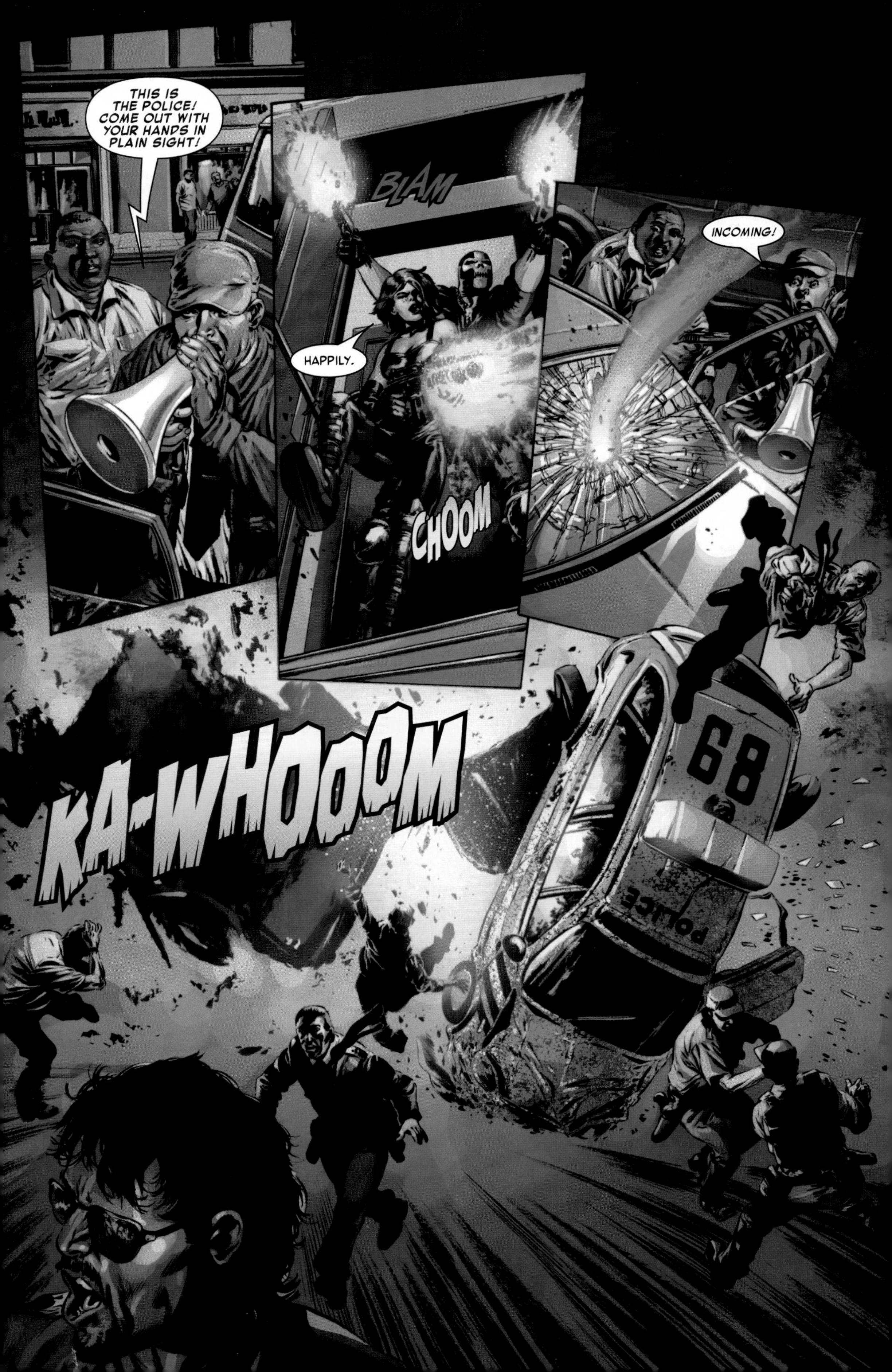
THIS IS THE POLICE! COME OUT WITH YOUR HANDS IN PLAIN SIGHT!
BLAM
HAPPILY.
CHOOM
INCOMING!
KA-WHOOOM
68
POLICE

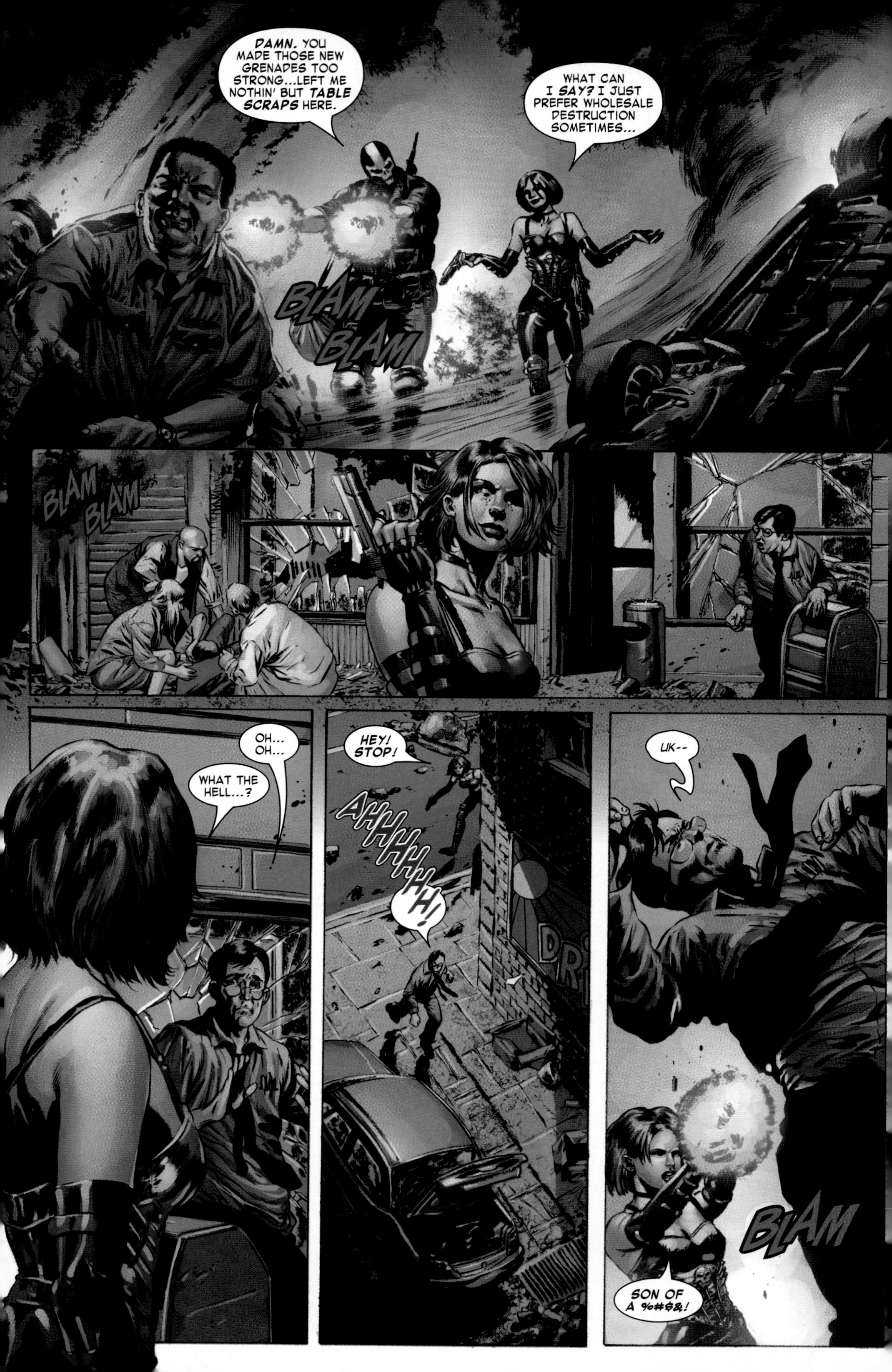
DAMN. YOU MADE THOSE NEW GRENADES TOO STRONG...LEFT ME NOTHIN' BUT TABLE SCRAPS HERE.
WHAT CAN I SAY? I JUST PREFER WHOLESALE DESTRUCTION SOMETIMES...
BLAM BLAM
BLAM BLAM
OH... OH...
WHAT THE HELL...?
HEY! STOP!
AHHHHHH!
UK--
BLAM
SON OF A %#$&!

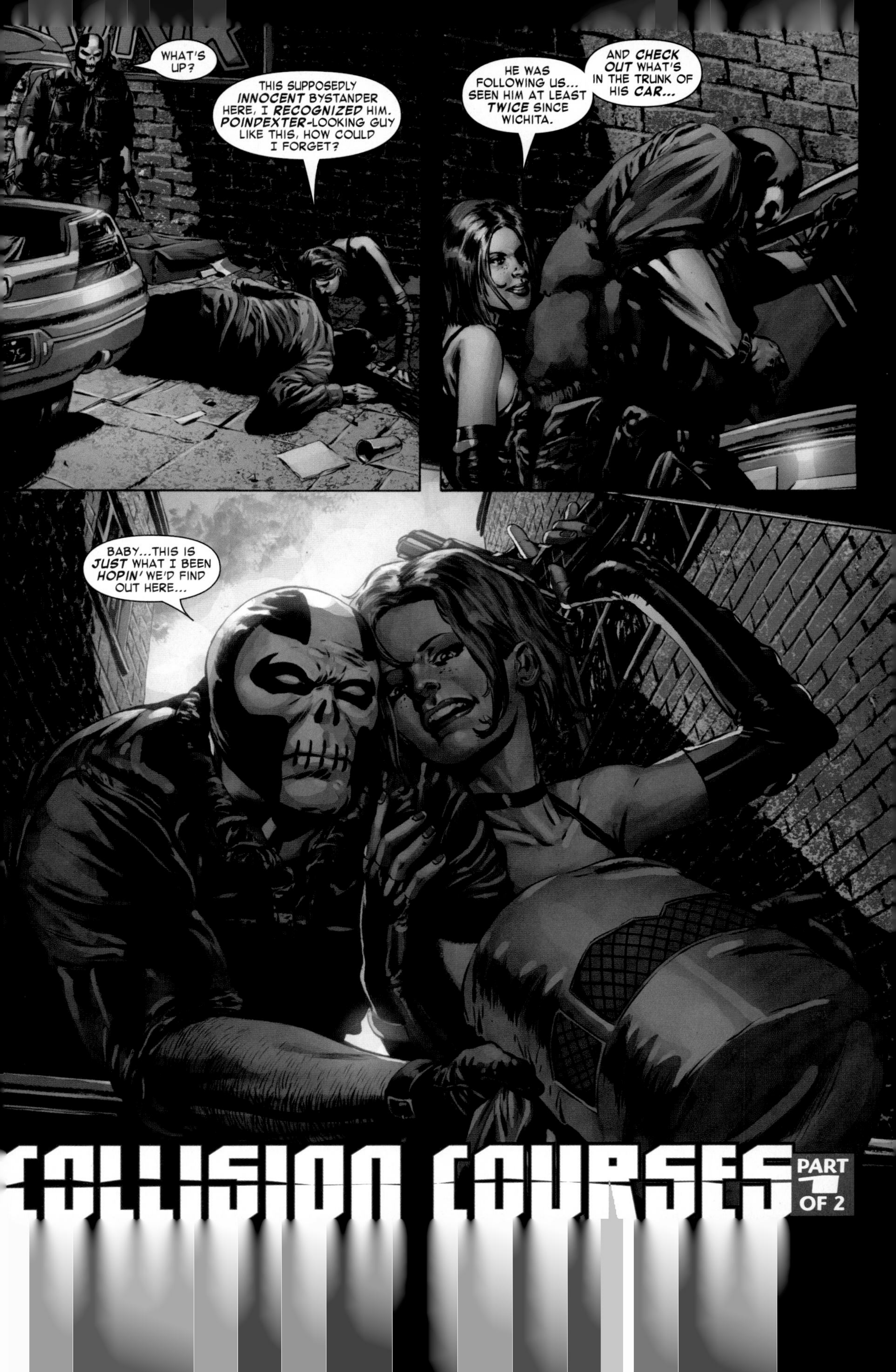
WHAT'S UP?
THIS SUPPOSEDLY INNOCENT BYSTANDER HERE, I RECOGNIZED HIM. POINDEXTER-LOOKING GUY LIKE THIS, HOW COULD I FORGET?
HE WAS FOLLOWING US... SEEN HIM AT LEAST TWICE SINCE WICHITA.
AND CHECK OUT WHAT'S IN THE TRUNK OF HIS CAR...
BABY...THIS IS JUST WHAT I BEEN HOPIN' WE'D FIND OUT HERE...
COLLISION COURSES
PART 1 OF 2

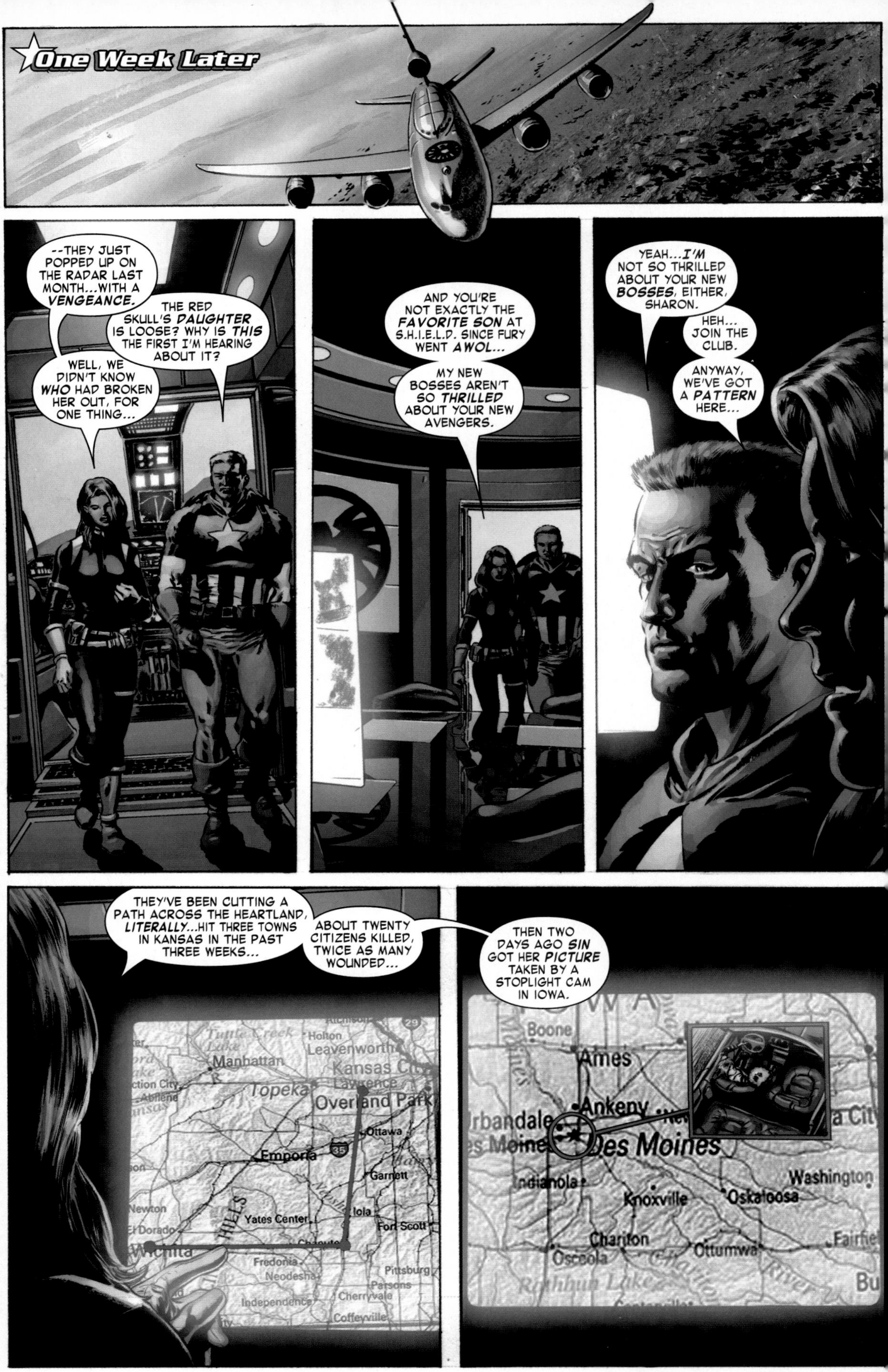
One Week Later
--THEY JUST POPPED UP ON THE RADAR LAST MONTH...WITH A VENGEANCE.
THE RED SKULL'S DAUGHTER IS LOOSE? WHY IS THIS THE FIRST I'M HEARING ABOUT IT?
WELL, WE DIDN'T KNOW WHO HAD BROKEN HER OUT, FOR ONE THING...
AND YOU'RE NOT EXACTLY THE FAVORITE SON AT S.H.I.E.L.D. SINCE FURY WENT AWOL...
MY NEW BOSSES AREN'T SO THRILLED ABOUT YOUR NEW AVENGERS.
YEAH...I'M NOT SO THRILLED ABOUT YOUR NEW BOSSES, EITHER, SHARON.
HEH... JOIN THE CLUB.
ANYWAY, WE'VE GOT A PATTERN HERE...
THEY'VE BEEN CUTTING A PATH ACROSS THE HEARTLAND, LITERALLY...HIT THREE TOWNS IN KANSAS IN THE PAST THREE WEEKS...
ABOUT TWENTY CITIZENS KILLED, TWICE AS MANY WOUNDED...
THEN TWO DAYS AGO SIN GOT HER PICTURE TAKEN BY A STOPLIGHT CAM IN IOWA.

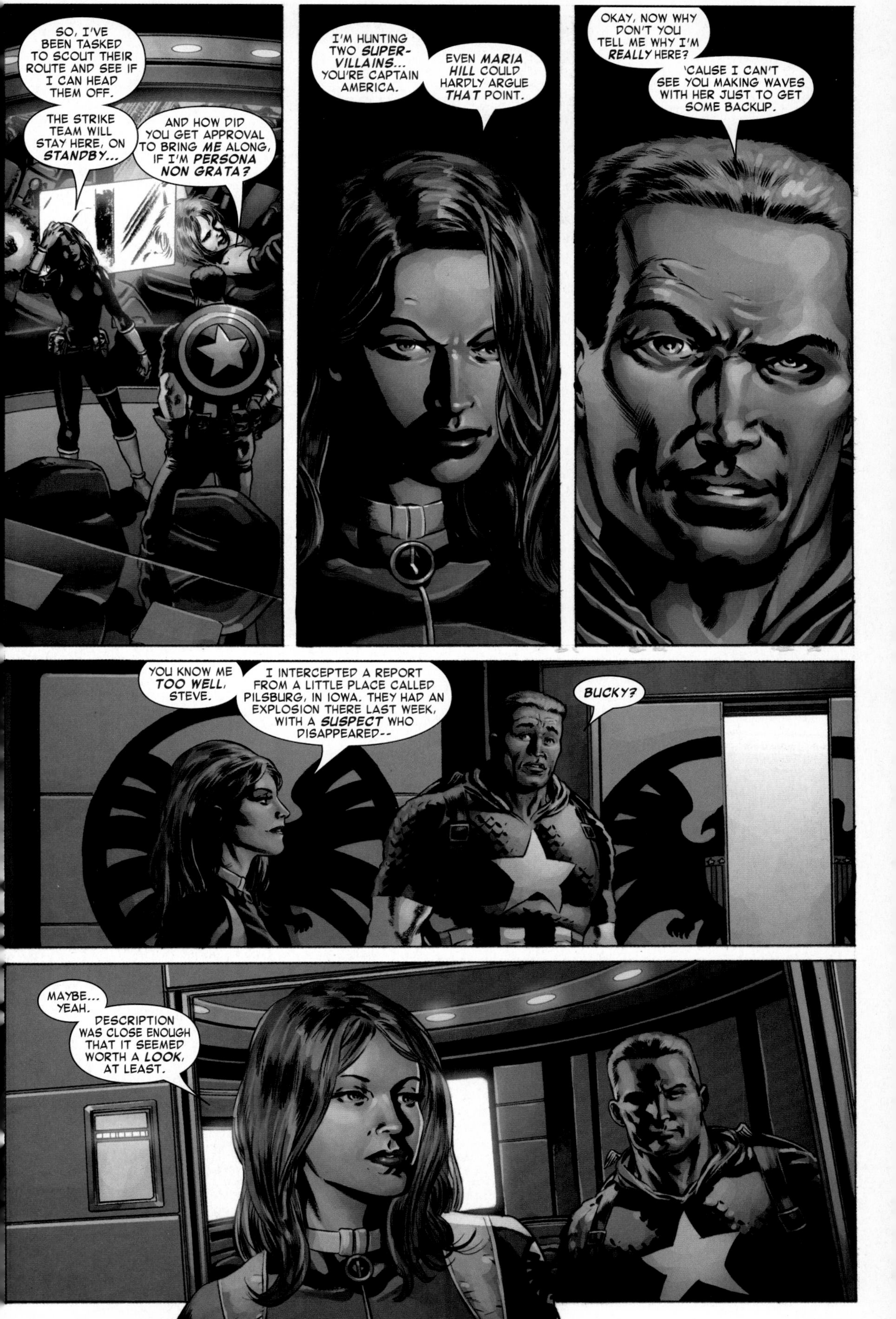
SO, I'VE BEEN TASKED TO SCOUT THEIR ROUTE AND SEE IF I CAN HEAD THEM OFF.
THE STRIKE TEAM WILL STAY HERE, ON STANDBY...
AND HOW DID YOU GET APPROVAL TO BRING ME ALONG, IF I'M PERSONA NON GRATA?
I'M HUNTING TWO SUPER-VILLAINS... YOU'RE CAPTAIN AMERICA.
EVEN MARIA HILL COULD HARDLY ARGUE THAT POINT.
OKAY, NOW WHY DON'T YOU TELL ME WHY I'M REALLY HERE?
'CAUSE I CAN'T SEE YOU MAKING WAVES WITH HER JUST TO GET SOME BACKUP.
YOU KNOW ME TOO WELL, STEVE.
I INTERCEPTED A REPORT FROM A LITTLE PLACE CALLED PILSBURG, IN IOWA. THEY HAD AN EXPLOSION THERE LAST WEEK, WITH A SUSPECT WHO DISAPPEARED--
BUCKY?
MAYBE... YEAH.
DESCRIPTION WAS CLOSE ENOUGH THAT IT SEEMED WORTH A LOOK, AT LEAST.

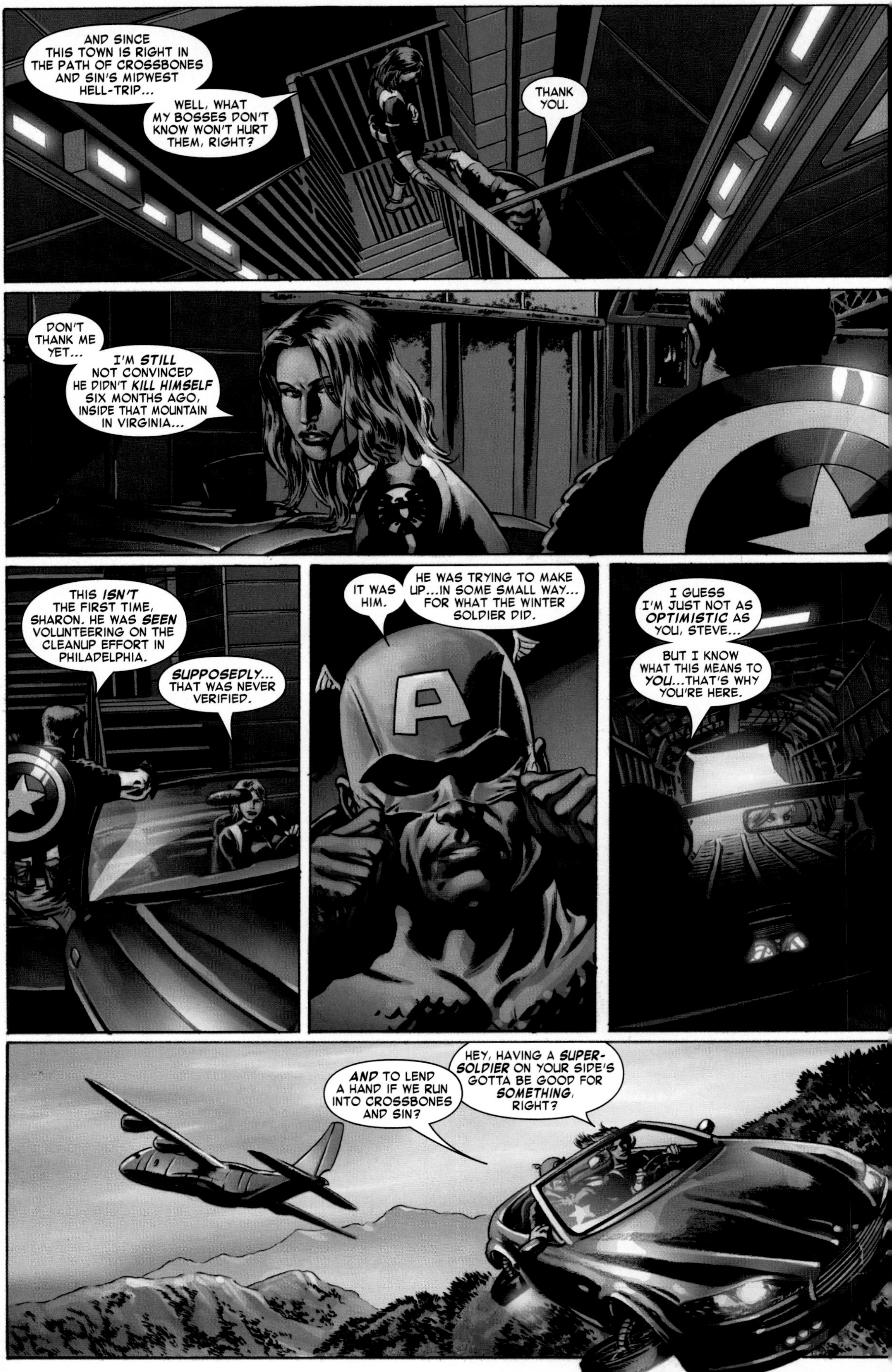

AND SINCE THIS TOWN IS RIGHT IN THE PATH OF CROSSBONES AND SIN'S MIDWEST HELL-TRIP...
WELL, WHAT MY BOSSES DON'T KNOW WON'T HURT THEM, RIGHT?
THANK YOU.
DON'T THANK ME YET...
I'M STILL NOT CONVINCED HE DIDN'T KILL HIMSELF SIX MONTHS AGO, INSIDE THAT MOUNTAIN IN VIRGINIA...
THIS ISN'T THE FIRST TIME, SHARON. HE WAS SEEN VOLUNTEERING ON THE CLEANUP EFFORT IN PHILADELPHIA.
SUPPOSEDLY... THAT WAS NEVER VERIFIED.
IT WAS HIM.
HE WAS TRYING TO MAKE UP...IN SOME SMALL WAY... FOR WHAT THE WINTER SOLDIER DID.
I GUESS I'M JUST NOT AS OPTIMISTIC AS YOU, STEVE...
BUT I KNOW WHAT THIS MEANS TO YOU...THAT'S WHY YOU'RE HERE.
AND TO LEND A HAND IF WE RUN INTO CROSSBONES AND SIN?
HEY, HAVING A SUPER-SOLDIER ON YOUR SIDE'S GOTTA BE GOOD FOR SOMETHING, RIGHT?

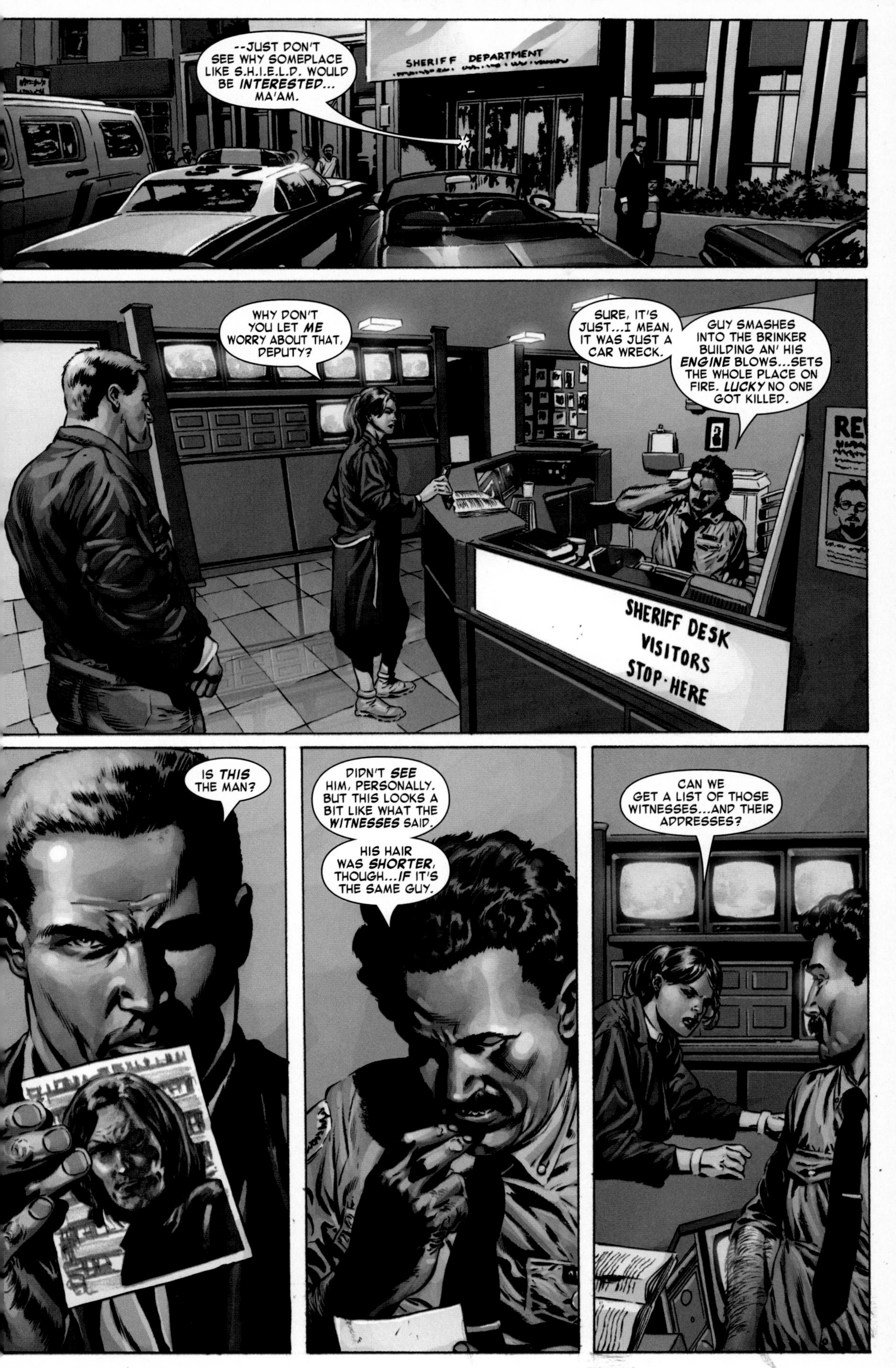
--JUST DON'T SEE WHY SOMEPLACE LIKE S.H.I.E.L.D. WOULD BE INTERESTED... MA'AM.
SHERIFF DEPARTMENT
WHY DON'T YOU LET ME WORRY ABOUT THAT, DEPUTY?
SURE, IT'S JUST...I MEAN, IT WAS JUST A CAR WRECK.
GUY SMASHES INTO THE BRINKER BUILDING AN' HIS ENGINE BLOWS...SETS THE WHOLE PLACE ON FIRE. LUCKY NO ONE GOT KILLED.
SHERIFF DESK
VISITORS
STOP·HERE
IS THIS THE MAN?
DIDN'T SEE HIM, PERSONALLY. BUT THIS LOOKS A BIT LIKE WHAT THE WITNESSES SAID.
HIS HAIR WAS SHORTER, THOUGH...IF IT'S THE SAME GUY.
CAN WE GET A LIST OF THOSE WITNESSES...AND THEIR ADDRESSES?

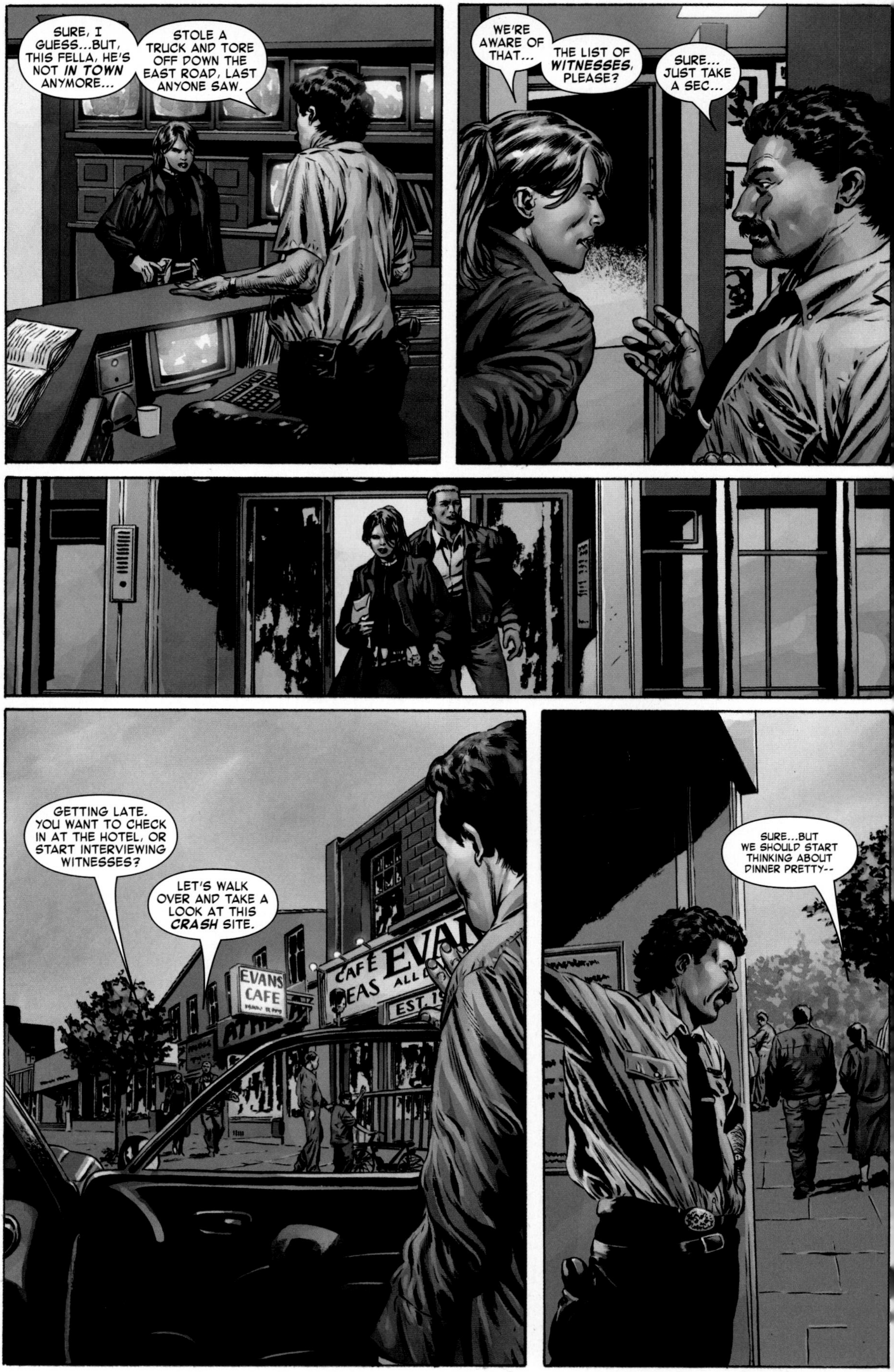
SURE, I GUESS...BUT, THIS FELLA, HE'S NOT *IN TOWN* ANYMORE...
STOLE A TRUCK AND TORE OFF DOWN THE EAST ROAD, LAST ANYONE SAW.
WE'RE AWARE OF THAT...
THE LIST OF *WITNESSES*, PLEASE?
SURE... JUST TAKE A SEC...
GETTING LATE. YOU WANT TO CHECK IN AT THE HOTEL, OR START INTERVIEWING WITNESSES?
LET'S WALK OVER AND TAKE A LOOK AT THIS *CRASH* SITE.
EVANS CAFE
SURE...BUT WE SHOULD START THINKING ABOUT DINNER PRETTY--

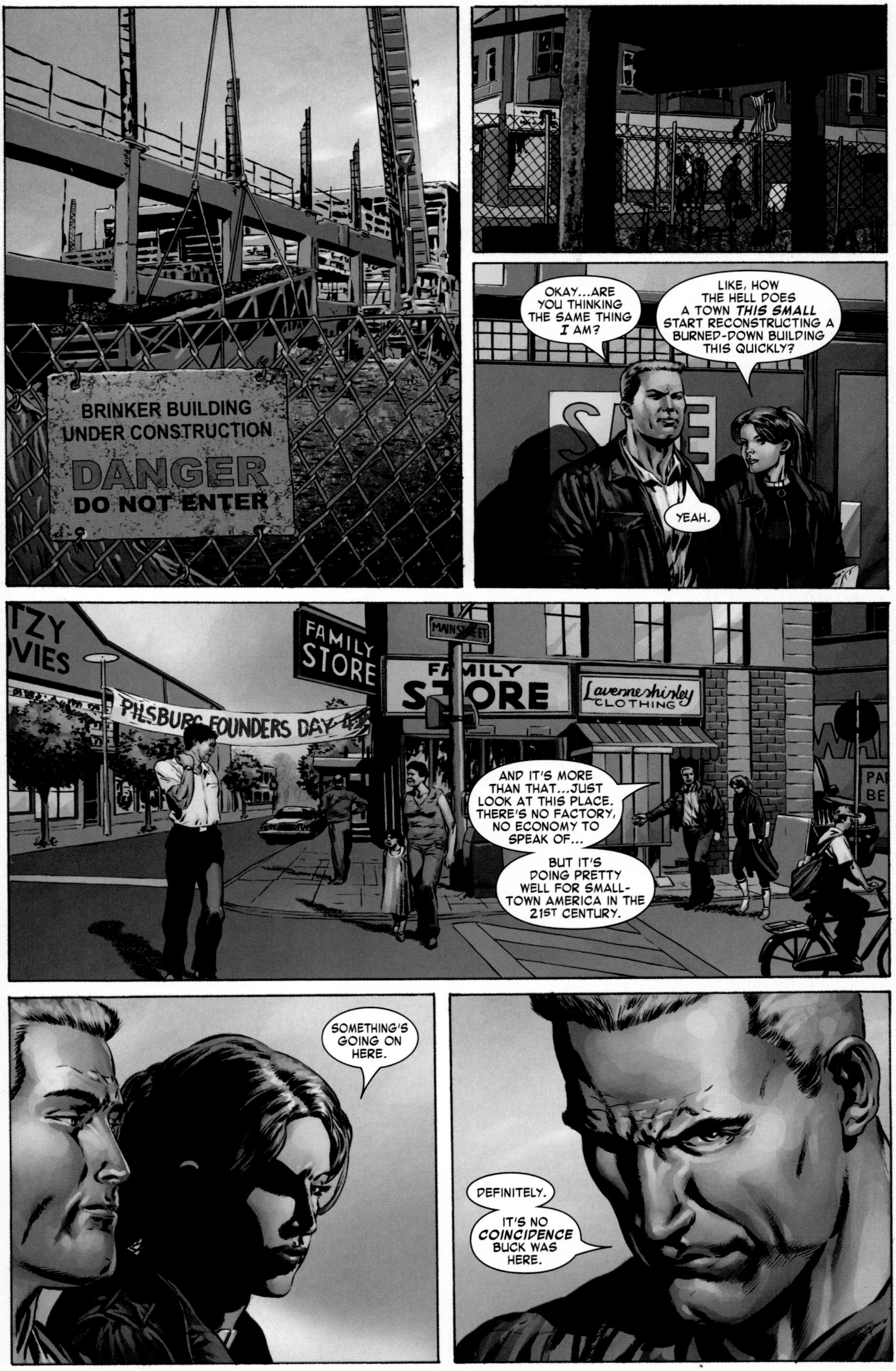
BRINKER BUILDING
UNDER CONSTRUCTION
DANGER
DO NOT ENTER
OKAY...ARE YOU THINKING THE SAME THING I AM?
LIKE, HOW THE HELL DOES A TOWN THIS SMALL START RECONSTRUCTING A BURNED-DOWN BUILDING THIS QUICKLY?
YEAH.
FAMILY STORE
MAIN STREET
FAMILY STORE
Lavernneshirley CLOTHING
PILSBURG FOUNDERS DAY
AND IT'S MORE THAN THAT...JUST LOOK AT THIS PLACE. THERE'S NO FACTORY, NO ECONOMY TO SPEAK OF...
BUT IT'S DOING PRETTY WELL FOR SMALL-TOWN AMERICA IN THE 21ST CENTURY.
SOMETHING'S GOING ON HERE.
DEFINITELY.
IT'S NO COINCIDENCE BUCK WAS HERE.

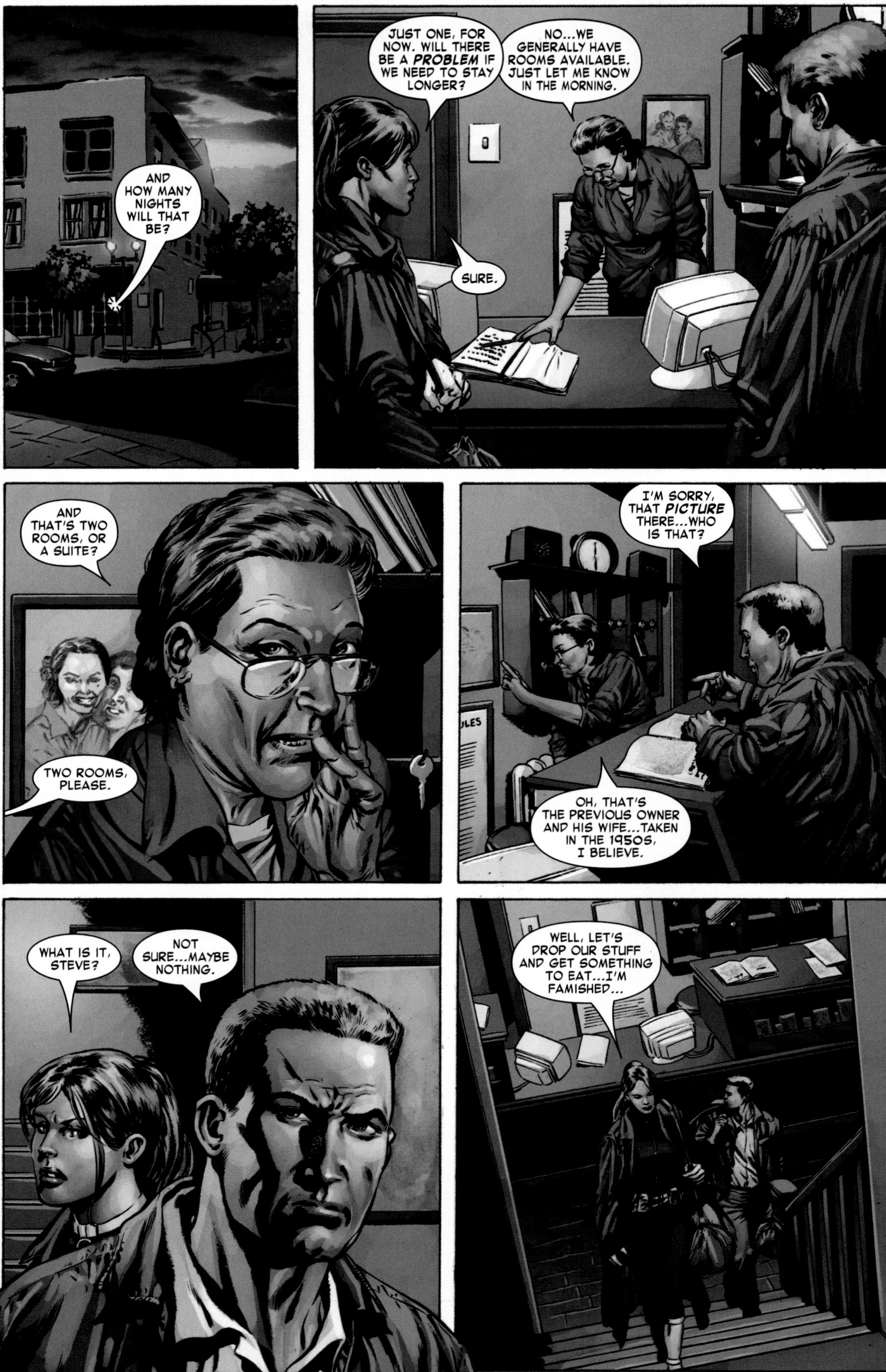
AND HOW MANY NIGHTS WILL THAT BE?
JUST ONE, FOR NOW. WILL THERE BE A PROBLEM IF WE NEED TO STAY LONGER?
SURE.
NO...WE GENERALLY HAVE ROOMS AVAILABLE. JUST LET ME KNOW IN THE MORNING.
AND THAT'S TWO ROOMS, OR A SUITE?
TWO ROOMS, PLEASE.
I'M SORRY, THAT PICTURE THERE...WHO IS THAT?
OH, THAT'S THE PREVIOUS OWNER AND HIS WIFE...TAKEN IN THE 1950S, I BELIEVE.
WHAT IS IT, STEVE?
NOT SURE...MAYBE NOTHING.
WELL, LET'S DROP OUR STUFF AND GET SOMETHING TO EAT...I'M FAMISHED...

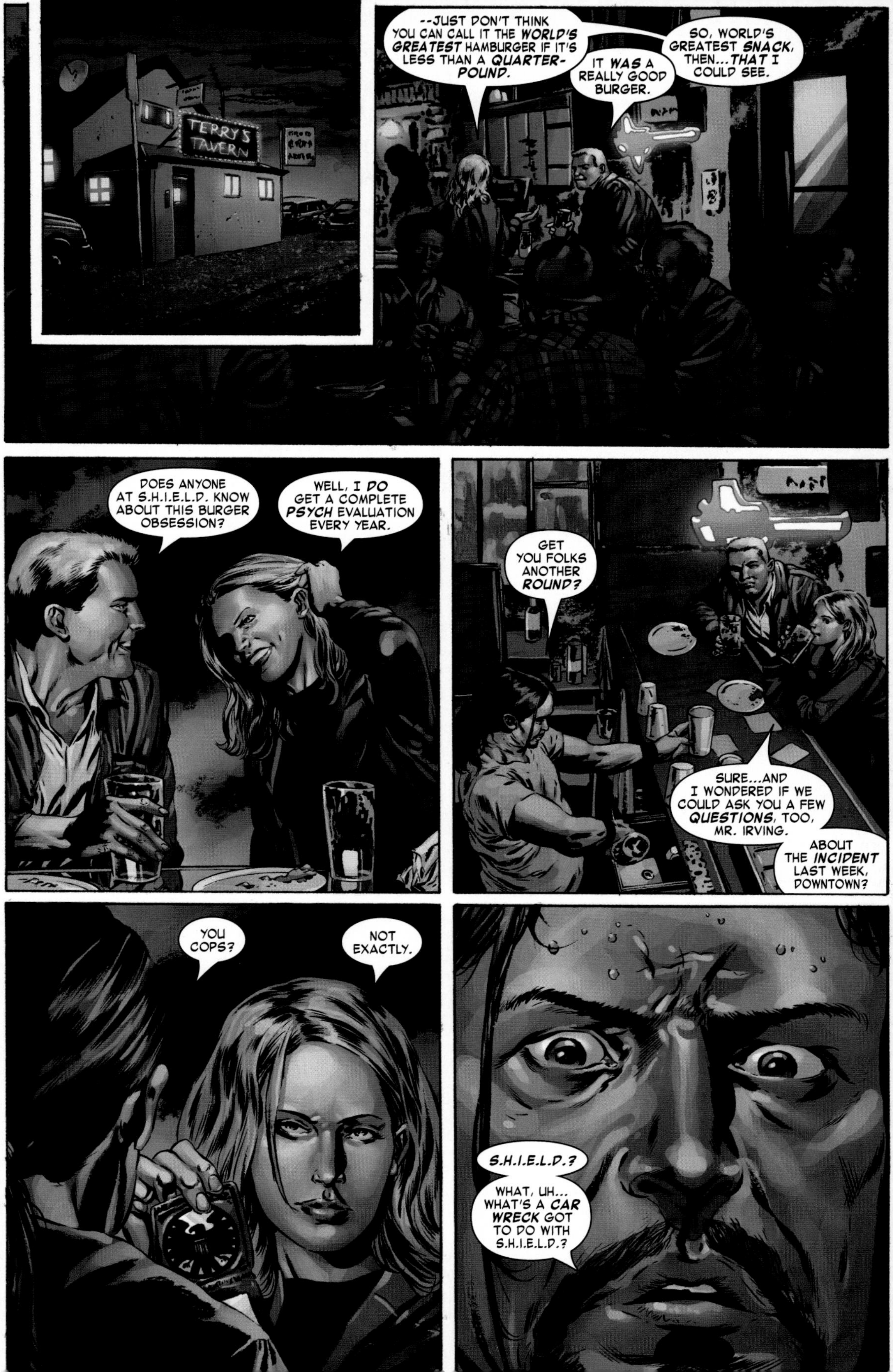
TERRY'S TAVERN
--JUST DON'T THINK YOU CAN CALL IT THE WORLD'S GREATEST HAMBURGER IF IT'S LESS THAN A QUARTER-POUND.
IT WAS A REALLY GOOD BURGER.
SO, WORLD'S GREATEST SNACK, THEN...THAT I COULD SEE.
DOES ANYONE AT S.H.I.E.L.D. KNOW ABOUT THIS BURGER OBSESSION?
WELL, I DO GET A COMPLETE PSYCH EVALUATION EVERY YEAR.
GET YOU FOLKS ANOTHER ROUND?
SURE...AND I WONDERED IF WE COULD ASK YOU A FEW QUESTIONS, TOO, MR. IRVING.
ABOUT THE INCIDENT LAST WEEK, DOWNTOWN?
YOU COPS?
NOT EXACTLY.
S.H.I.E.L.D.?
WHAT, UH... WHAT'S A CAR WRECK GOT TO DO WITH S.H.I.E.L.D.?

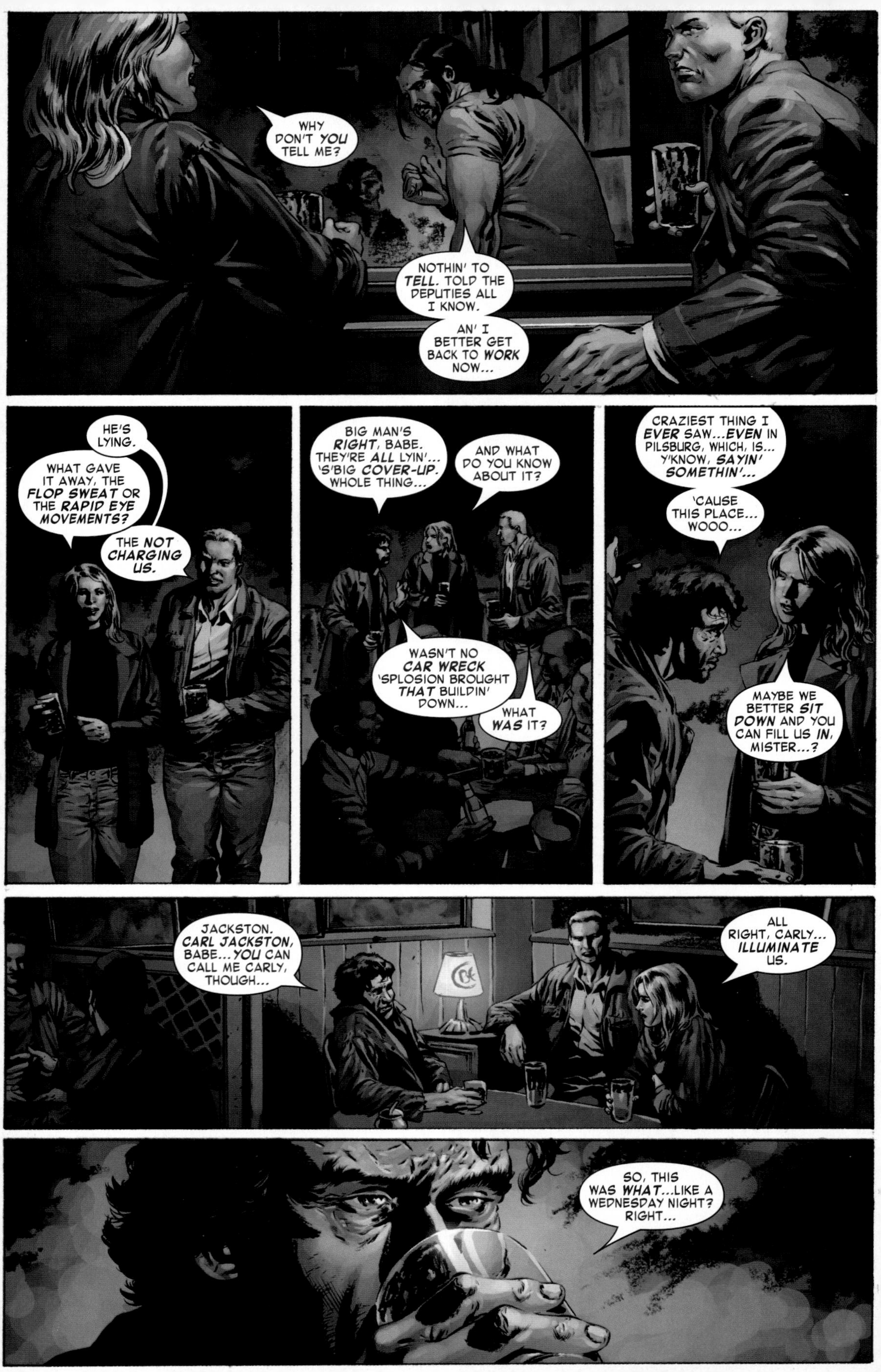
WHY DON'T YOU TELL ME?
NOTHIN' TO TELL. TOLD THE DEPUTIES ALL I KNOW.
AN' I BETTER GET BACK TO WORK NOW...
HE'S LYING.
WHAT GAVE IT AWAY, THE FLOP SWEAT OR THE RAPID EYE MOVEMENTS?
THE NOT CHARGING US.
BIG MAN'S RIGHT, BABE. THEY'RE ALL LYIN'... 'S'BIG COVER-UP. WHOLE THING...
AND WHAT DO YOU KNOW ABOUT IT?
WASN'T NO CAR WRECK 'SPLOSION BROUGHT THAT BUILDIN' DOWN...
WHAT WAS IT?
CRAZIEST THING I EVER SAW...EVEN IN PILSBURG, WHICH, IS... Y'KNOW, SAYIN' SOMETHIN'...
'CAUSE THIS PLACE... WOOO...
MAYBE WE BETTER SIT DOWN AND YOU CAN FILL US IN, MISTER...?
JACKSTON. CARL JACKSTON, BABE...YOU CAN CALL ME CARLY, THOUGH...
ALL RIGHT, CARLY... ILLUMINATE US.
SO, THIS WAS WHAT...LIKE A WEDNESDAY NIGHT? RIGHT...

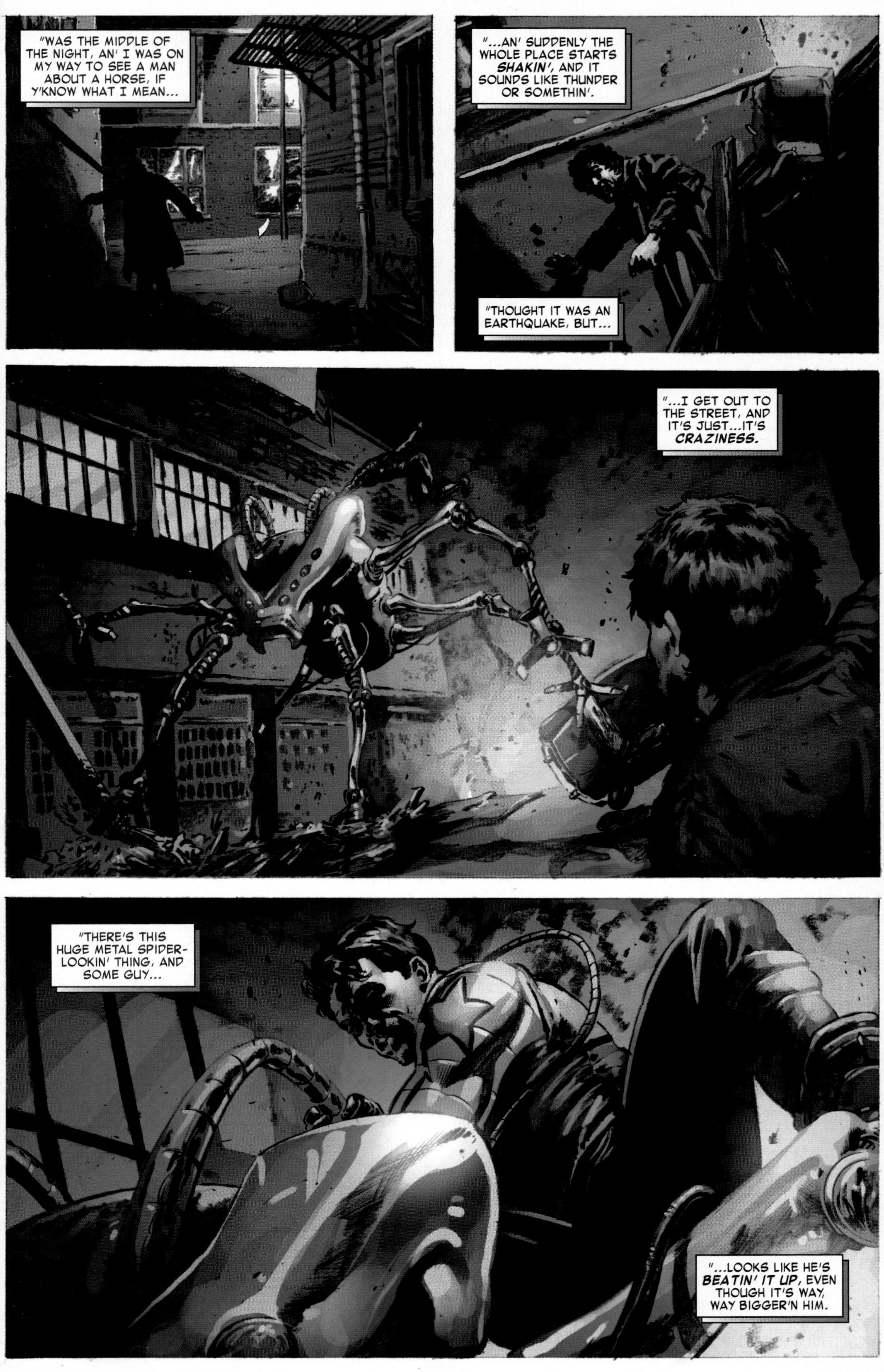
"WAS THE MIDDLE OF THE NIGHT, AN' I WAS ON MY WAY TO SEE A MAN ABOUT A HORSE, IF Y'KNOW WHAT I MEAN...
"...AN' SUDDENLY THE WHOLE PLACE STARTS SHAKIN', AND IT SOUNDS LIKE THUNDER OR SOMETHIN'.
"THOUGHT IT WAS AN EARTHQUAKE, BUT...
"...I GET OUT TO THE STREET, AND IT'S JUST...IT'S CRAZINESS.
"THERE'S THIS HUGE METAL SPIDER-LOOKIN' THING, AND SOME GUY...
"...LOOKS LIKE HE'S BEATIN' IT UP, EVEN THOUGH IT'S WAY, WAY BIGGER'N HIM.

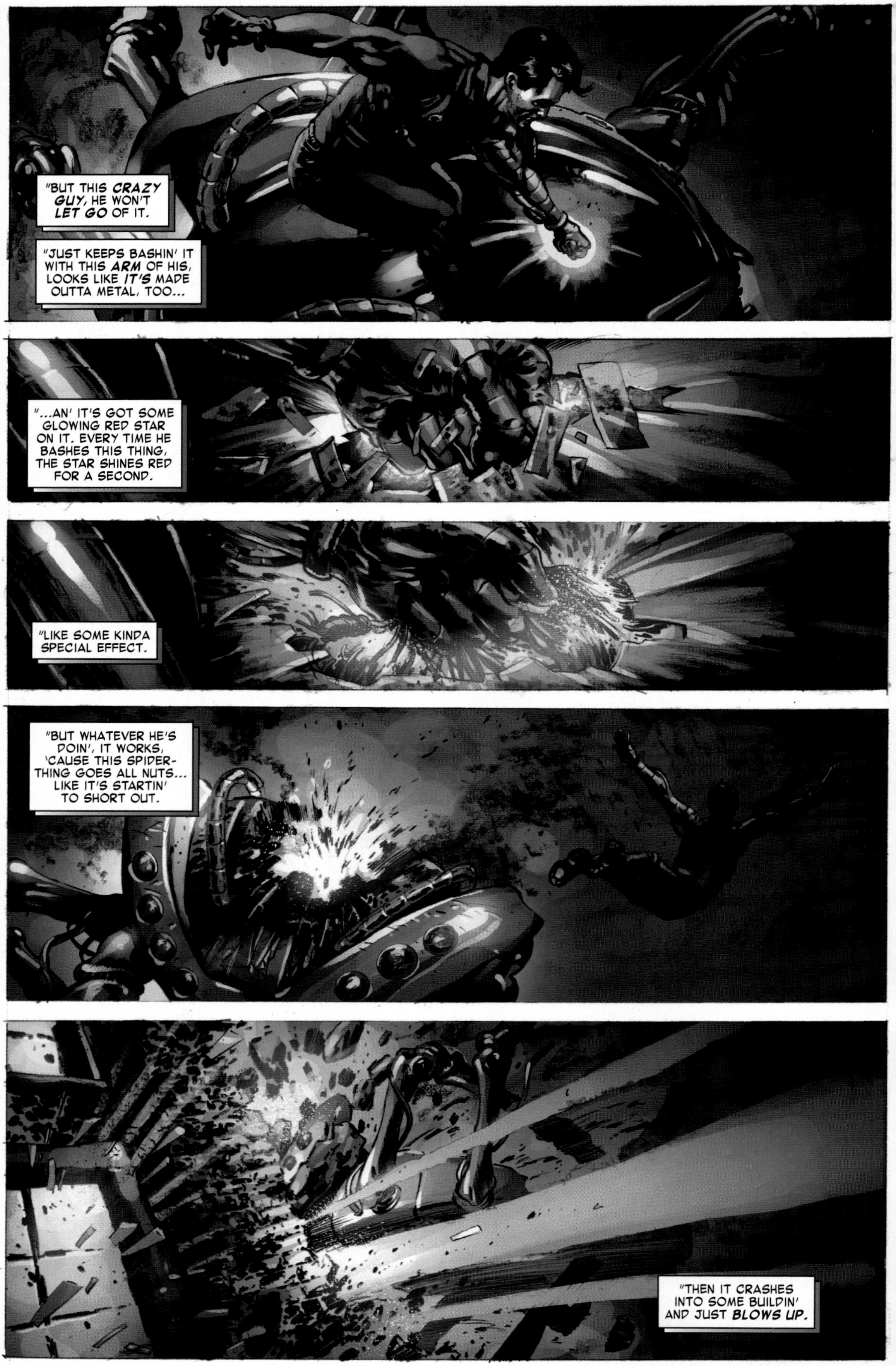
"BUT THIS ***CRAZY GUY,*** HE WON'T ***LET GO*** OF IT.
"JUST KEEPS BASHIN' IT WITH THIS ***ARM*** OF HIS, LOOKS LIKE ***IT'S*** MADE OUTTA METAL, TOO...
"...AN' IT'S GOT SOME GLOWING RED STAR ON IT. EVERY TIME HE BASHES THIS THING, THE STAR SHINES RED FOR A SECOND.
"LIKE SOME KINDA SPECIAL EFFECT.
"BUT WHATEVER HE'S DOIN', IT WORKS, 'CAUSE THIS SPIDER-THING GOES ALL NUTS... LIKE IT'S STARTIN' TO SHORT OUT.
"THEN IT CRASHES INTO SOME BUILDIN' AND JUST ***BLOWS UP.***

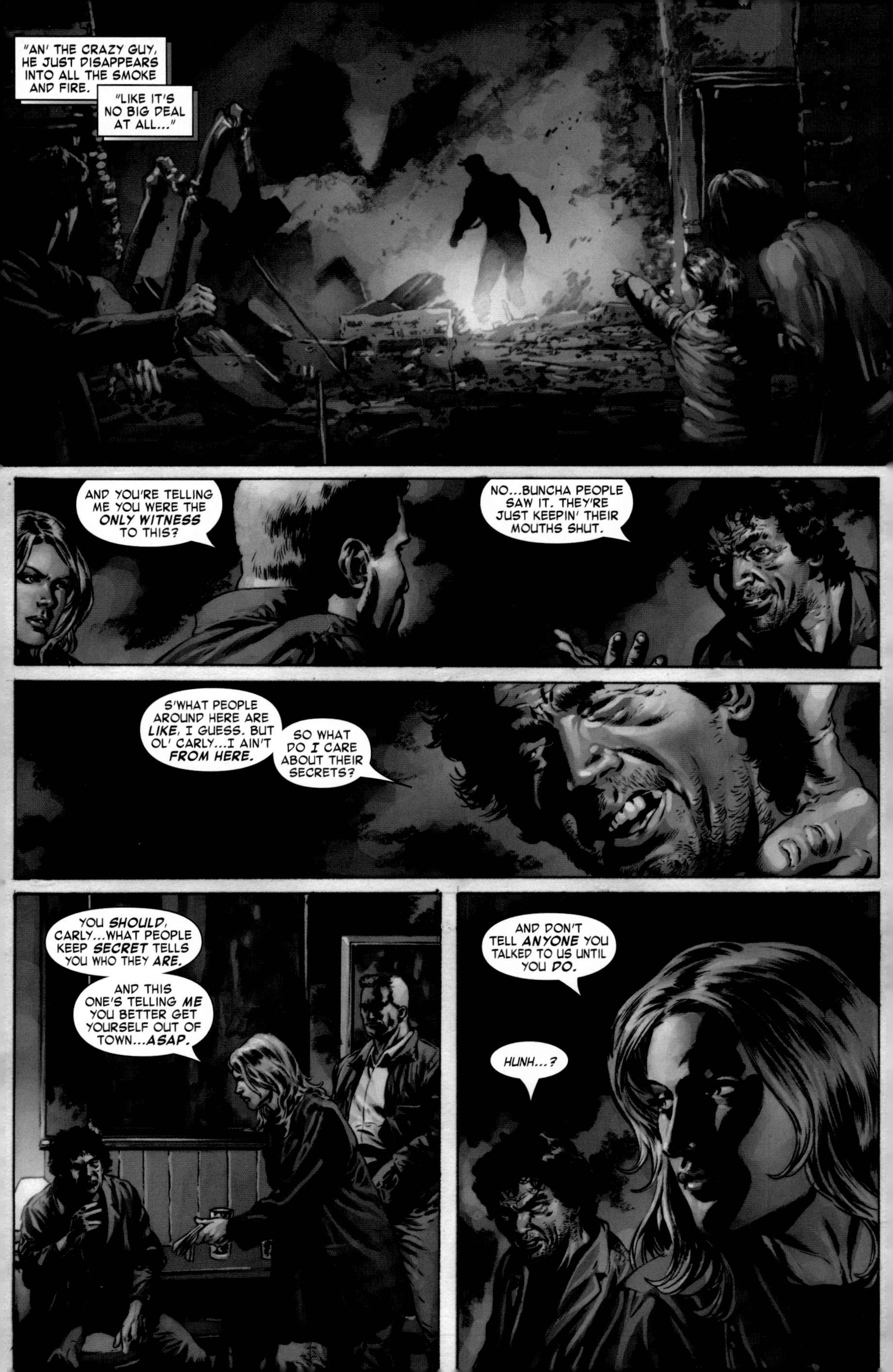
"AN' THE CRAZY GUY, HE JUST DISAPPEARS INTO ALL THE SMOKE AND FIRE.
"LIKE IT'S NO BIG DEAL AT ALL..."
AND YOU'RE TELLING ME YOU WERE THE ONLY WITNESS TO THIS?
NO...BUNCHA PEOPLE SAW IT. THEY'RE JUST KEEPIN' THEIR MOUTHS SHUT.
S'WHAT PEOPLE AROUND HERE ARE LIKE, I GUESS. BUT OL' CARLY...I AIN'T FROM HERE.
SO WHAT DO I CARE ABOUT THEIR SECRETS?
YOU SHOULD, CARLY...WHAT PEOPLE KEEP SECRET TELLS YOU WHO THEY ARE.
AND THIS ONE'S TELLING ME YOU BETTER GET YOURSELF OUT OF TOWN...ASAP.
AND DON'T TELL ANYONE YOU TALKED TO US UNTIL YOU DO.
HUNH...?

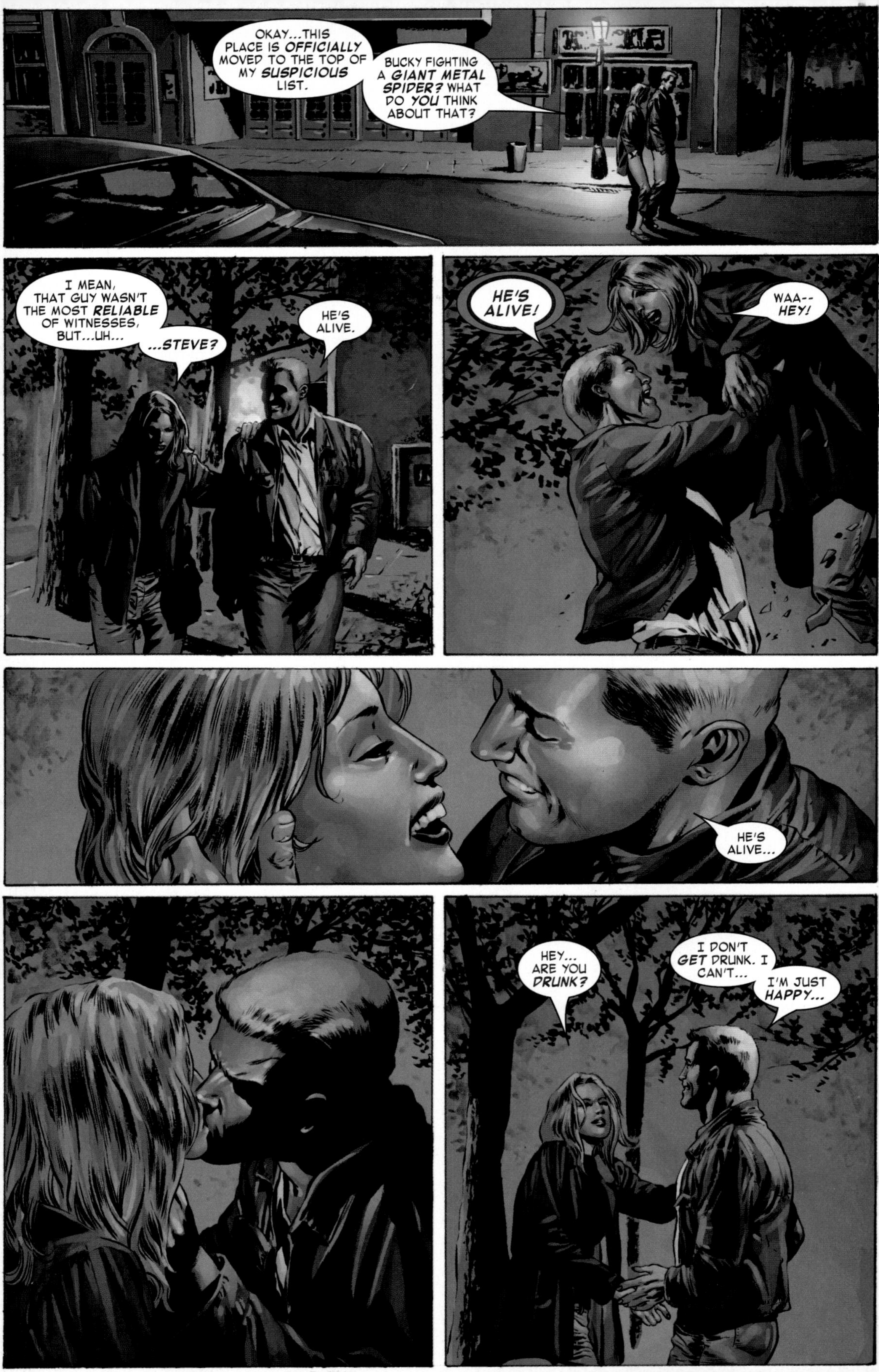
OKAY...THIS PLACE IS OFFICIALLY MOVED TO THE TOP OF MY SUSPICIOUS LIST.
BUCKY FIGHTING A GIANT METAL SPIDER? WHAT DO YOU THINK ABOUT THAT?
I MEAN, THAT GUY WASN'T THE MOST RELIABLE OF WITNESSES, BUT...UH...
...STEVE?
HE'S ALIVE.
HE'S ALIVE!
WAA-- HEY!
HE'S ALIVE...
HEY... ARE YOU DRUNK?
I DON'T GET DRUNK. I CAN'T...
I'M JUST HAPPY...

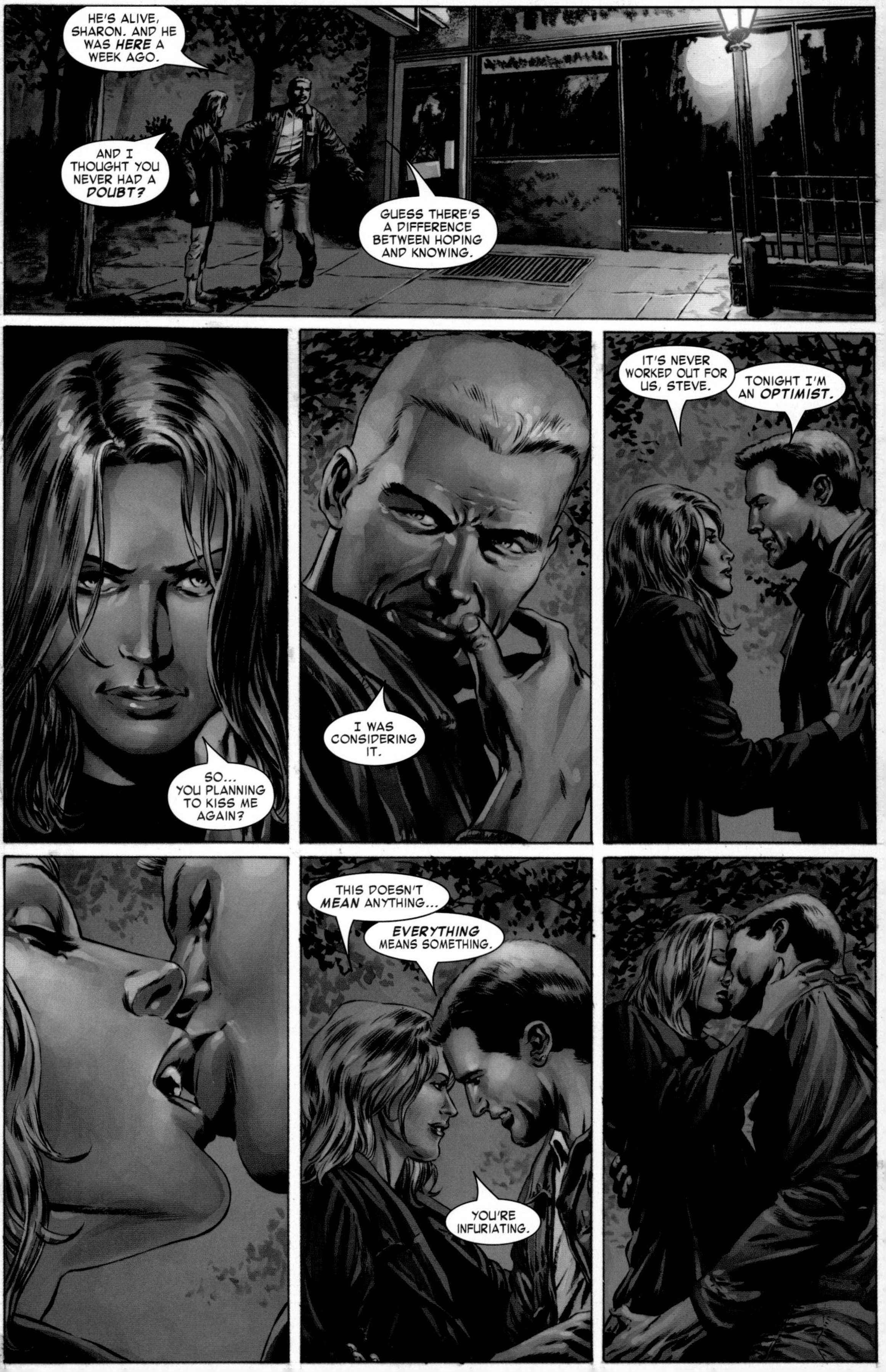
HE'S ALIVE, SHARON. AND HE WAS HERE A WEEK AGO.
AND I THOUGHT YOU NEVER HAD A DOUBT?
GUESS THERE'S A DIFFERENCE BETWEEN HOPING AND KNOWING.
SO... YOU PLANNING TO KISS ME AGAIN?
I WAS CONSIDERING IT.
IT'S NEVER WORKED OUT FOR US, STEVE.
TONIGHT I'M AN OPTIMIST.
THIS DOESN'T MEAN ANYTHING...
EVERYTHING MEANS SOMETHING.
YOU'RE INFURIATING.

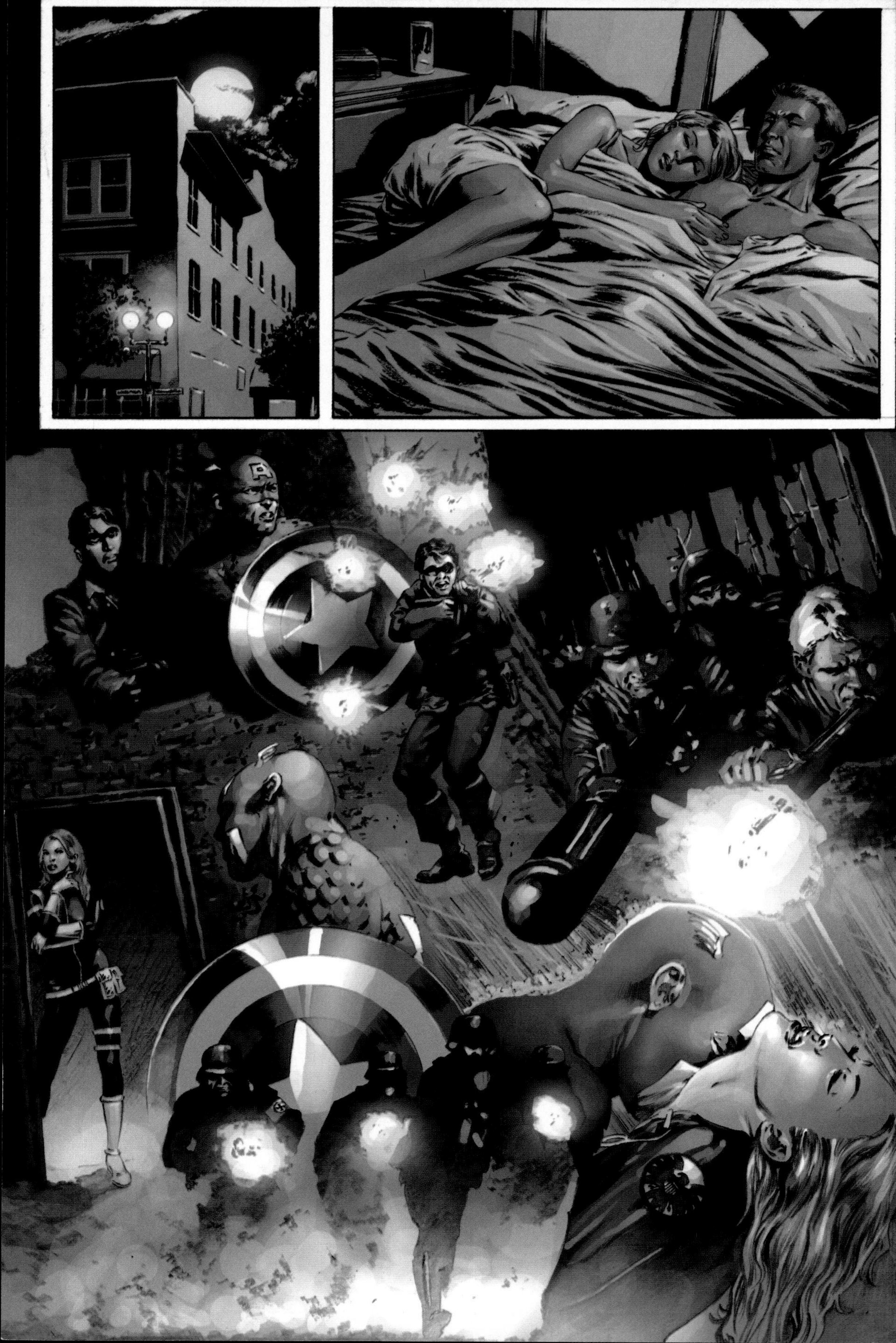

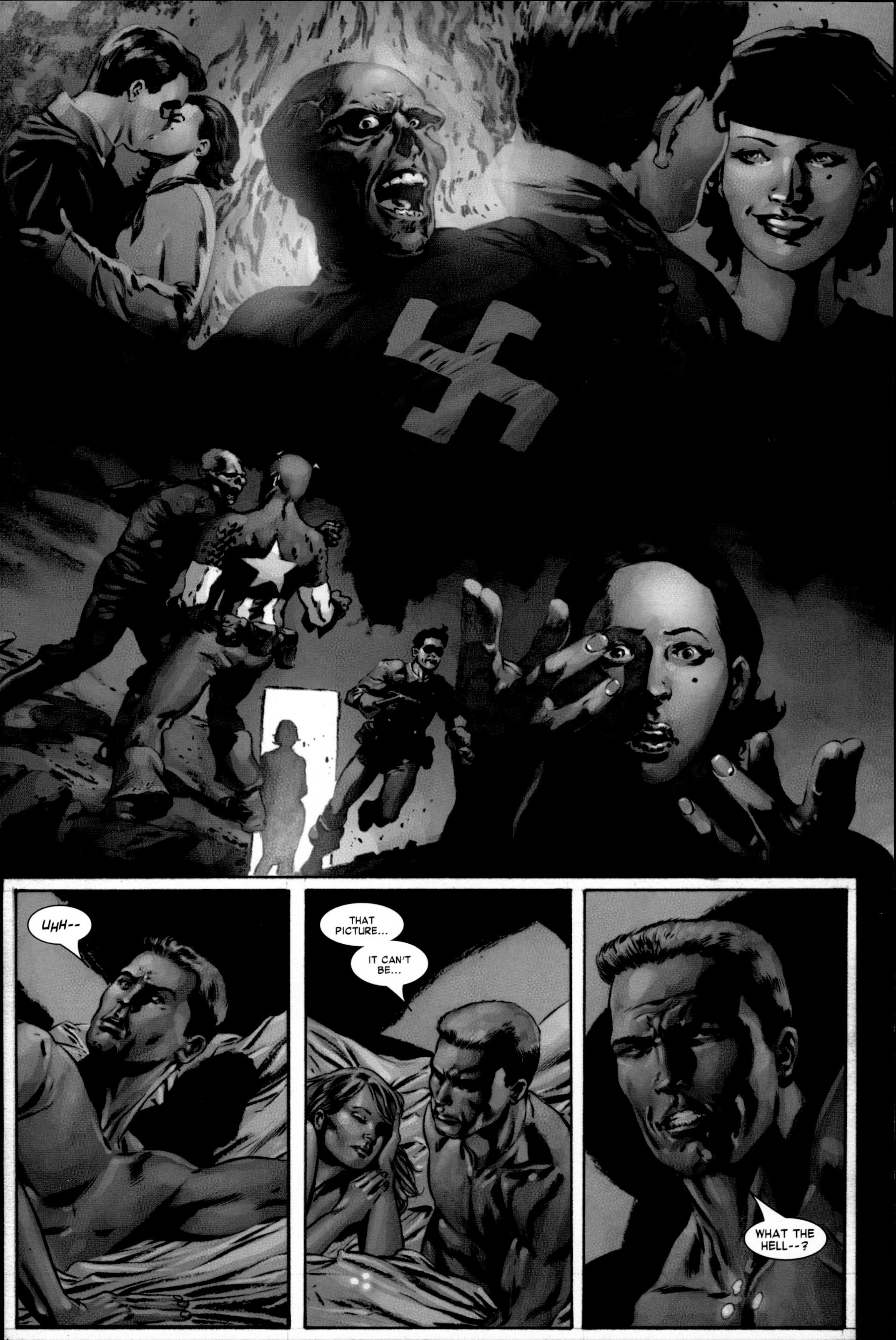
UHH--
THAT PICTURE...
IT CAN'T BE...
WHAT THE HELL--?

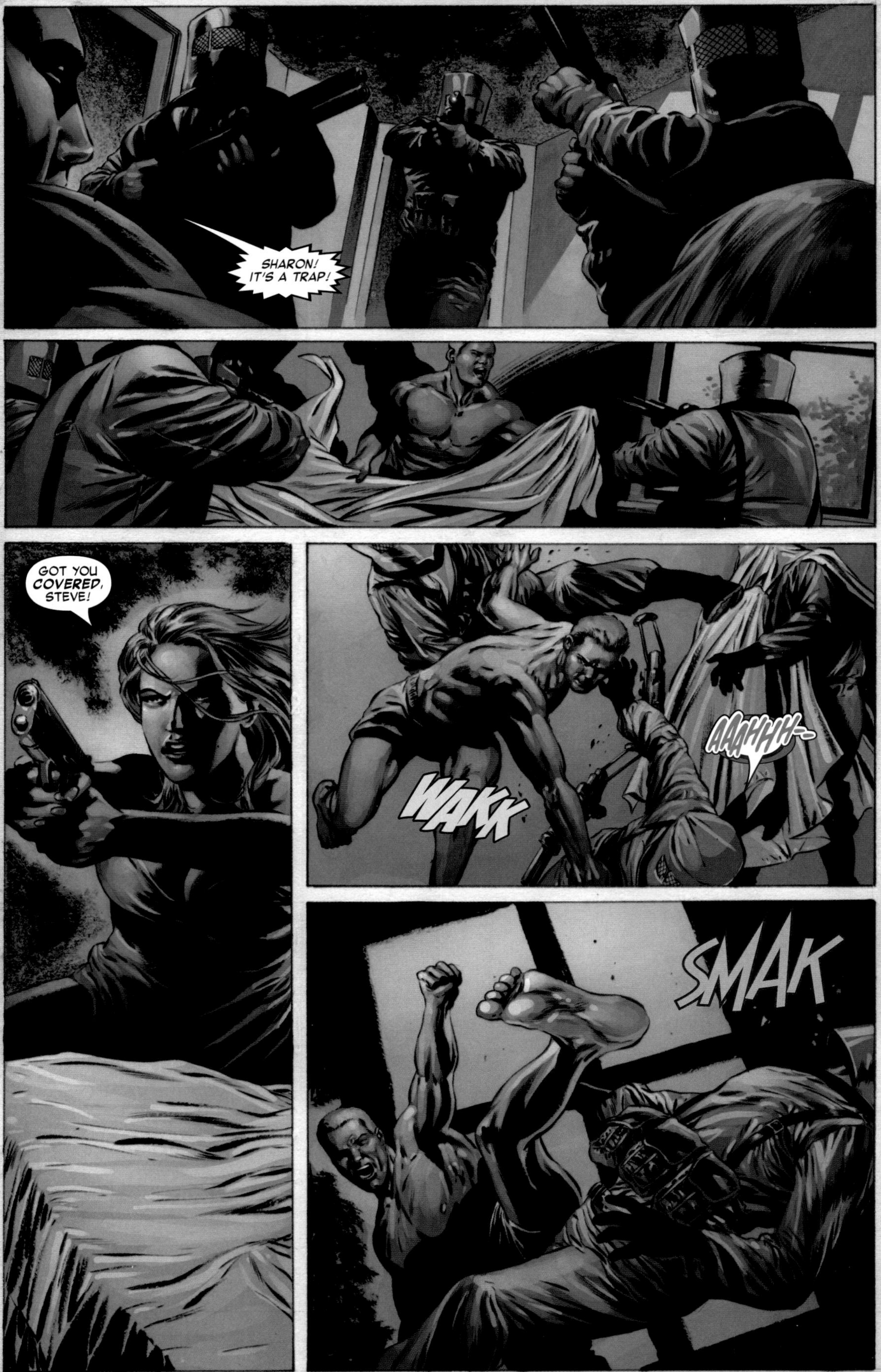
SHARON! IT'S A TRAP!
GOT YOU COVERED, STEVE!
WAKK
AAAHHH--
SMAK

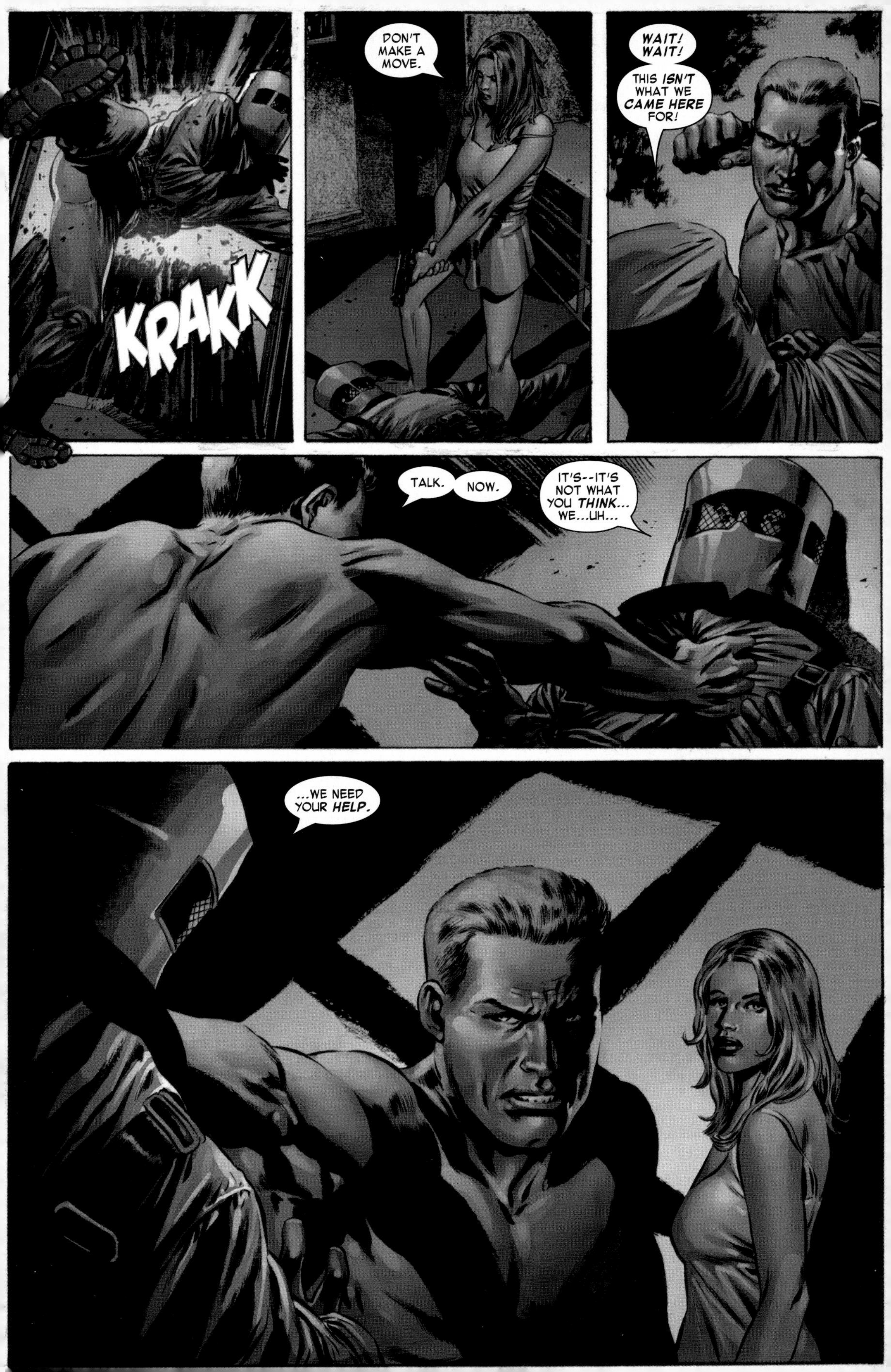
KRAKK
DON'T MAKE A MOVE.
WAIT! WAIT!
THIS ISN'T WHAT WE CAME HERE FOR!
TALK.
NOW.
IT'S--IT'S NOT WHAT YOU THINK... WE...UH...
...WE NEED YOUR HELP.

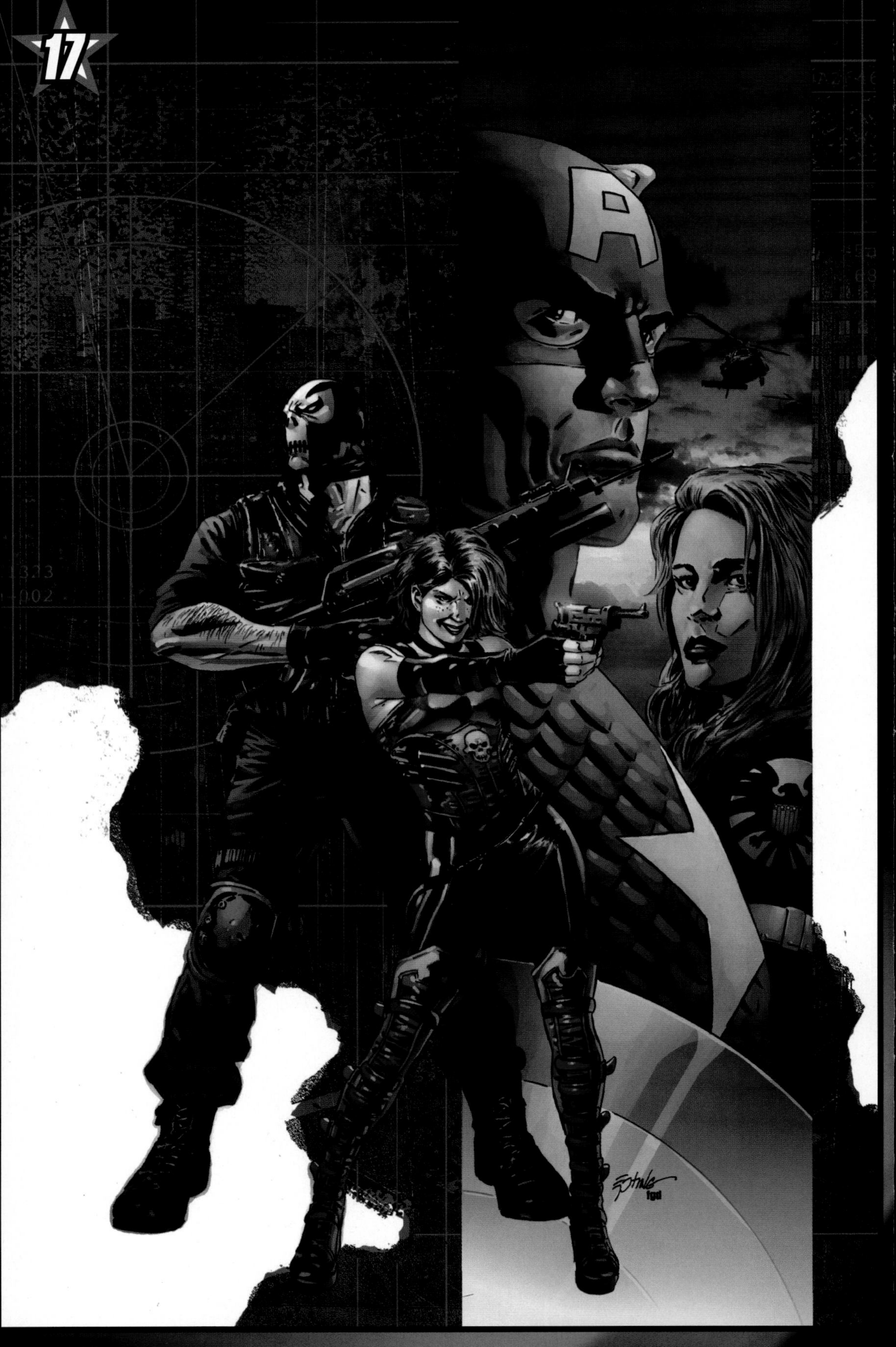
17

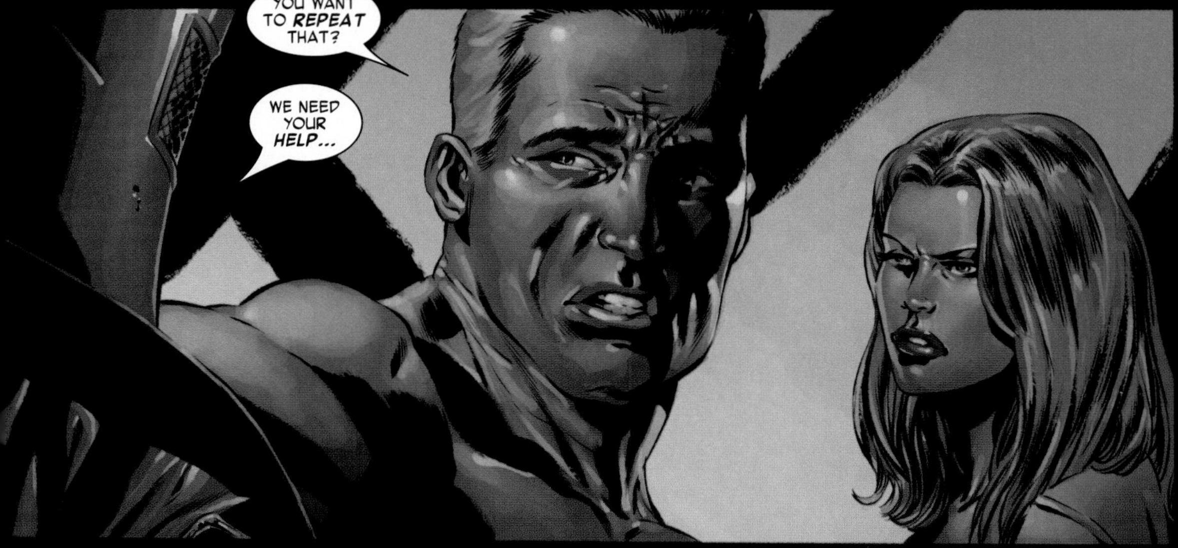
YOU WANT TO REPEAT THAT?
WE NEED YOUR HELP...

COLLISION COURSES PART 2 OF 2

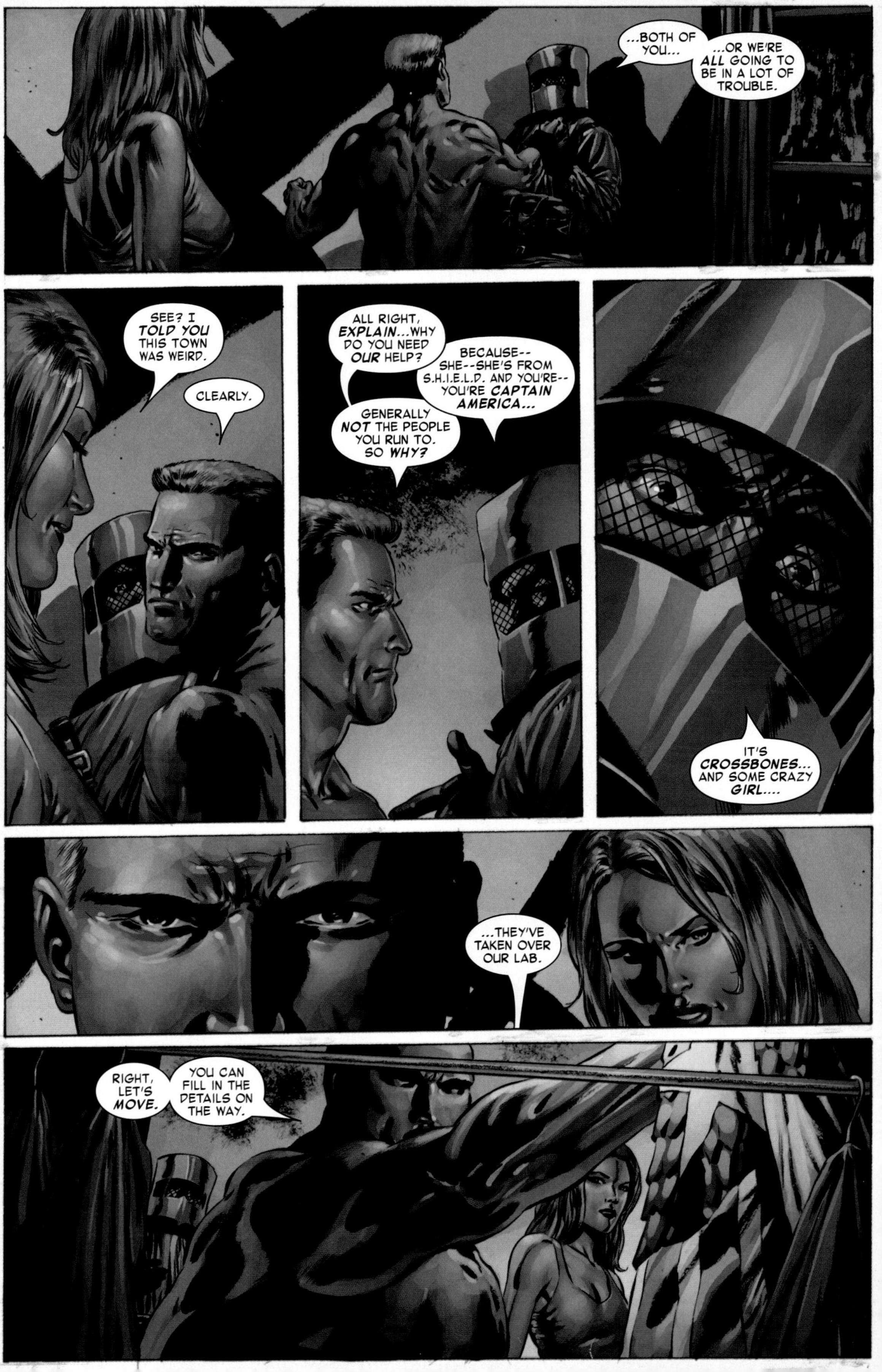
...BOTH OF YOU...
...OR WE'RE ALL GOING TO BE IN A LOT OF TROUBLE.
SEE? I TOLD YOU THIS TOWN WAS WEIRD.
CLEARLY.
ALL RIGHT, EXPLAIN...WHY DO YOU NEED OUR HELP?
BECAUSE-- SHE--SHE'S FROM S.H.I.E.L.D. AND YOU'RE-- YOU'RE CAPTAIN AMERICA...
GENERALLY NOT THE PEOPLE YOU RUN TO. SO WHY?
IT'S CROSSBONES... AND SOME CRAZY GIRL....
...THEY'VE TAKEN OVER OUR LAB.
RIGHT, LET'S MOVE.
YOU CAN FILL IN THE DETAILS ON THE WAY.

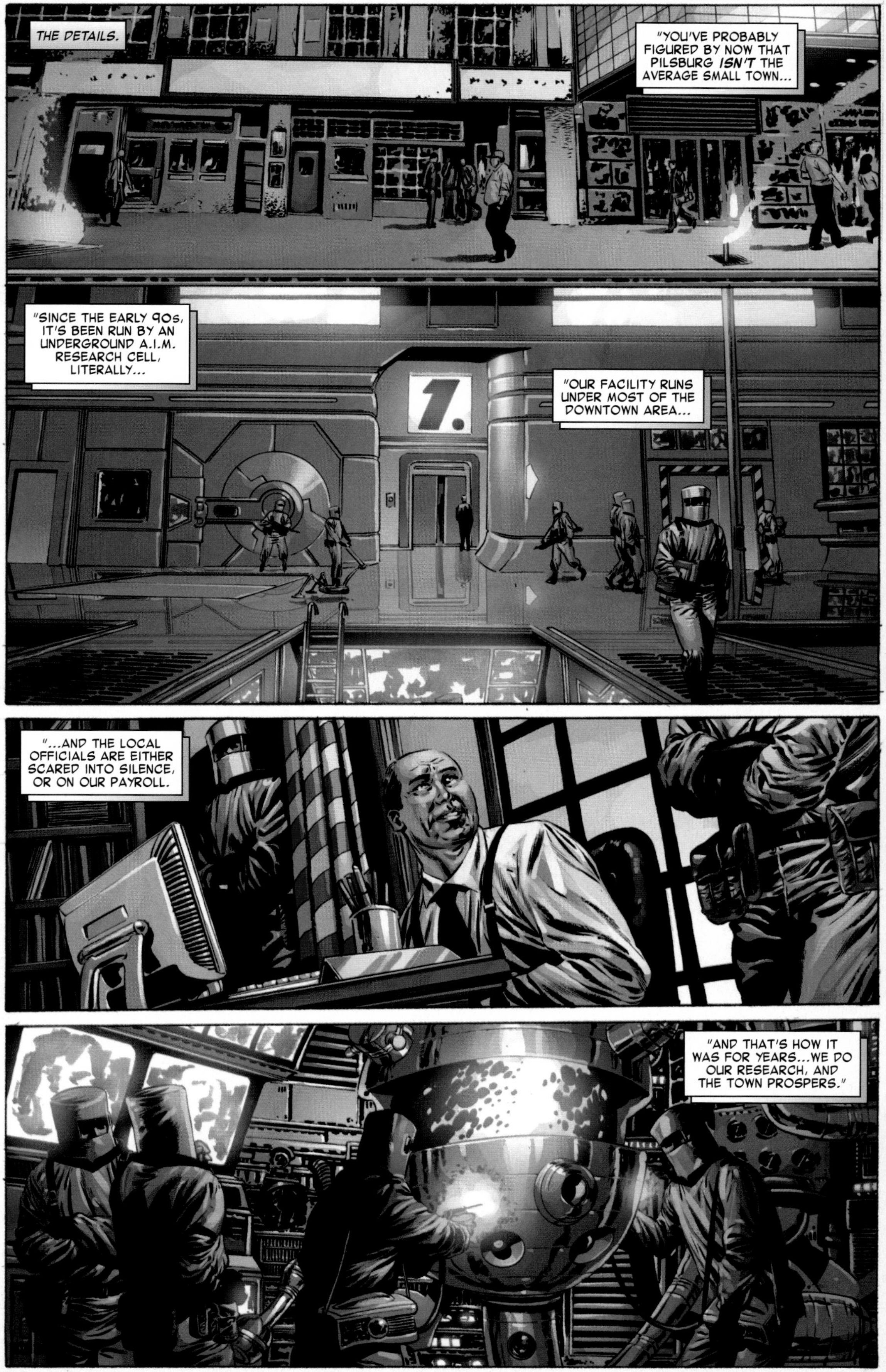
THE DETAILS.
"YOU'VE PROBABLY FIGURED BY NOW THAT PILSBURG ISN'T THE AVERAGE SMALL TOWN...
"SINCE THE EARLY 90s, IT'S BEEN RUN BY AN UNDERGROUND A.I.M. RESEARCH CELL, LITERALLY...
1.
"OUR FACILITY RUNS UNDER MOST OF THE DOWNTOWN AREA...
"...AND THE LOCAL OFFICIALS ARE EITHER SCARED INTO SILENCE, OR ON OUR PAYROLL.
"AND THAT'S HOW IT WAS FOR YEARS...WE DO OUR RESEARCH, AND THE TOWN PROSPERS."

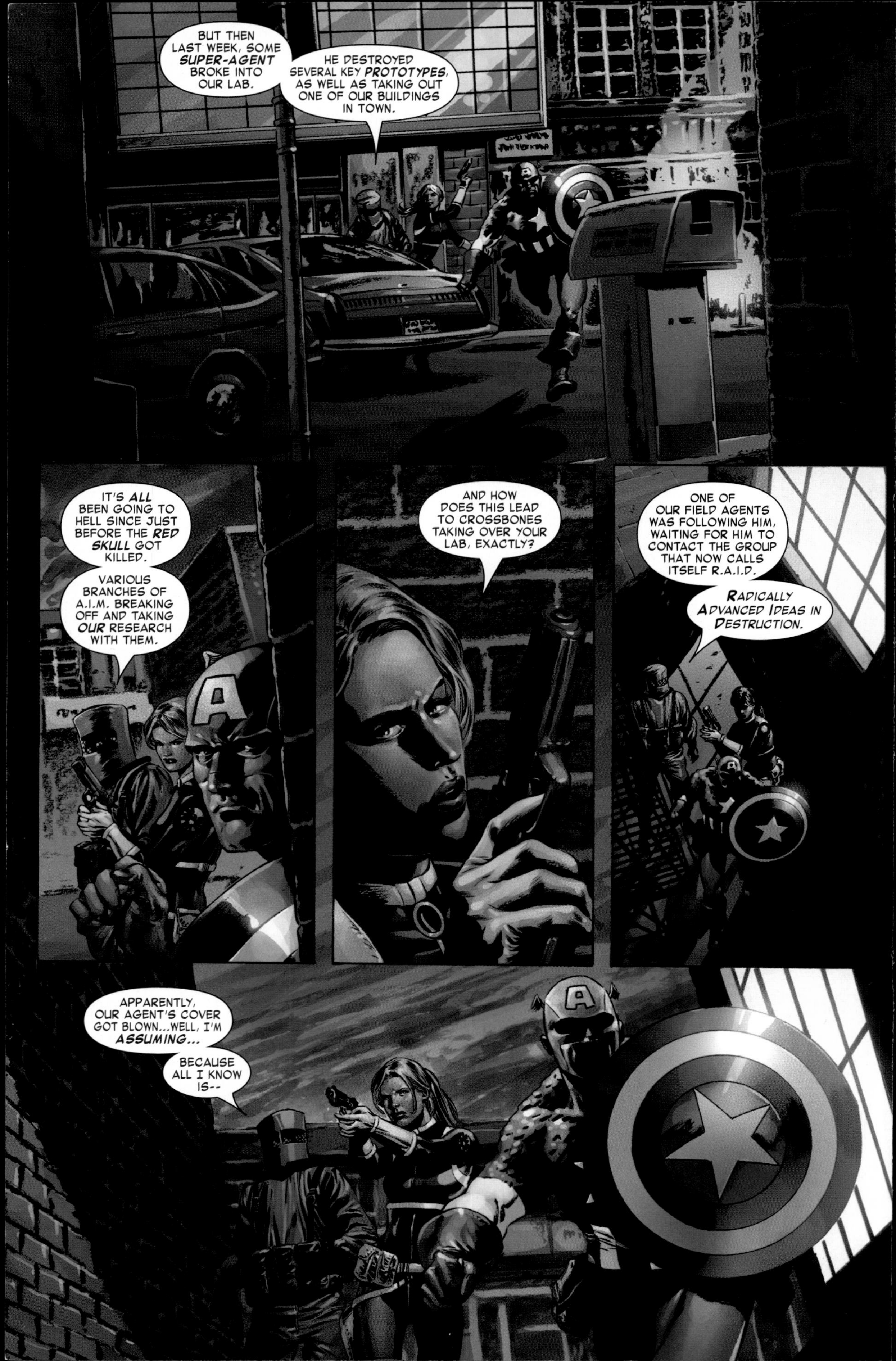
BUT THEN LAST WEEK, SOME SUPER-AGENT BROKE INTO OUR LAB.
HE DESTROYED SEVERAL KEY PROTOTYPES, AS WELL AS TAKING OUT ONE OF OUR BUILDINGS IN TOWN.
IT'S ALL BEEN GOING TO HELL SINCE JUST BEFORE THE RED SKULL GOT KILLED.
VARIOUS BRANCHES OF A.I.M. BREAKING OFF AND TAKING OUR RESEARCH WITH THEM.
AND HOW DOES THIS LEAD TO CROSSBONES TAKING OVER YOUR LAB, EXACTLY?
ONE OF OUR FIELD AGENTS WAS FOLLOWING HIM, WAITING FOR HIM TO CONTACT THE GROUP THAT NOW CALLS ITSELF R.A.I.D.
RADICALLY ADVANCED IDEAS IN DESTRUCTION.
APPARENTLY, OUR AGENT'S COVER GOT BLOWN...WELL, I'M ASSUMING...
BECAUSE ALL I KNOW IS--

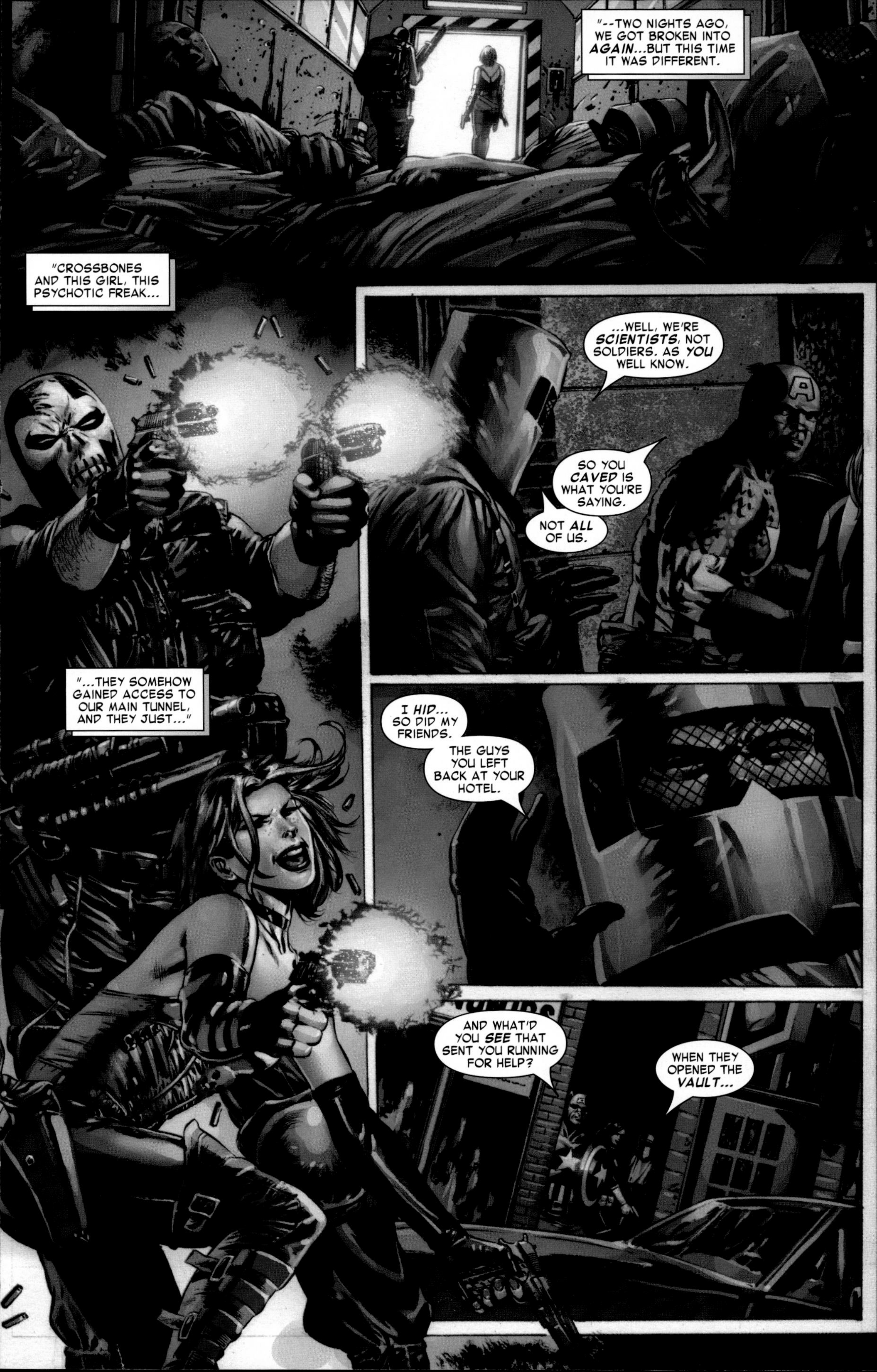
"--TWO NIGHTS AGO, WE GOT BROKEN INTO AGAIN...BUT THIS TIME IT WAS DIFFERENT.
"CROSSBONES AND THIS GIRL, THIS PSYCHOTIC FREAK...
"...THEY SOMEHOW GAINED ACCESS TO OUR MAIN TUNNEL, AND THEY JUST..."
...WELL, WE'RE SCIENTISTS, NOT SOLDIERS. AS YOU WELL KNOW.
SO YOU CAVED IS WHAT YOU'RE SAYING.
NOT ALL OF US.
I HID... SO DID MY FRIENDS.
THE GUYS YOU LEFT BACK AT YOUR HOTEL.
AND WHAT'D YOU SEE THAT SENT YOU RUNNING FOR HELP?
WHEN THEY OPENED THE VAULT...

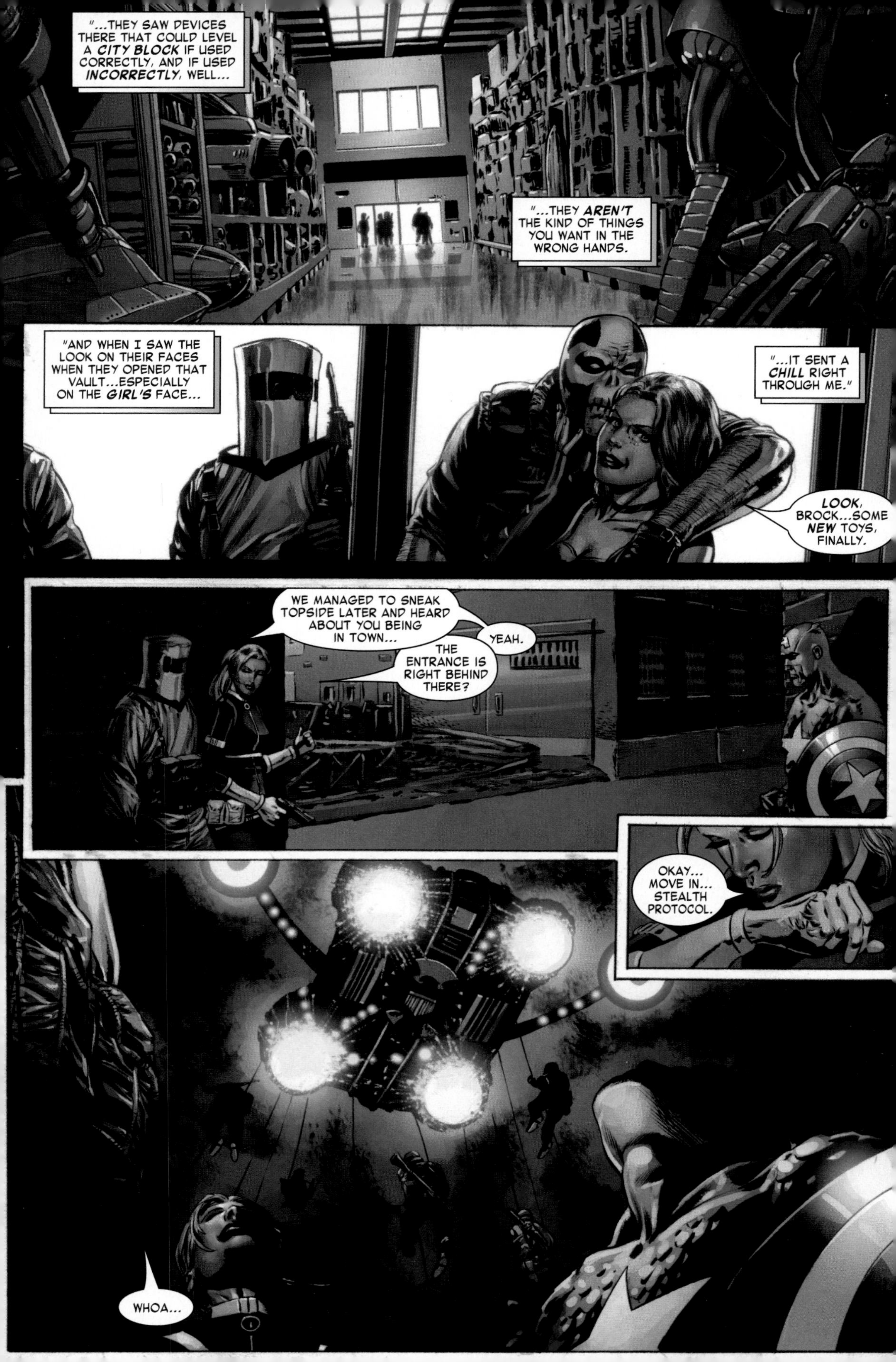
"...THEY SAW DEVICES THERE THAT COULD LEVEL A CITY BLOCK IF USED CORRECTLY, AND IF USED INCORRECTLY, WELL...
"...THEY AREN'T THE KIND OF THINGS YOU WANT IN THE WRONG HANDS.
"AND WHEN I SAW THE LOOK ON THEIR FACES WHEN THEY OPENED THAT VAULT...ESPECIALLY ON THE GIRL'S FACE...
"...IT SENT A CHILL RIGHT THROUGH ME."
LOOK, BROCK...SOME NEW TOYS, FINALLY.
WE MANAGED TO SNEAK TOPSIDE LATER AND HEARD ABOUT YOU BEING IN TOWN...
YEAH.
THE ENTRANCE IS RIGHT BEHIND THERE?
OKAY... MOVE IN... STEALTH PROTOCOL.
WHOA...

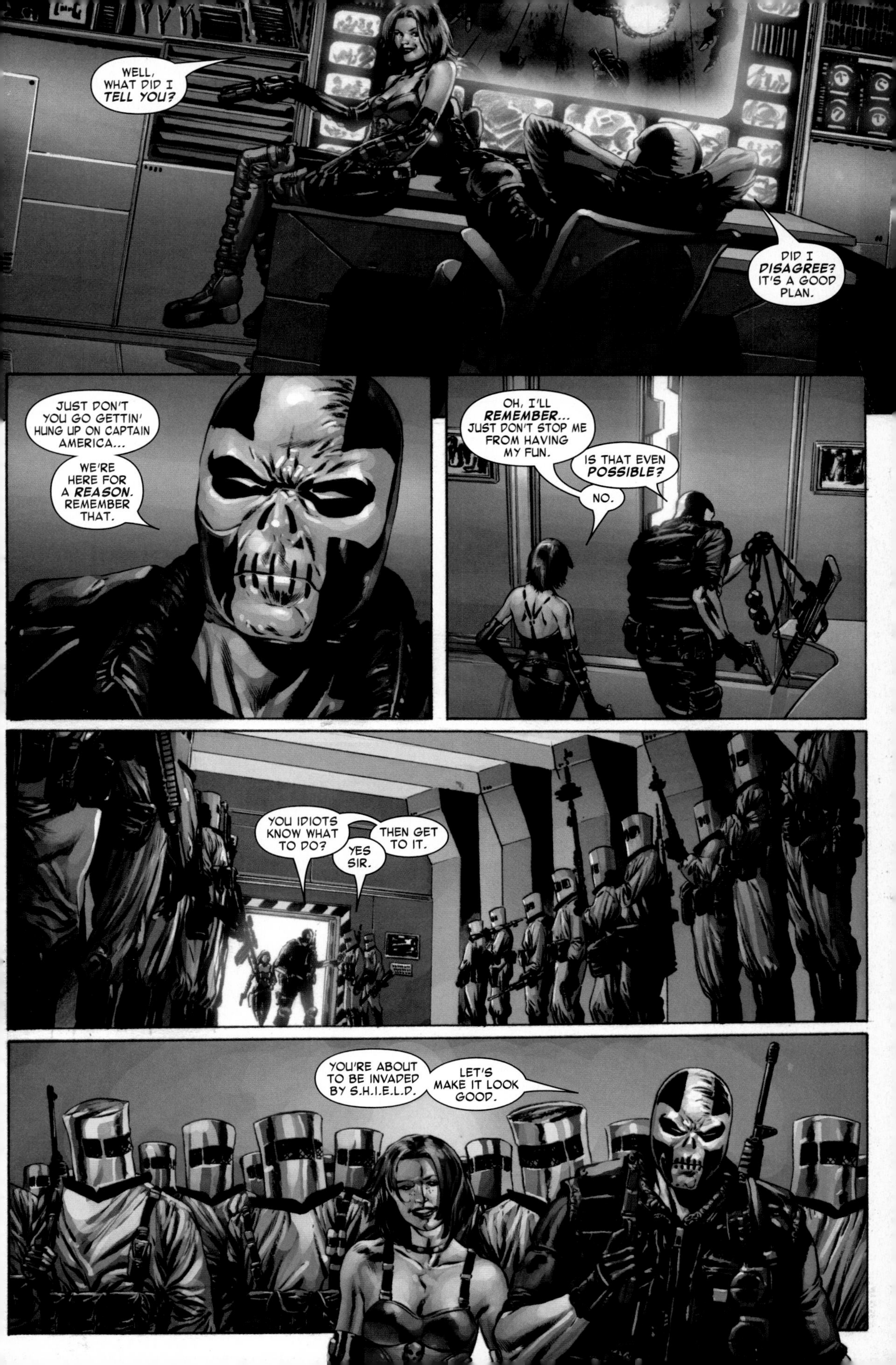
WELL, WHAT DID I TELL YOU?
DID I DISAGREE? IT'S A GOOD PLAN.
JUST DON'T YOU GO GETTIN' HUNG UP ON CAPTAIN AMERICA...
WE'RE HERE FOR A REASON. REMEMBER THAT.
OH, I'LL REMEMBER... JUST DON'T STOP ME FROM HAVING MY FUN.
IS THAT EVEN POSSIBLE?
NO.
YOU IDIOTS KNOW WHAT TO DO?
YES SIR.
THEN GET TO IT.
YOU'RE ABOUT TO BE INVADED BY S.H.I.E.L.D.
LET'S MAKE IT LOOK GOOD.

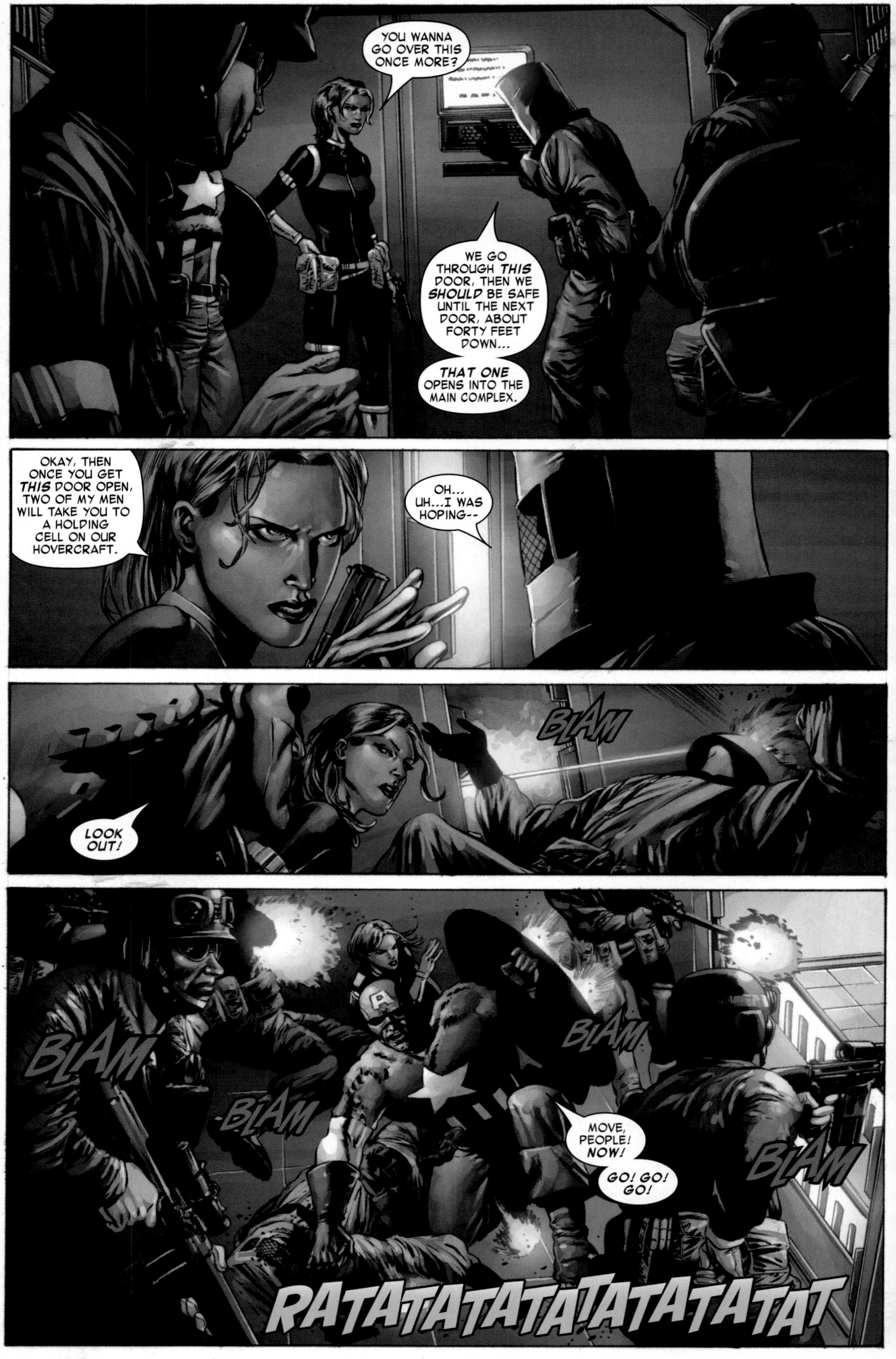
YOU WANNA GO OVER THIS ONCE MORE?
WE GO THROUGH THIS DOOR, THEN WE SHOULD BE SAFE UNTIL THE NEXT DOOR, ABOUT FORTY FEET DOWN...
THAT ONE OPENS INTO THE MAIN COMPLEX.
OKAY, THEN ONCE YOU GET THIS DOOR OPEN, TWO OF MY MEN WILL TAKE YOU TO A HOLDING CELL ON OUR HOVERCRAFT.
OH... UH...I WAS HOPING--
BLAM
LOOK OUT!
BLAM
BLAM
BLAM
MOVE, PEOPLE! NOW!
GO! GO! GO!
BLAM
BLAM
RATATATATATATATATATATAT

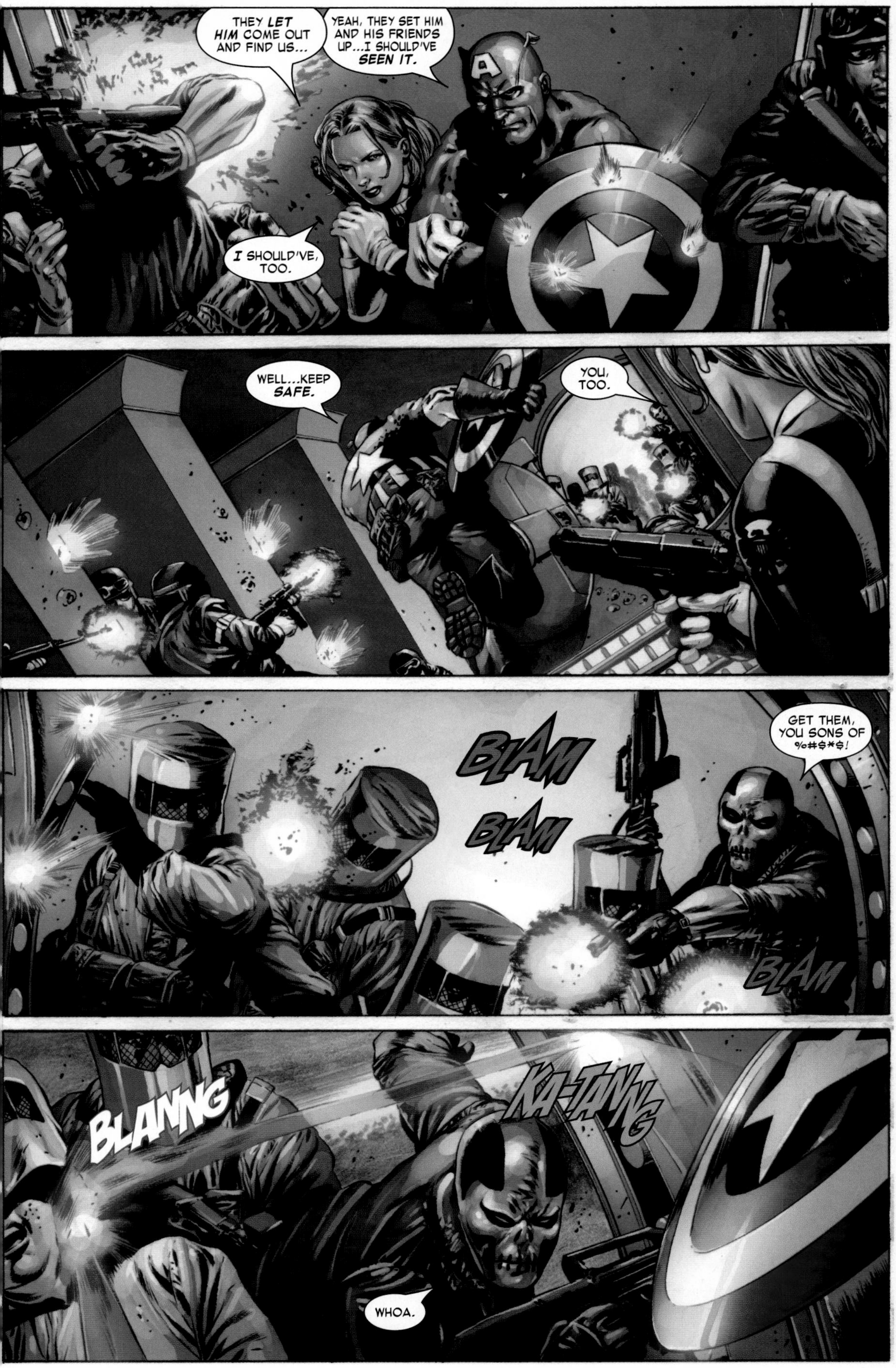
THEY LET HIM COME OUT AND FIND US...
YEAH, THEY SET HIM AND HIS FRIENDS UP...I SHOULD'VE SEEN IT.
I SHOULD'VE, TOO.
WELL...KEEP SAFE.
YOU, TOO.
BLAM
BLAM
GET THEM, YOU SONS OF %#$*$!
BLAM
BLANNG
KA-TANNG
WHOA.

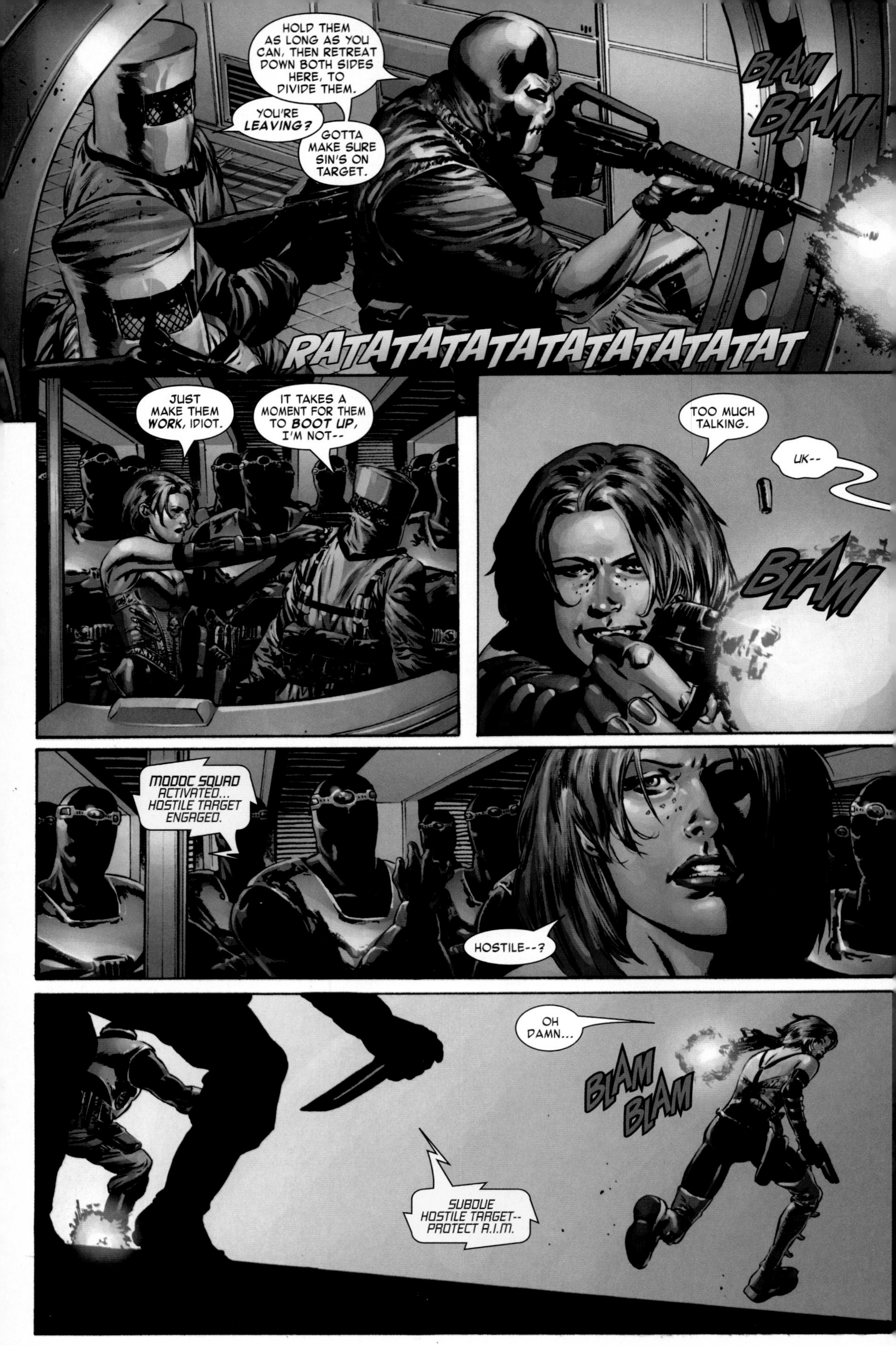
HOLD THEM AS LONG AS YOU CAN, THEN RETREAT DOWN BOTH SIDES HERE, TO DIVIDE THEM.
YOU'RE LEAVING?
GOTTA MAKE SURE SIN'S ON TARGET.
BLAM
BLAM
RATATATATATATATATATATATAT
JUST MAKE THEM WORK, IDIOT.
IT TAKES A MOMENT FOR THEM TO BOOT UP, I'M NOT--
TOO MUCH TALKING.
UK--
BLAM
MODOC SQUAD ACTIVATED... HOSTILE TARGET ENGAGED.
HOSTILE--?
OH DAMN...
BLAM
BLAM
SUBDUE HOSTILE TARGET-- PROTECT A.I.M.

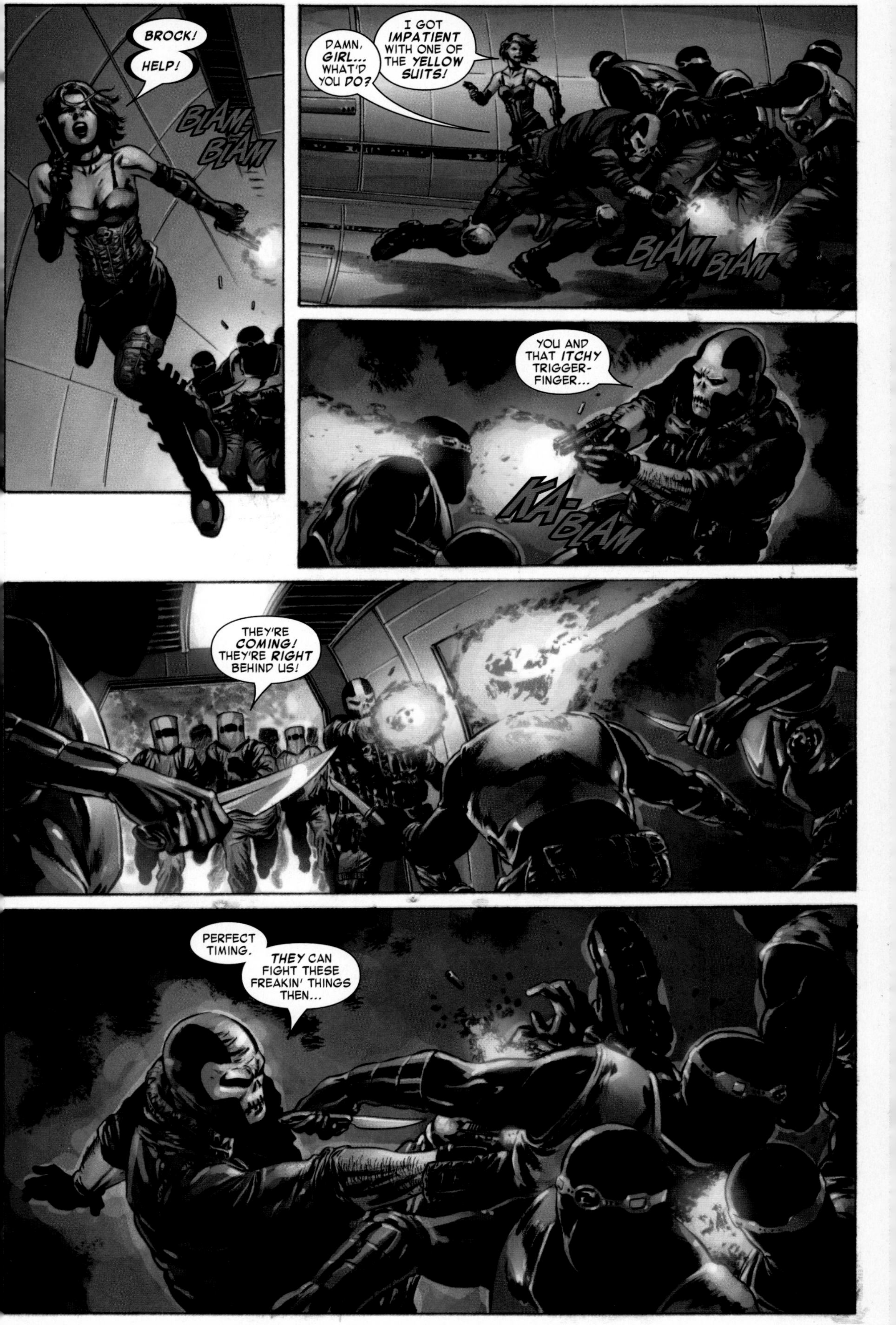
BROCK!
HELP!
BLAM-BLAM
I GOT IMPATIENT WITH ONE OF THE YELLOW SUITS!
DAMN, GIRL... WHAT'D YOU DO?
BLAM BLAM
YOU AND THAT ITCHY TRIGGER-FINGER...
KA-BLAM
THEY'RE COMING! THEY'RE RIGHT BEHIND US!
PERFECT TIMING. THEY CAN FIGHT THESE FREAKIN' THINGS THEN...

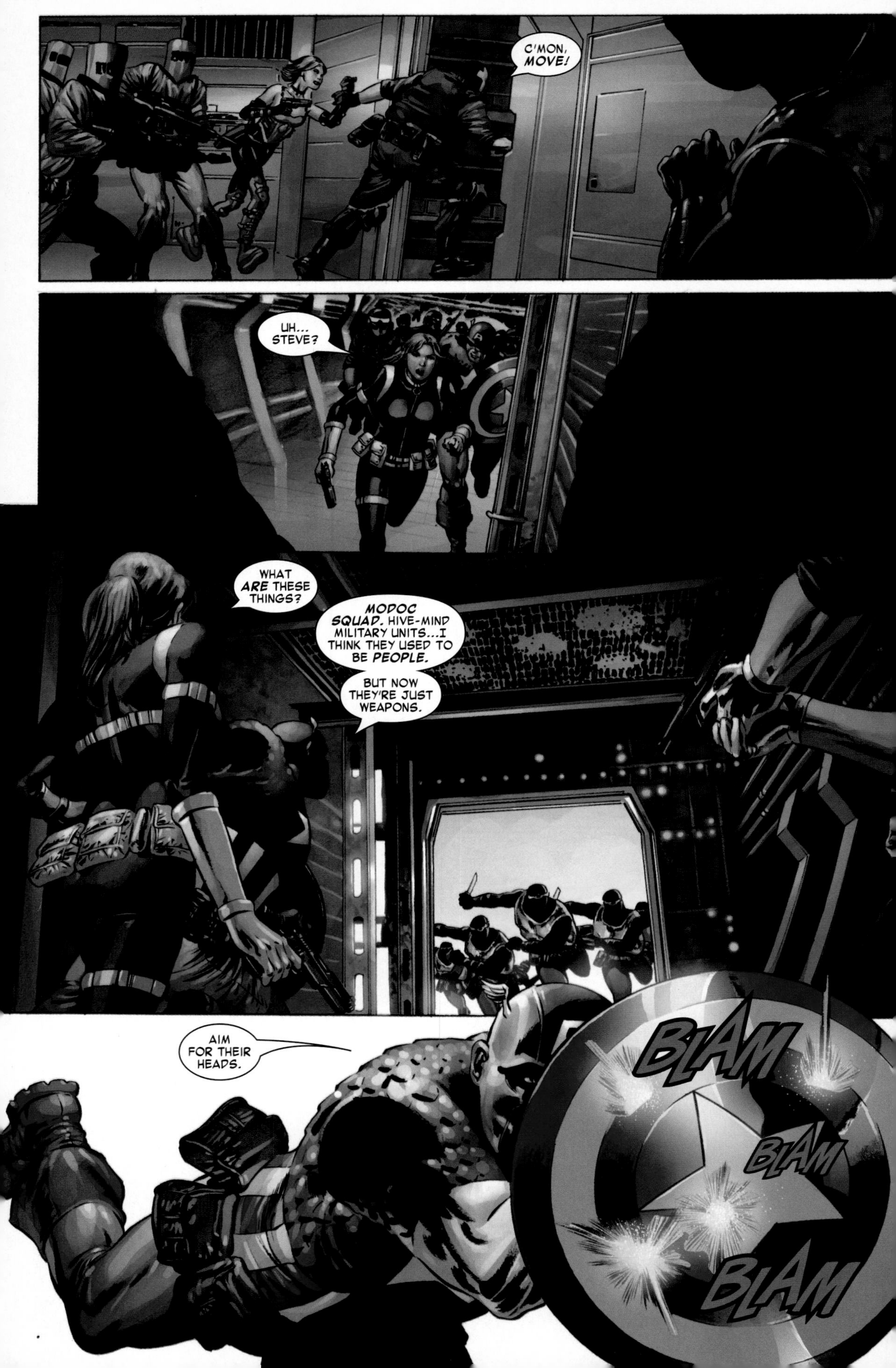
C'MON, MOVE!
UH... STEVE?
WHAT ARE THESE THINGS?
MODOC SQUAD. HIVE-MIND MILITARY UNITS...I THINK THEY USED TO BE PEOPLE.
BUT NOW THEY'RE JUST WEAPONS.
AIM FOR THEIR HEADS.
BLAM
BLAM
BLAM

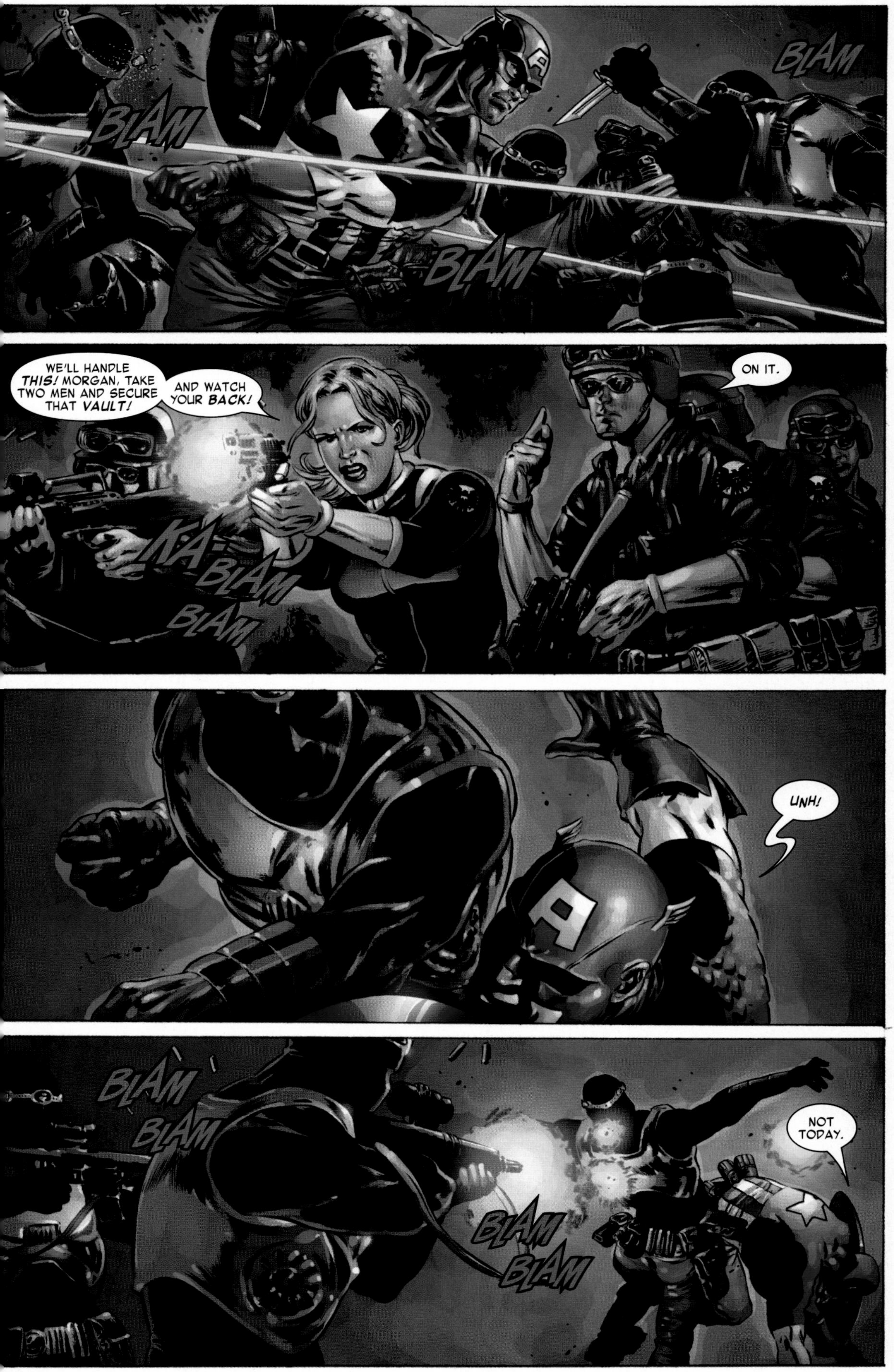
BLAM
BLAM
BLAM
WE'LL HANDLE THIS! MORGAN, TAKE TWO MEN AND SECURE THAT VAULT!
AND WATCH YOUR BACK!
ON IT.
KA-BLAM
BLAM
UNH!
BLAM
BLAM
BLAM
BLAM
NOT TODAY.

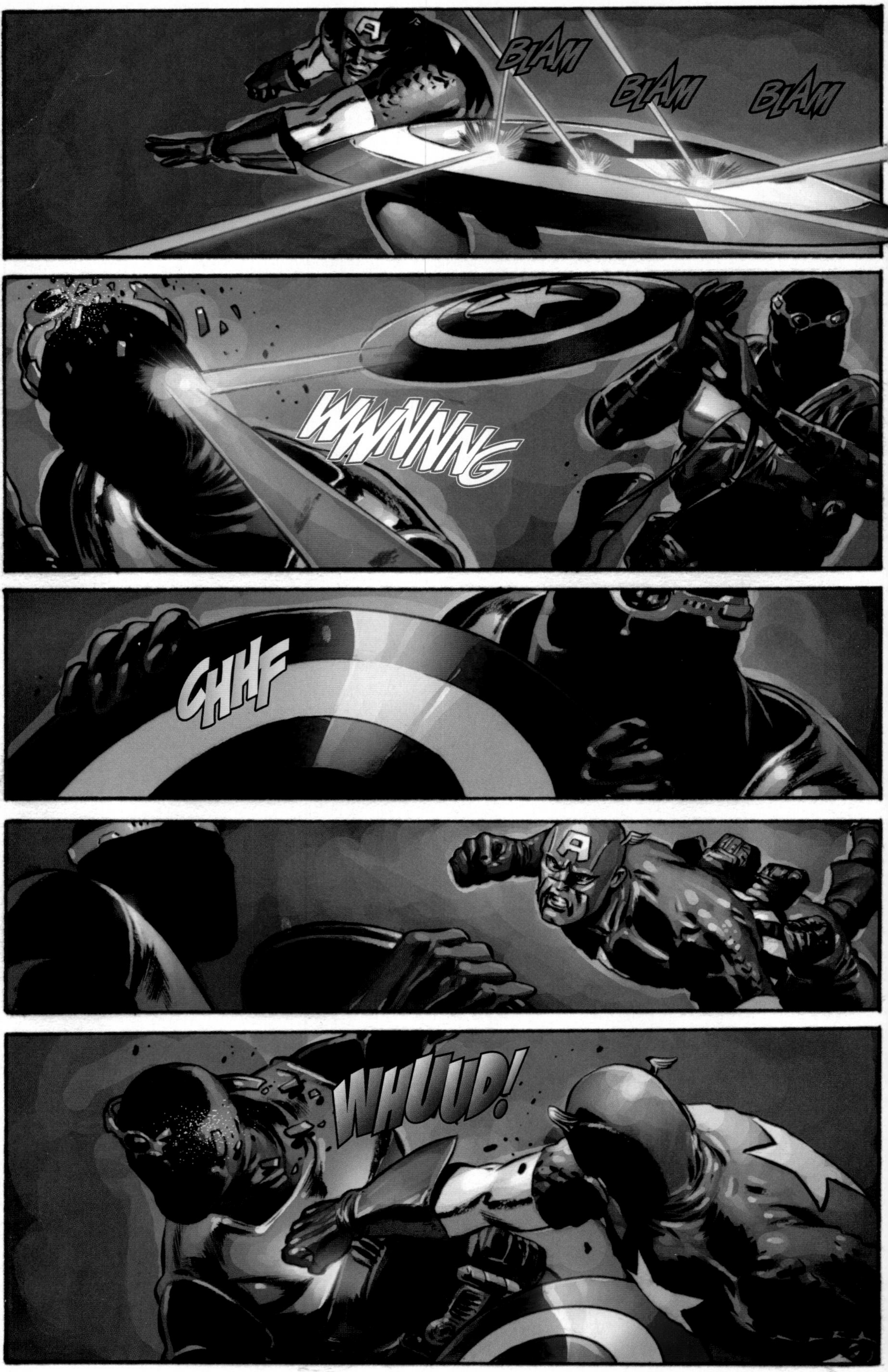
BLAM
BLAM
BLAM
WWNNNG
CHHF
WHUUD!

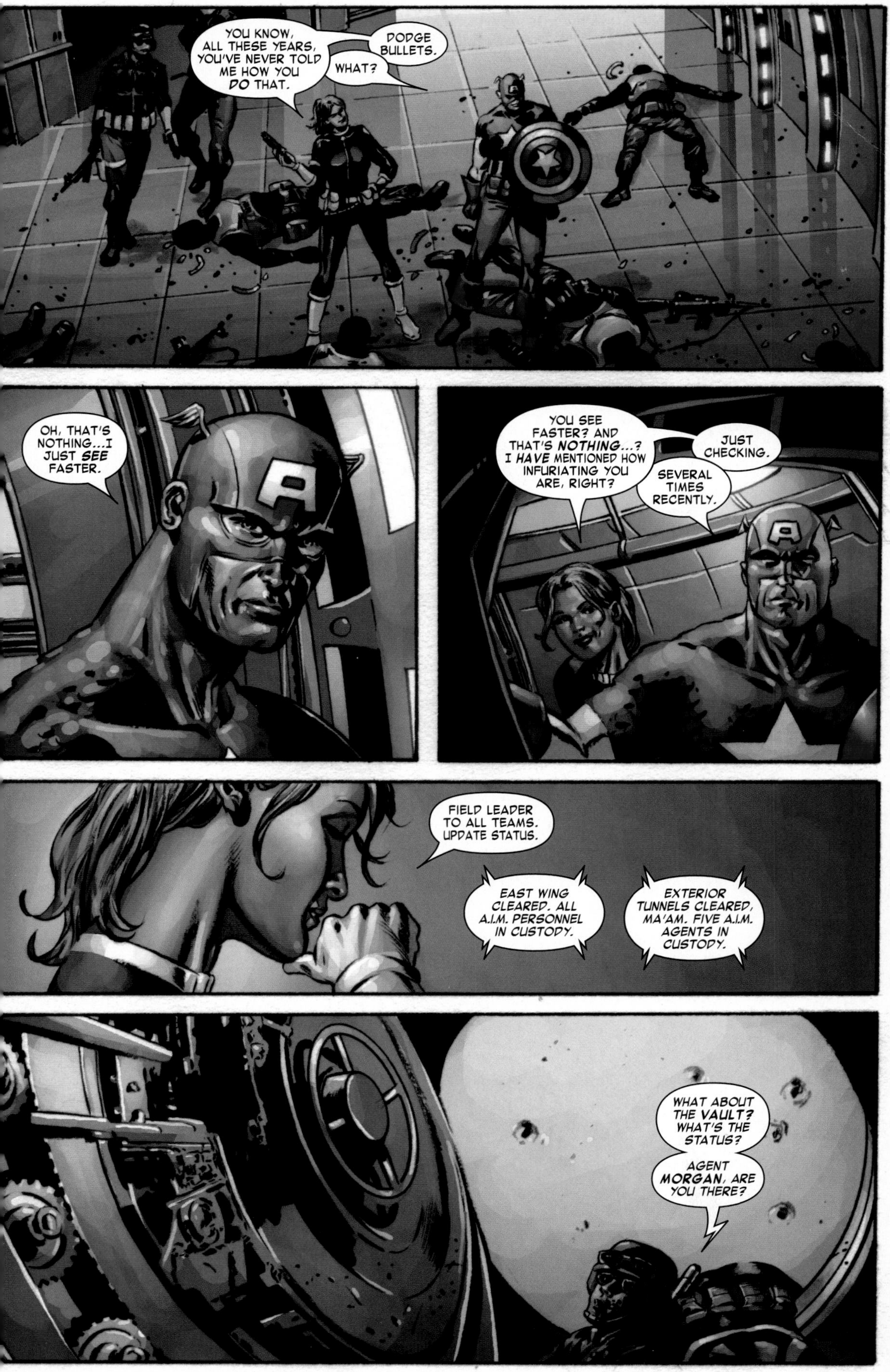
YOU KNOW, ALL THESE YEARS, YOU'VE NEVER TOLD ME HOW YOU DO THAT.
WHAT?
DODGE BULLETS.
OH, THAT'S NOTHING...I JUST SEE FASTER.
YOU SEE FASTER? AND THAT'S NOTHING...? I HAVE MENTIONED HOW INFURIATING YOU ARE, RIGHT?
SEVERAL TIMES RECENTLY.
JUST CHECKING.
FIELD LEADER TO ALL TEAMS. UPDATE STATUS.
EAST WING CLEARED. ALL A.I.M. PERSONNEL IN CUSTODY.
EXTERIOR TUNNELS CLEARED, MA'AM. FIVE A.I.M. AGENTS IN CUSTODY.
WHAT ABOUT THE VAULT? WHAT'S THE STATUS?
AGENT MORGAN, ARE YOU THERE?

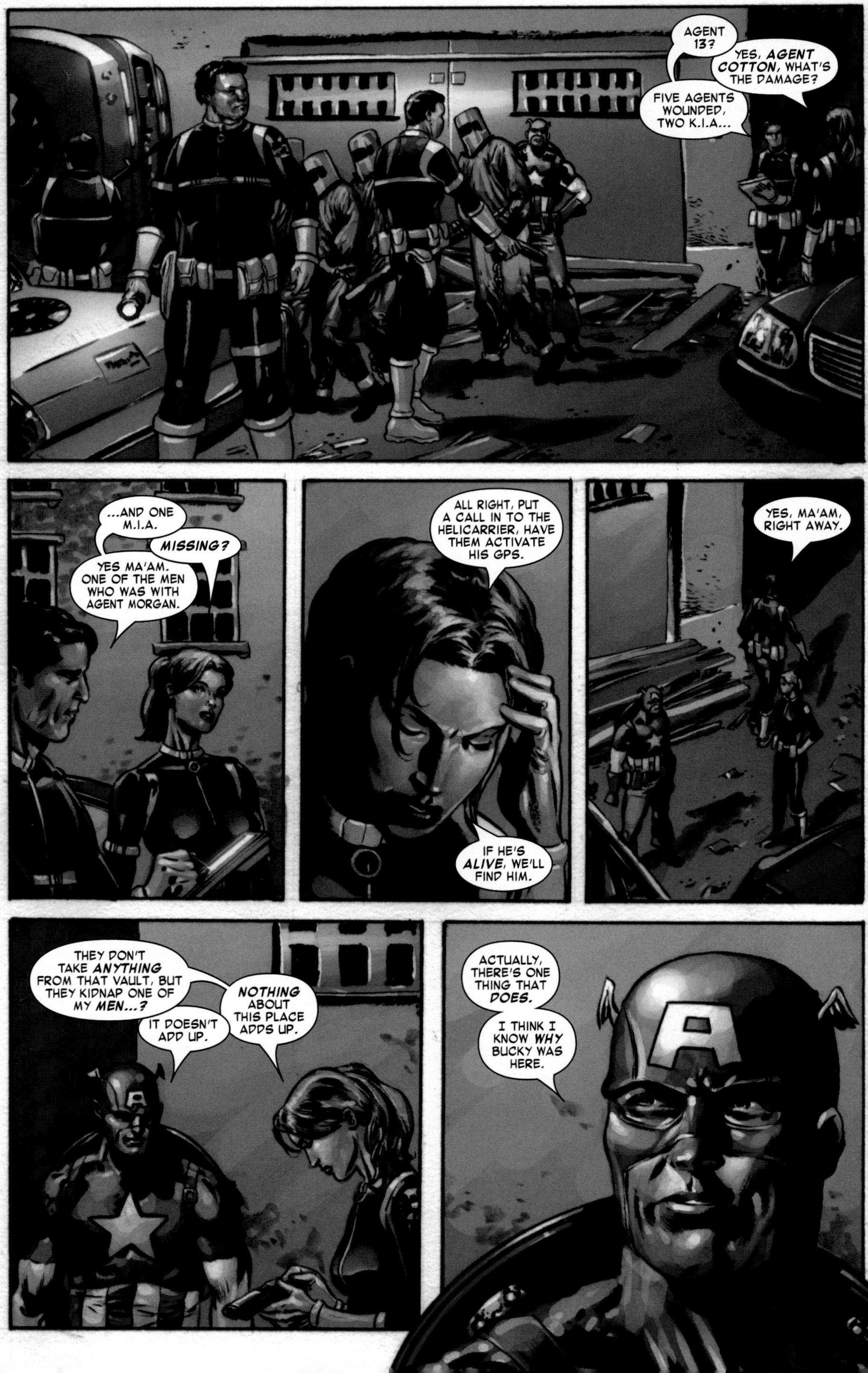
AGENT 13?
YES, AGENT COTTON, WHAT'S THE DAMAGE?
FIVE AGENTS WOUNDED, TWO K.I.A...
...AND ONE M.I.A.
MISSING?
YES MA'AM. ONE OF THE MEN WHO WAS WITH AGENT MORGAN.
ALL RIGHT, PUT A CALL IN TO THE HELICARRIER, HAVE THEM ACTIVATE HIS GPS.
IF HE'S ALIVE, WE'LL FIND HIM.
YES, MA'AM, RIGHT AWAY.
THEY DON'T TAKE ANYTHING FROM THAT VAULT, BUT THEY KIDNAP ONE OF MY MEN...?
IT DOESN'T ADD UP.
NOTHING ABOUT THIS PLACE ADDS UP.
ACTUALLY, THERE'S ONE THING THAT DOES.
I THINK I KNOW WHY BUCKY WAS HERE.

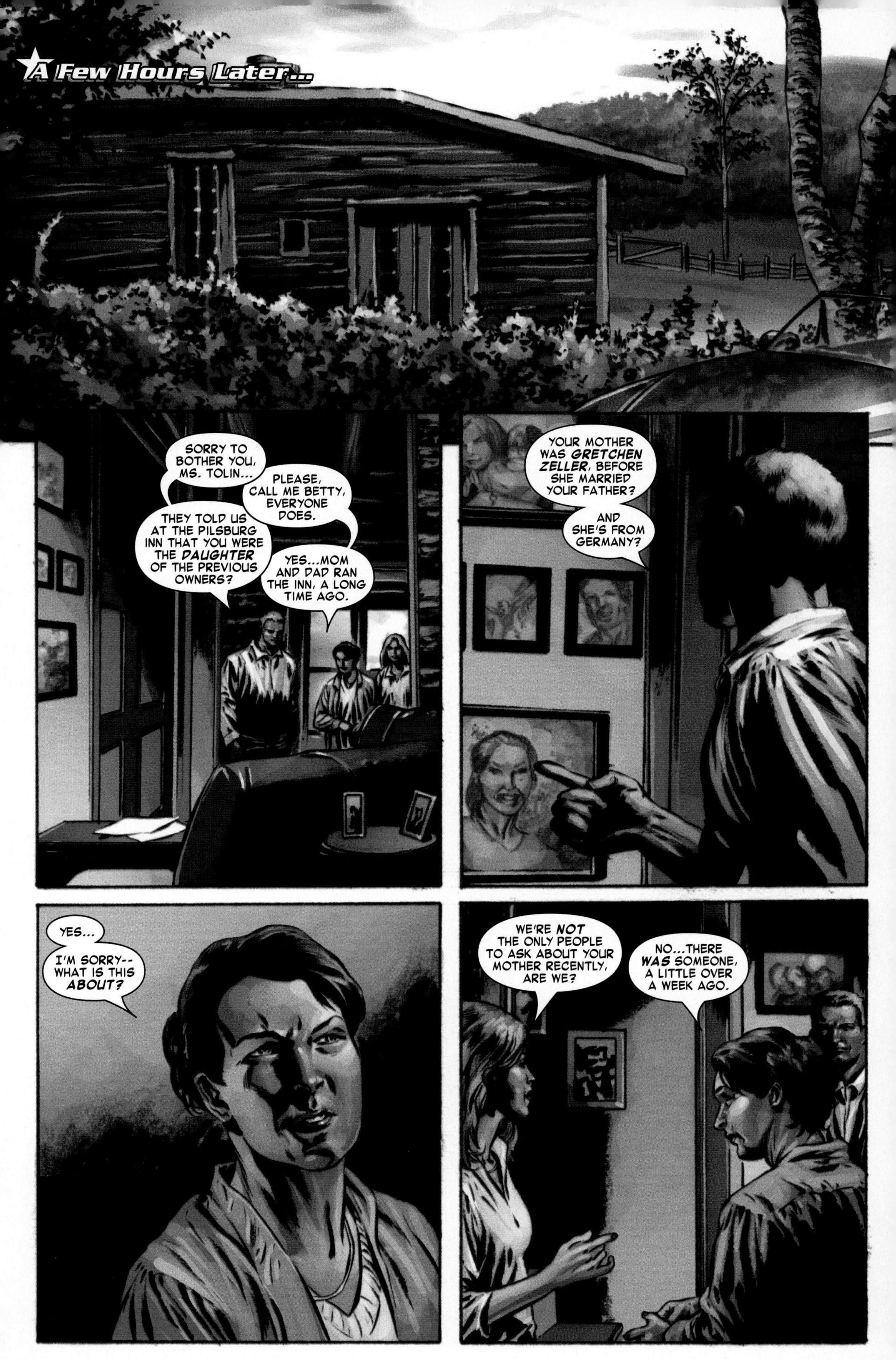
A Few Hours Later...
SORRY TO BOTHER YOU, MS. TOLIN...
PLEASE, CALL ME BETTY, EVERYONE DOES.
THEY TOLD US AT THE PILSBURG INN THAT YOU WERE THE DAUGHTER OF THE PREVIOUS OWNERS?
YES...MOM AND DAD RAN THE INN, A LONG TIME AGO.
YOUR MOTHER WAS GRETCHEN ZELLER, BEFORE SHE MARRIED YOUR FATHER?
AND SHE'S FROM GERMANY?
YES...
I'M SORRY-- WHAT IS THIS ABOUT?
WE'RE NOT THE ONLY PEOPLE TO ASK ABOUT YOUR MOTHER RECENTLY, ARE WE?
NO...THERE WAS SOMEONE, A LITTLE OVER A WEEK AGO.

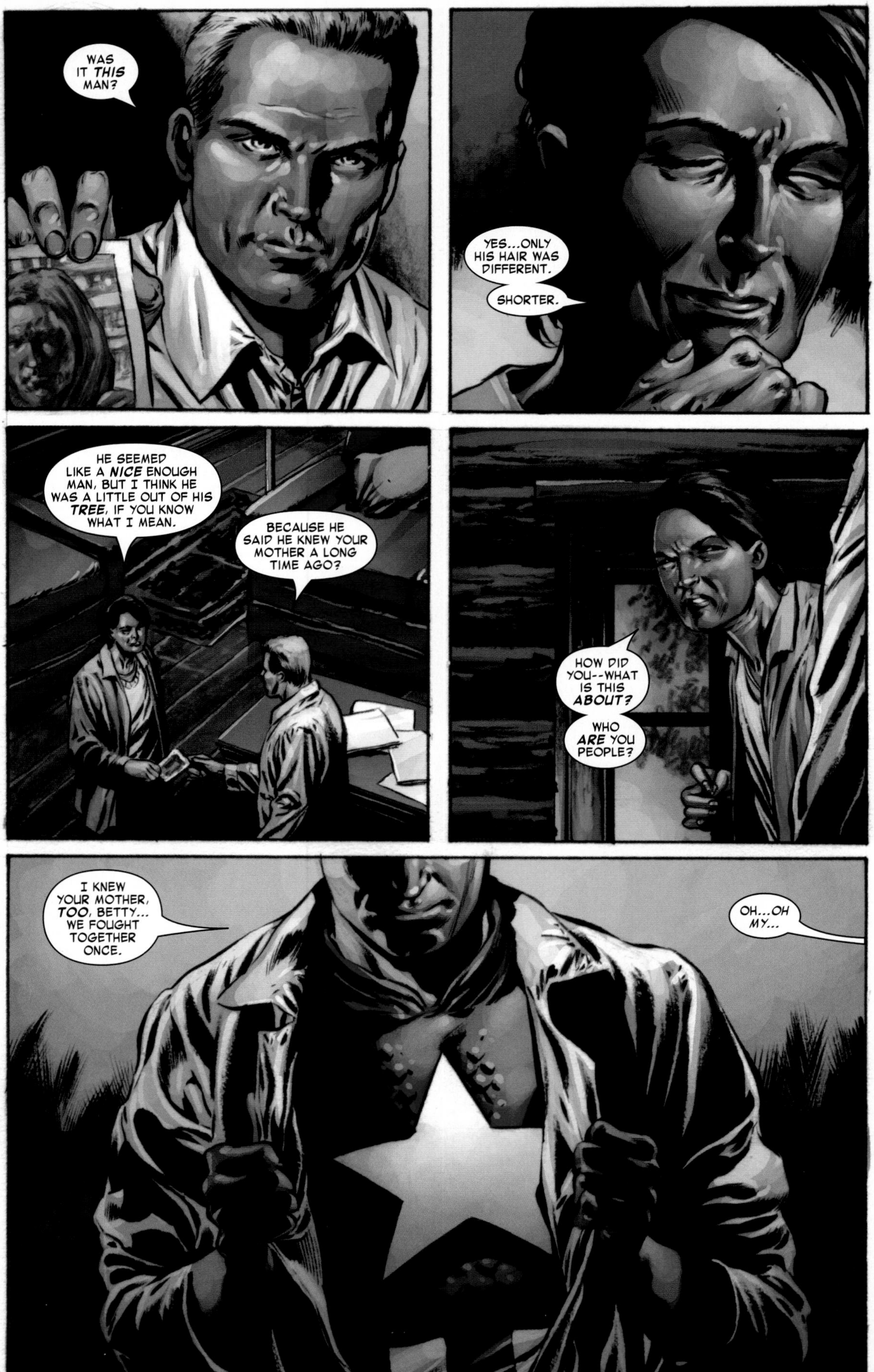
WAS IT THIS MAN?
YES...ONLY HIS HAIR WAS DIFFERENT.
SHORTER.
HE SEEMED LIKE A NICE ENOUGH MAN, BUT I THINK HE WAS A LITTLE OUT OF HIS TREE, IF YOU KNOW WHAT I MEAN.
BECAUSE HE SAID HE KNEW YOUR MOTHER A LONG TIME AGO?
HOW DID YOU--WHAT IS THIS ABOUT?
WHO ARE YOU PEOPLE?
I KNEW YOUR MOTHER, TOO, BETTY... WE FOUGHT TOGETHER ONCE.
OH...OH MY...

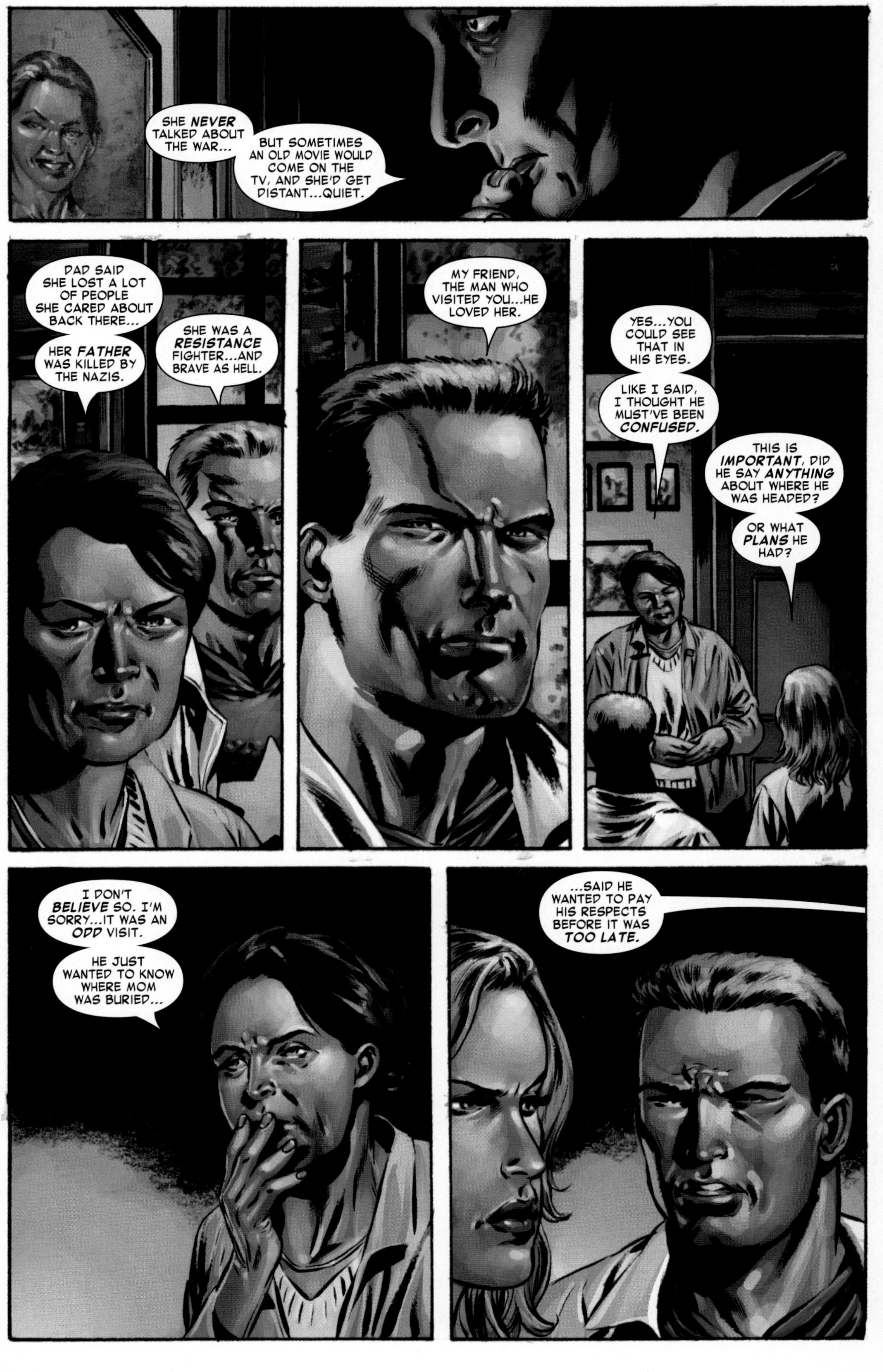
SHE NEVER TALKED ABOUT THE WAR...
BUT SOMETIMES AN OLD MOVIE WOULD COME ON THE TV, AND SHE'D GET DISTANT...QUIET.
DAD SAID SHE LOST A LOT OF PEOPLE SHE CARED ABOUT BACK THERE...
HER FATHER WAS KILLED BY THE NAZIS.
SHE WAS A RESISTANCE FIGHTER...AND BRAVE AS HELL.
MY FRIEND, THE MAN WHO VISITED YOU...HE LOVED HER.
YES...YOU COULD SEE THAT IN HIS EYES.
LIKE I SAID, I THOUGHT HE MUST'VE BEEN CONFUSED.
THIS IS IMPORTANT, DID HE SAY ANYTHING ABOUT WHERE HE WAS HEADED?
OR WHAT PLANS HE HAD?
I DON'T BELIEVE SO. I'M SORRY...IT WAS AN ODD VISIT.
HE JUST WANTED TO KNOW WHERE MOM WAS BURIED...
...SAID HE WANTED TO PAY HIS RESPECTS BEFORE IT WAS TOO LATE.

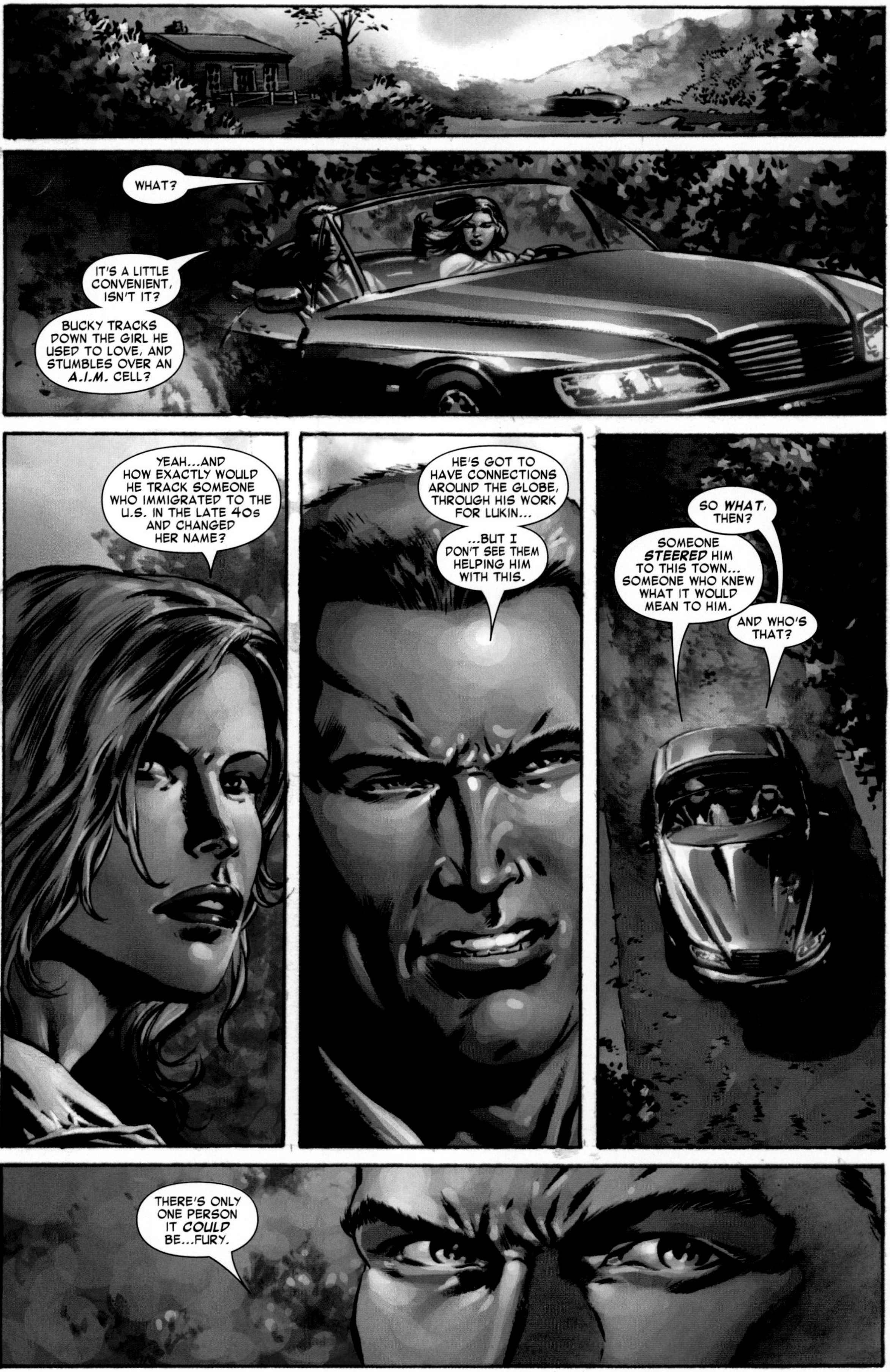
WHAT?
IT'S A LITTLE CONVENIENT, ISN'T IT?
BUCKY TRACKS DOWN THE GIRL HE USED TO LOVE, AND STUMBLES OVER AN A.I.M. CELL?
YEAH...AND HOW EXACTLY WOULD HE TRACK SOMEONE WHO IMMIGRATED TO THE U.S. IN THE LATE 40s AND CHANGED HER NAME?
HE'S GOT TO HAVE CONNECTIONS AROUND THE GLOBE, THROUGH HIS WORK FOR LUKIN...
...BUT I DON'T SEE THEM HELPING HIM WITH THIS.
SO WHAT, THEN?
SOMEONE STEERED HIM TO THIS TOWN... SOMEONE WHO KNEW WHAT IT WOULD MEAN TO HIM.
AND WHO'S THAT?
THERE'S ONLY ONE PERSON IT COULD BE...FURY.

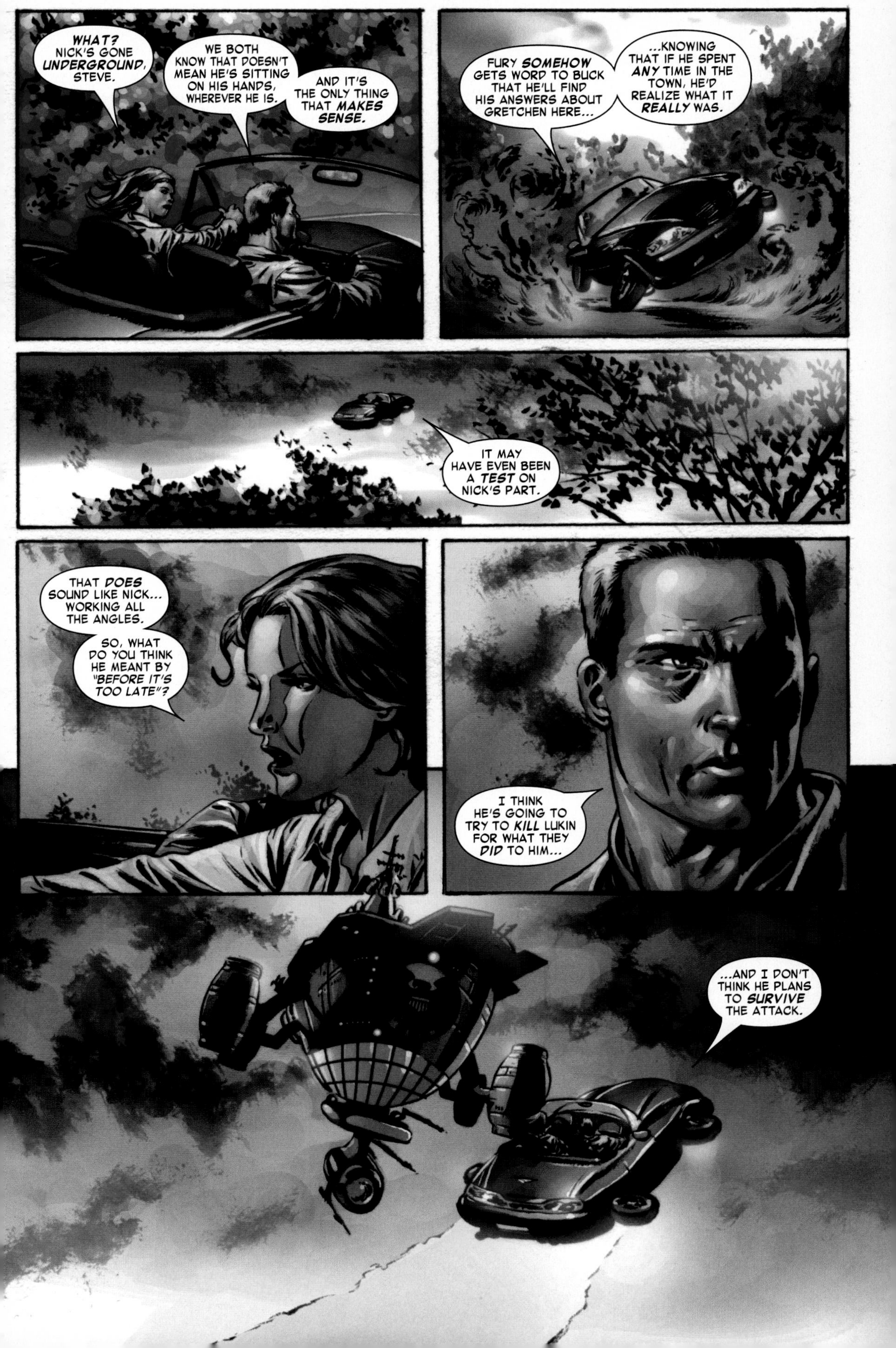
WHAT? NICK'S GONE UNDERGROUND, STEVE.
WE BOTH KNOW THAT DOESN'T MEAN HE'S SITTING ON HIS HANDS, WHEREVER HE IS.
AND IT'S THE ONLY THING THAT MAKES SENSE.
FURY SOMEHOW GETS WORD TO BUCK THAT HE'LL FIND HIS ANSWERS ABOUT GRETCHEN HERE...
...KNOWING THAT IF HE SPENT ANY TIME IN THE TOWN, HE'D REALIZE WHAT IT REALLY WAS.
IT MAY HAVE EVEN BEEN A TEST ON NICK'S PART.
THAT DOES SOUND LIKE NICK... WORKING ALL THE ANGLES.
SO, WHAT DO YOU THINK HE MEANT BY "BEFORE IT'S TOO LATE"?
I THINK HE'S GOING TO TRY TO KILL LUKIN FOR WHAT THEY DID TO HIM...
...AND I DON'T THINK HE PLANS TO SURVIVE THE ATTACK.

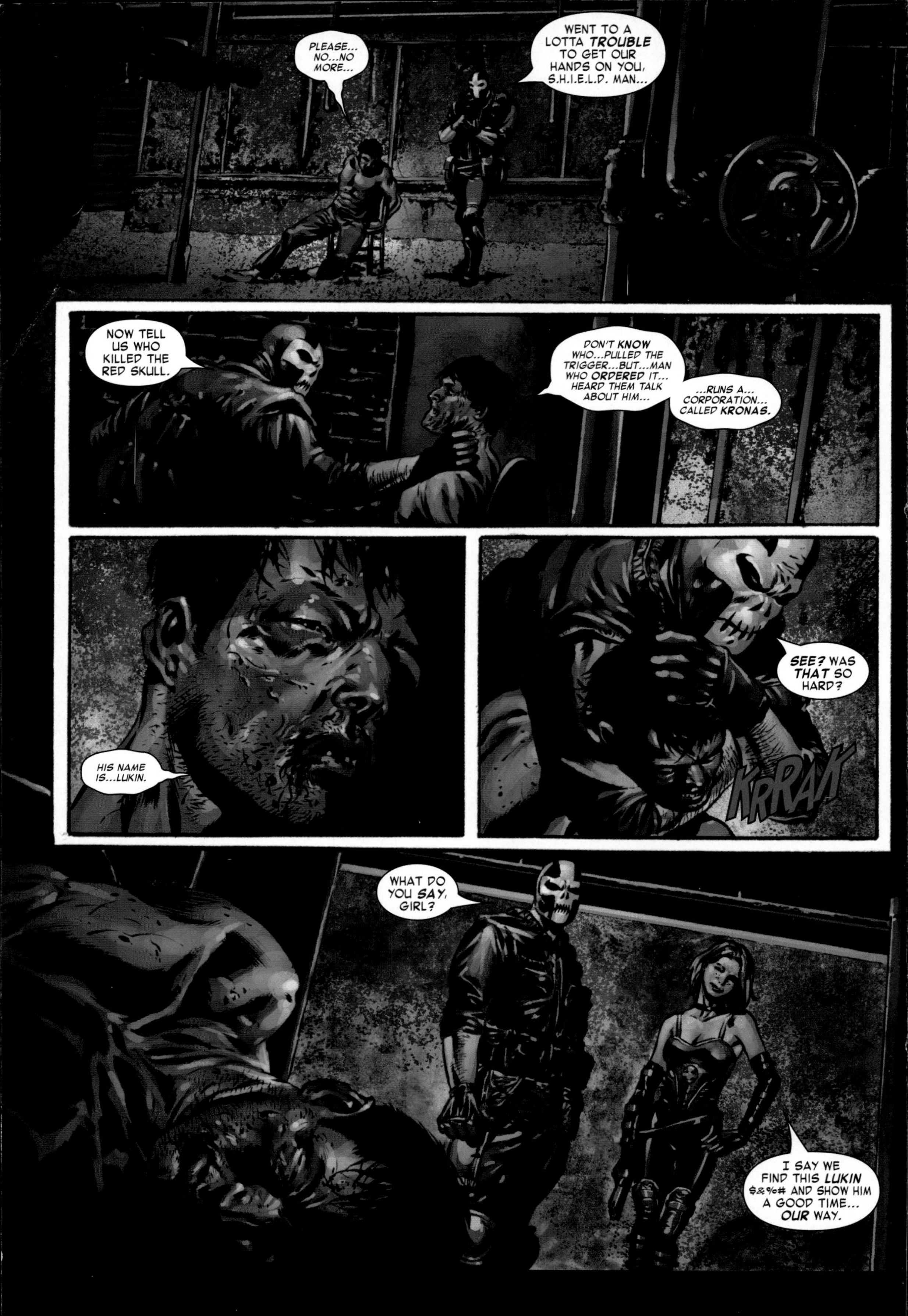
PLEASE... NO...NO MORE...
WENT TO A LOTTA TROUBLE TO GET OUR HANDS ON YOU, S.H.I.E.L.D. MAN...
NOW TELL US WHO KILLED THE RED SKULL.
DON'T KNOW WHO...PULLED THE TRIGGER...BUT...MAN WHO ORDERED IT... HEARD THEM TALK ABOUT HIM...
...RUNS A... CORPORATION... CALLED KRONAS.
HIS NAME IS...LUKIN.
SEE? WAS THAT SO HARD?
KRRAK
WHAT DO YOU SAY, GIRL?
I SAY WE FIND THIS LUKIN $&%# AND SHOW HIM A GOOD TIME... OUR WAY.

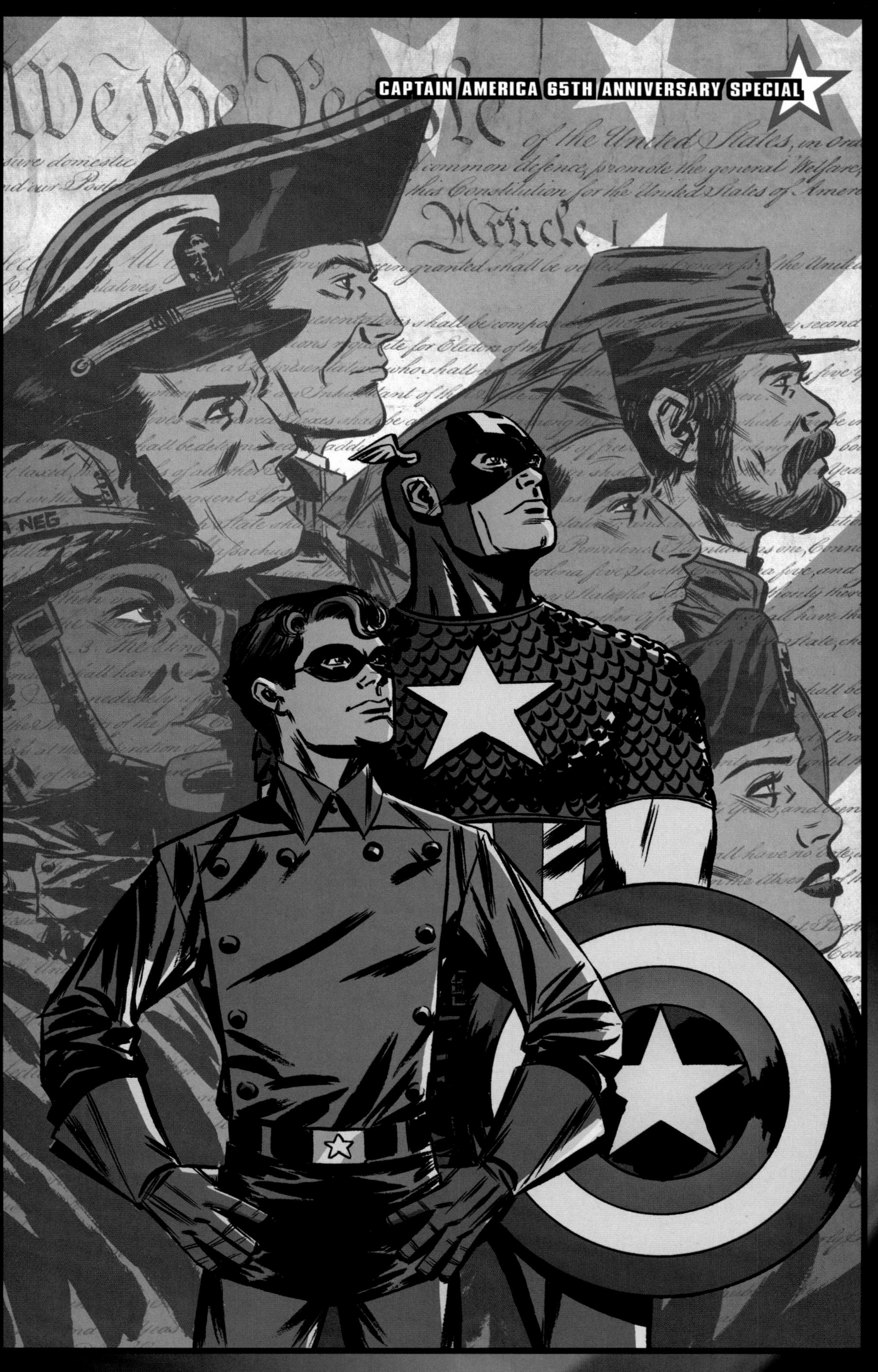
CAPTAIN AMERICA 65TH ANNIVERSARY SPECIAL
of the United States, in Orde
common defence, promote the general Welfare,
this Constitution for the United States of Amer
Article I
NEG

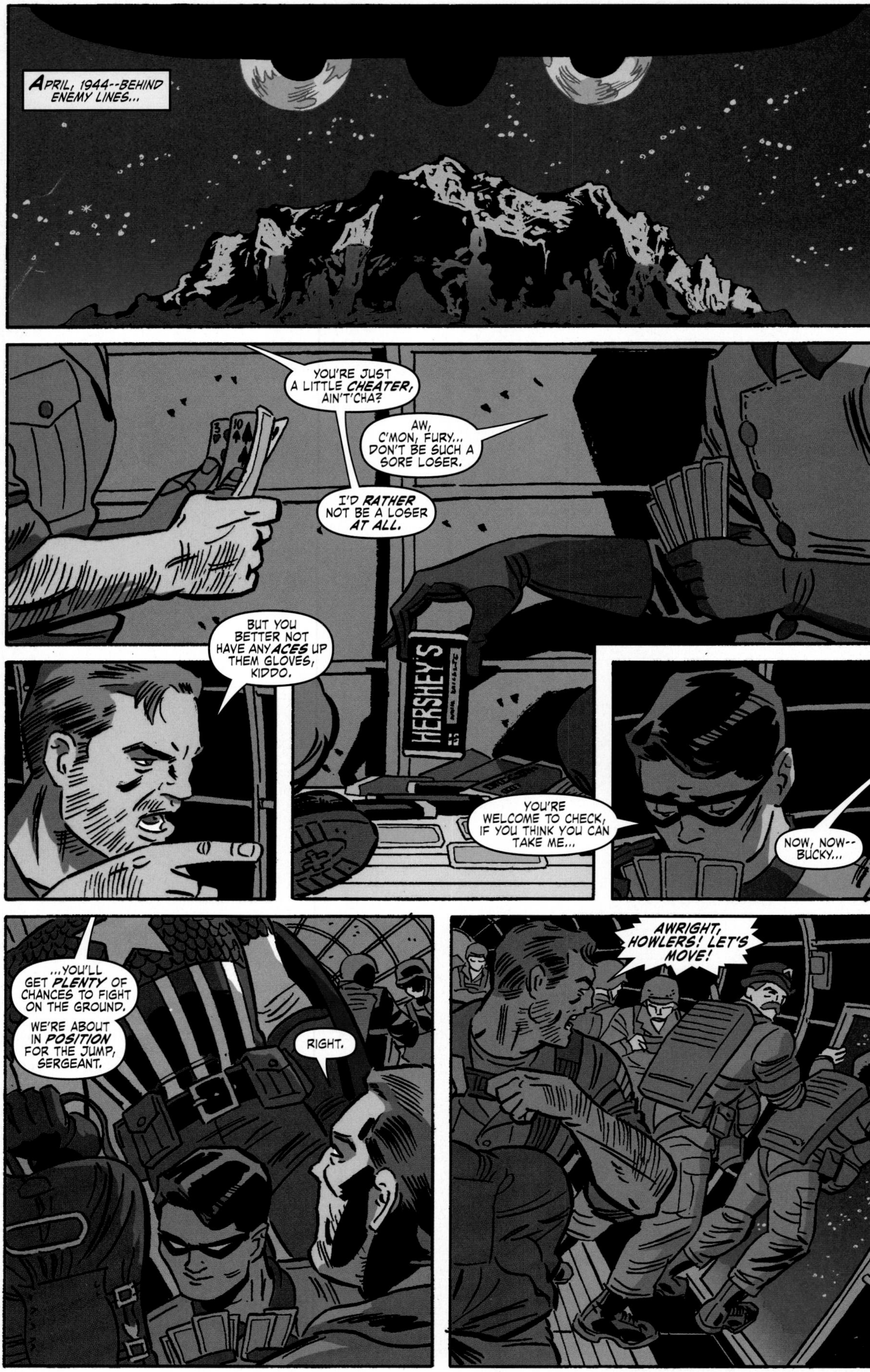
APRIL, 1944--BEHIND ENEMY LINES...
YOU'RE JUST A LITTLE *CHEATER,* AIN'T'CHA?
AW, C'MON, FURY... DON'T BE SUCH A SORE LOSER.
I'D *RATHER* NOT BE A LOSER *AT ALL.*
BUT YOU BETTER NOT HAVE ANY *ACES* UP THEM GLOVES, KIDDO.
HERSHEY'S
YOU'RE WELCOME TO CHECK, IF YOU THINK YOU CAN TAKE ME...
NOW, NOW-- BUCKY...
...YOU'LL GET *PLENTY* OF CHANCES TO FIGHT ON THE GROUND.
WE'RE ABOUT IN *POSITION* FOR THE JUMP, SERGEANT.
RIGHT.
AWRIGHT, HOWLERS! LET'S MOVE!

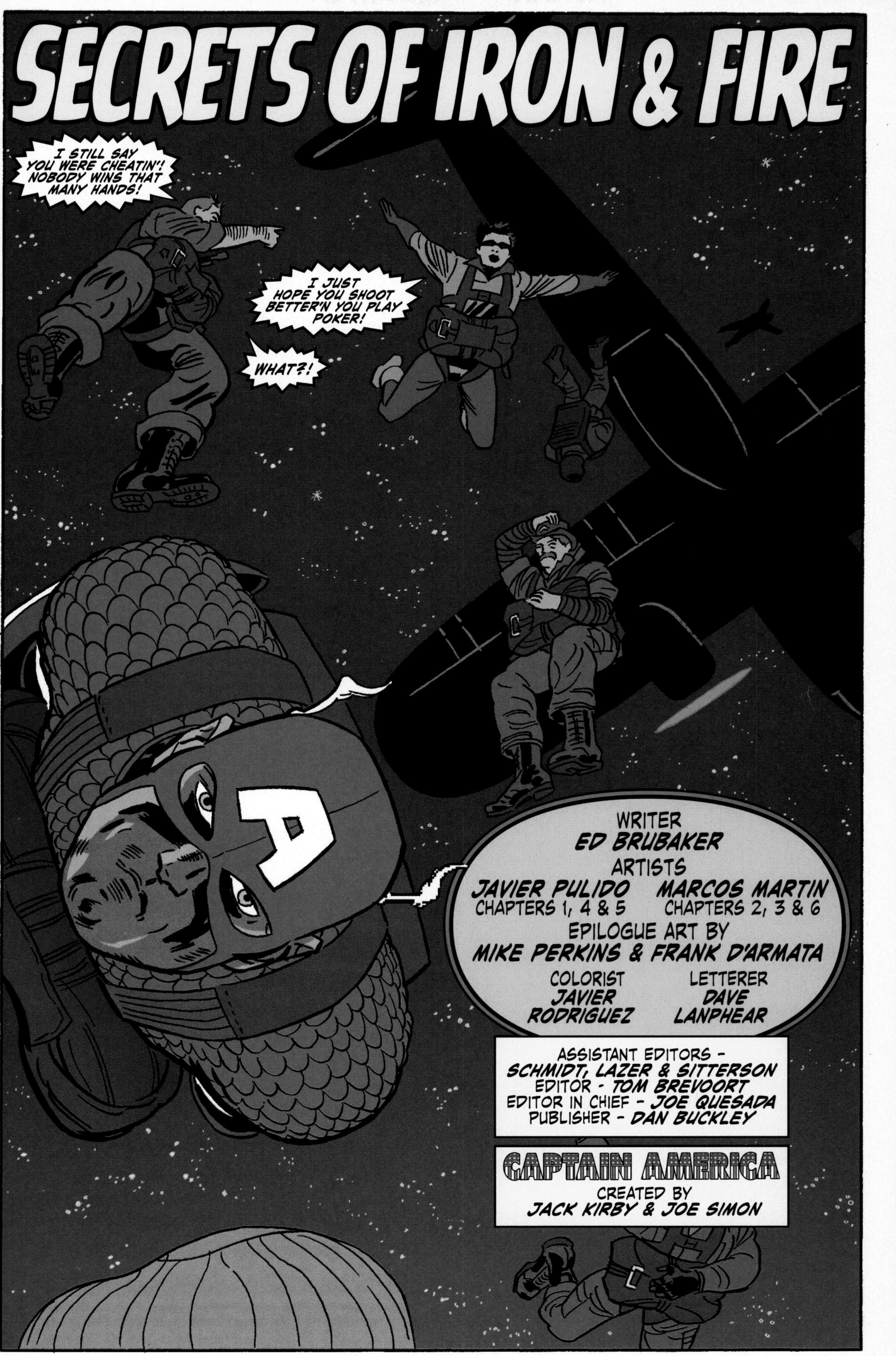
SECRETS OF IRON & FIRE
I STILL SAY YOU WERE CHEATIN'! NOBODY WINS THAT MANY HANDS!
I JUST HOPE YOU SHOOT BETTER'N YOU PLAY POKER!
WHAT?!
WRITER
ED BRUBAKER
ARTISTS
JAVIER PULIDO CHAPTERS 1, 4 & 5
MARCOS MARTIN CHAPTERS 2, 3 & 6
EPILOGUE ART BY
MIKE PERKINS & FRANK D'ARMATA
COLORIST JAVIER RODRIGUEZ
LETTERER DAVE LANPHEAR
ASSISTANT EDITORS - SCHMIDT, LAZER & SITTERSON
EDITOR - TOM BREVOORT
EDITOR IN CHIEF - JOE QUESADA
PUBLISHER - DAN BUCKLEY
CAPTAIN AMERICA
CREATED BY
JACK KIRBY & JOE SIMON

THIS WASN'T OUR FIRST MISSION WITH FURY AND HIS HOWLERS, AND WHILE NORMALLY WE'D HAVE BEEN WITH THE REST OF THE INVADERS...

...THIS TIME, WE NEEDED SOMETHING A LITTLE LESS CONSPICUOUS.

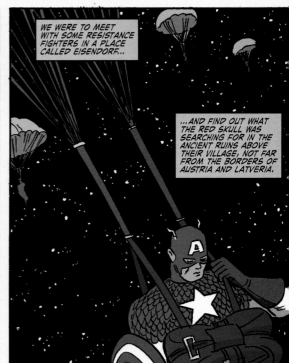

WE WERE TO MEET WITH SOME RESISTANCE FIGHTERS IN A PLACE CALLED EISENDORF...

...AND FIND OUT WHAT THE RED SKULL WAS SEARCHING FOR IN THE ANCIENT RUINS ABOVE THEIR VILLAGE, NOT FAR FROM THE BORDERS OF AUSTRIA AND LATVERIA.

WORD HAD LEAKED FROM THESE ANTI-NAZI SPIES THAT THE SKULL CLAIMED WHAT HE WAS SEEKING HERE HELD THE SECRET TO CRUSHING THE ALLIED FORCES...

...AND WE WERE TO PREVENT THAT COMING TO PASS, BY ANY MEANS NECESSARY.

GET THOSE CHUTES BUNDLED AND *BURIED!*

LAST THING WE NEED IS SOME GOOSE-STEPPER FINDIN'--

RATATATATATATATATATATATATATATATATATATATATAT

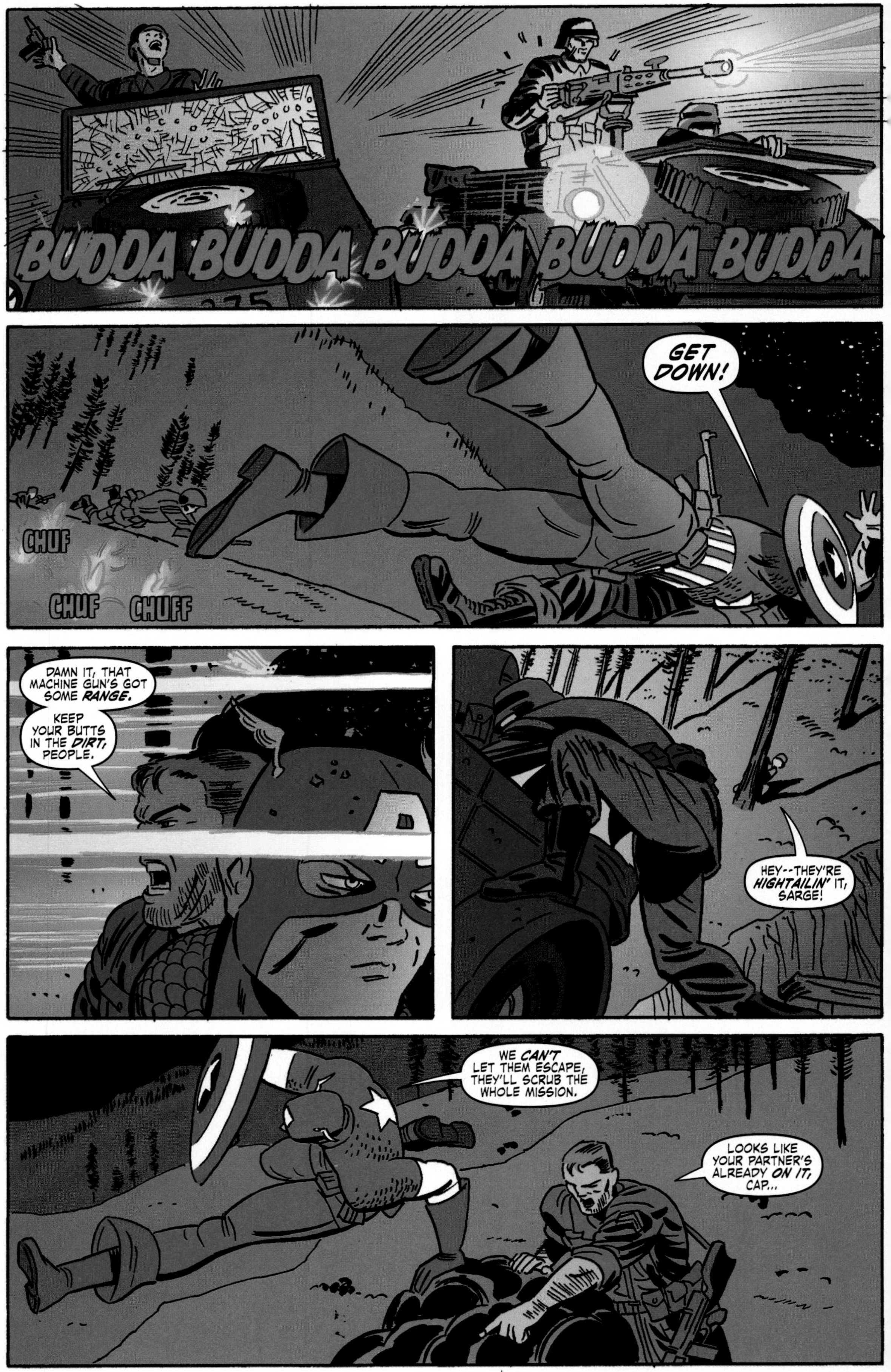
BUDDA BUDDA BUDDA BUDDA BUDDA
GET DOWN!
CHUF
CHUF CHUFF
DAMN IT, THAT MACHINE GUN'S GOT SOME *RANGE.*
KEEP YOUR BUTTS IN THE *DIRT,* PEOPLE.
HEY--THEY'RE *HIGHTAILIN'* IT, SARGE!
WE *CAN'T* LET THEM ESCAPE, THEY'LL SCRUB THE WHOLE MISSION.
LOOKS LIKE YOUR PARTNER'S ALREADY *ON IT,* CAP...

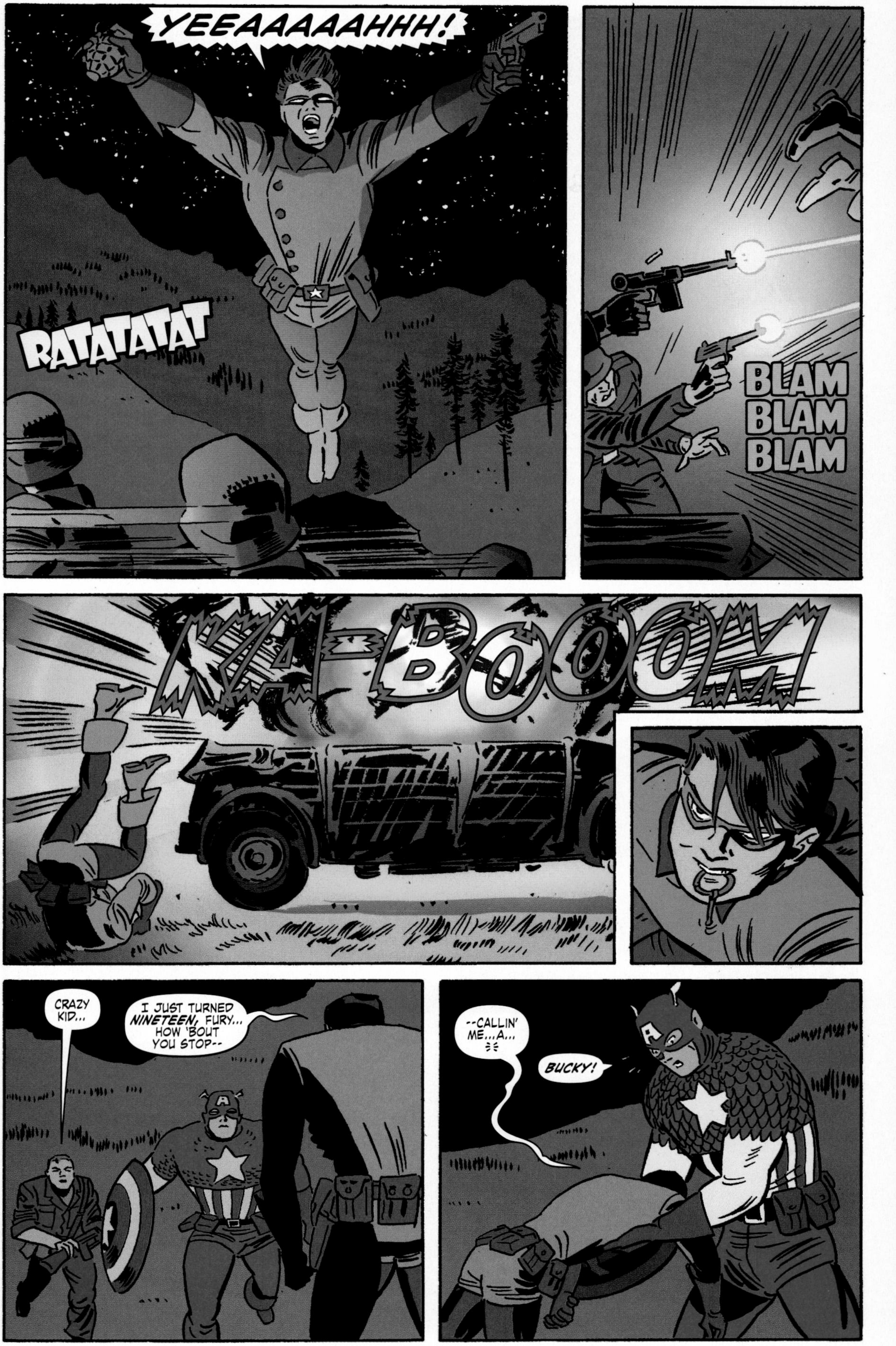
YEEAAAAAHHH!
RATATATAT
BLAM
BLAM
BLAM
KA-BOOOOM
CRAZY KID...
I JUST TURNED NINETEEN, FURY... HOW 'BOUT YOU STOP--
--CALLIN' ME...A...
BUCKY!

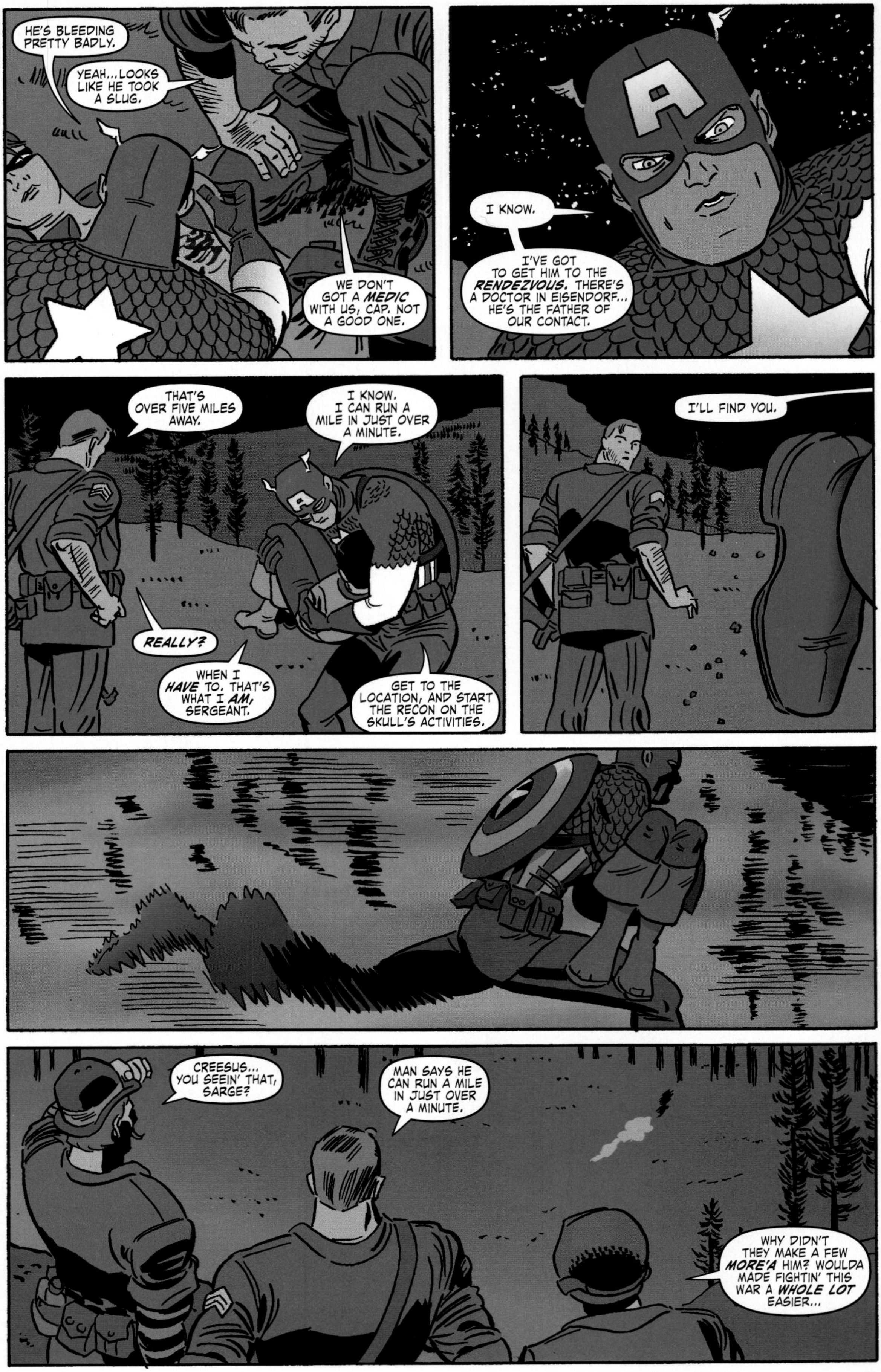
HE'S BLEEDING PRETTY BADLY.
YEAH...LOOKS LIKE HE TOOK A SLUG.
WE DON'T GOT A MEDIC WITH US, CAP. NOT A GOOD ONE.
I KNOW.
I'VE GOT TO GET HIM TO THE RENDEZVOUS. THERE'S A DOCTOR IN EISENDORF... HE'S THE FATHER OF OUR CONTACT.
THAT'S OVER FIVE MILES AWAY.
I KNOW. I CAN RUN A MILE IN JUST OVER A MINUTE.
REALLY?
WHEN I HAVE TO. THAT'S WHAT I AM, SERGEANT.
GET TO THE LOCATION, AND START THE RECON ON THE SKULL'S ACTIVITIES.
I'LL FIND YOU.
CREESUS... YOU SEEIN' THAT, SARGE?
MAN SAYS HE CAN RUN A MILE IN JUST OVER A MINUTE.
WHY DIDN'T THEY MAKE A FEW MORE'A HIM? WOULDA MADE FIGHTIN' THIS WAR A WHOLE LOT EASIER...

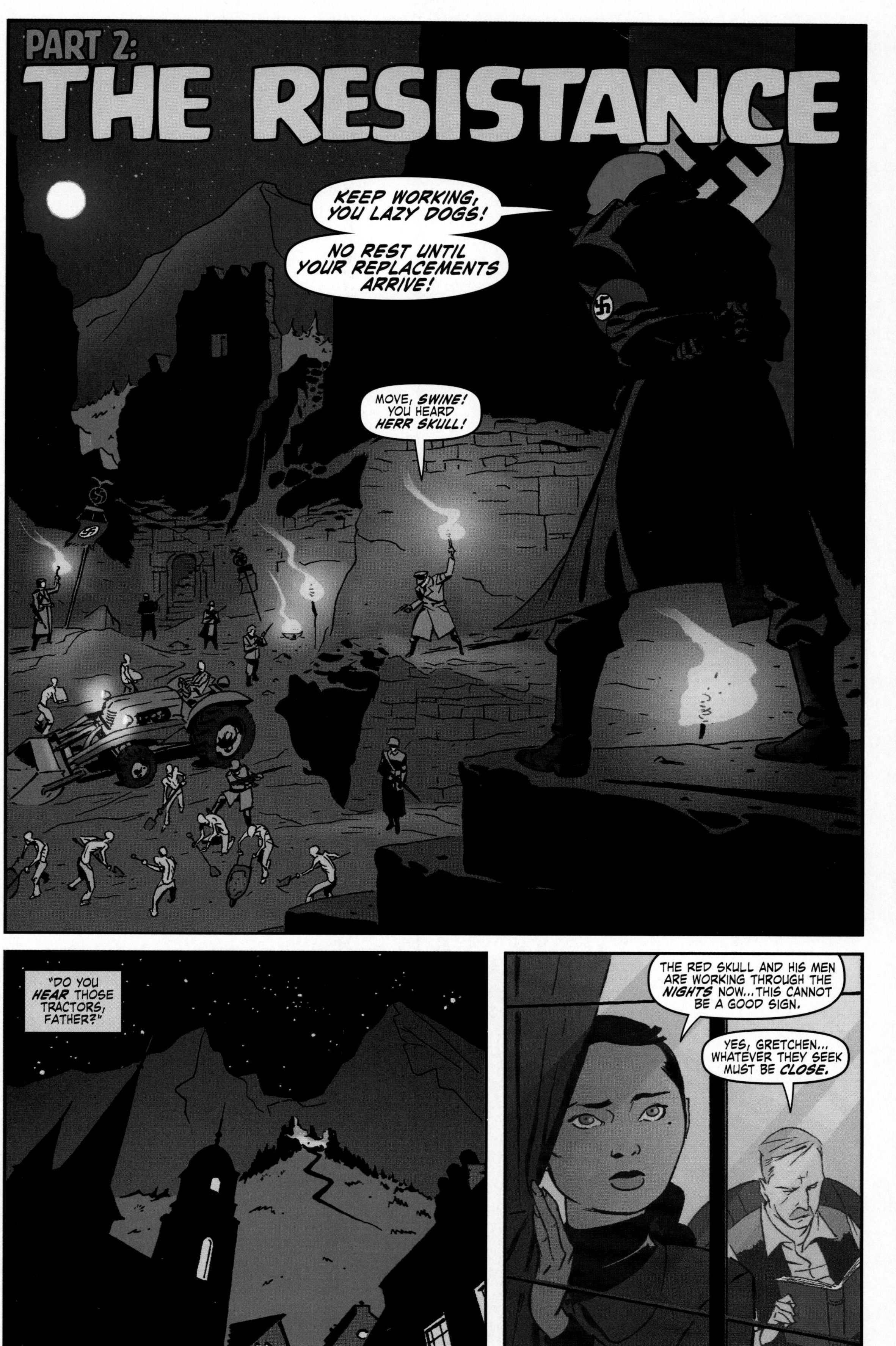
PART 2:
THE RESISTANCE
KEEP WORKING, YOU LAZY DOGS!
NO REST UNTIL YOUR REPLACEMENTS ARRIVE!
MOVE, SWINE! YOU HEARD HERR SKULL!
"DO YOU HEAR THOSE TRACTORS, FATHER?"
THE RED SKULL AND HIS MEN ARE WORKING THROUGH THE NIGHTS NOW... THIS CANNOT BE A GOOD SIGN.
YES, GRETCHEN... WHATEVER THEY SEEK MUST BE CLOSE.

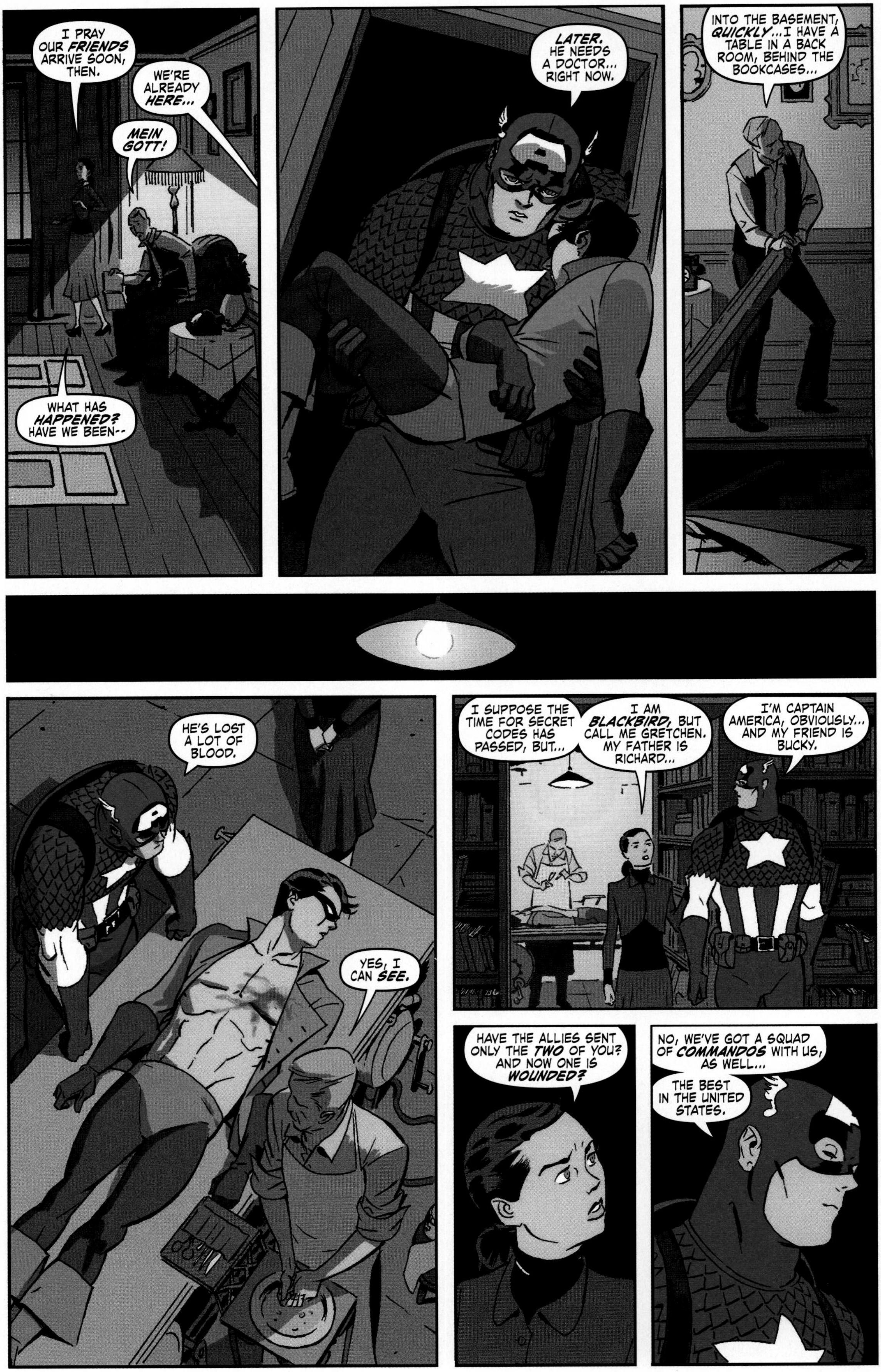
I PRAY OUR *FRIENDS* ARRIVE SOON, THEN.
WE'RE ALREADY *HERE...*
MEIN GOTT!
WHAT HAS *HAPPENED?* HAVE WE BEEN--
LATER. HE NEEDS A DOCTOR... RIGHT NOW.
INTO THE BASEMENT, *QUICKLY*...I HAVE A TABLE IN A BACK ROOM, BEHIND THE BOOKCASES...
HE'S LOST A LOT OF BLOOD.
YES, I CAN *SEE.*
I SUPPOSE THE TIME FOR SECRET CODES HAS PASSED, BUT...
I AM *BLACKBIRD,* BUT CALL ME GRETCHEN. MY FATHER IS RICHARD...
I'M CAPTAIN AMERICA, OBVIOUSLY... AND MY FRIEND IS BUCKY.
HAVE THE ALLIES SENT ONLY THE *TWO* OF YOU? AND NOW ONE IS *WOUNDED?*
NO, WE'VE GOT A SQUAD OF *COMMANDOS* WITH US, AS WELL...
THE BEST IN THE UNITED STATES.

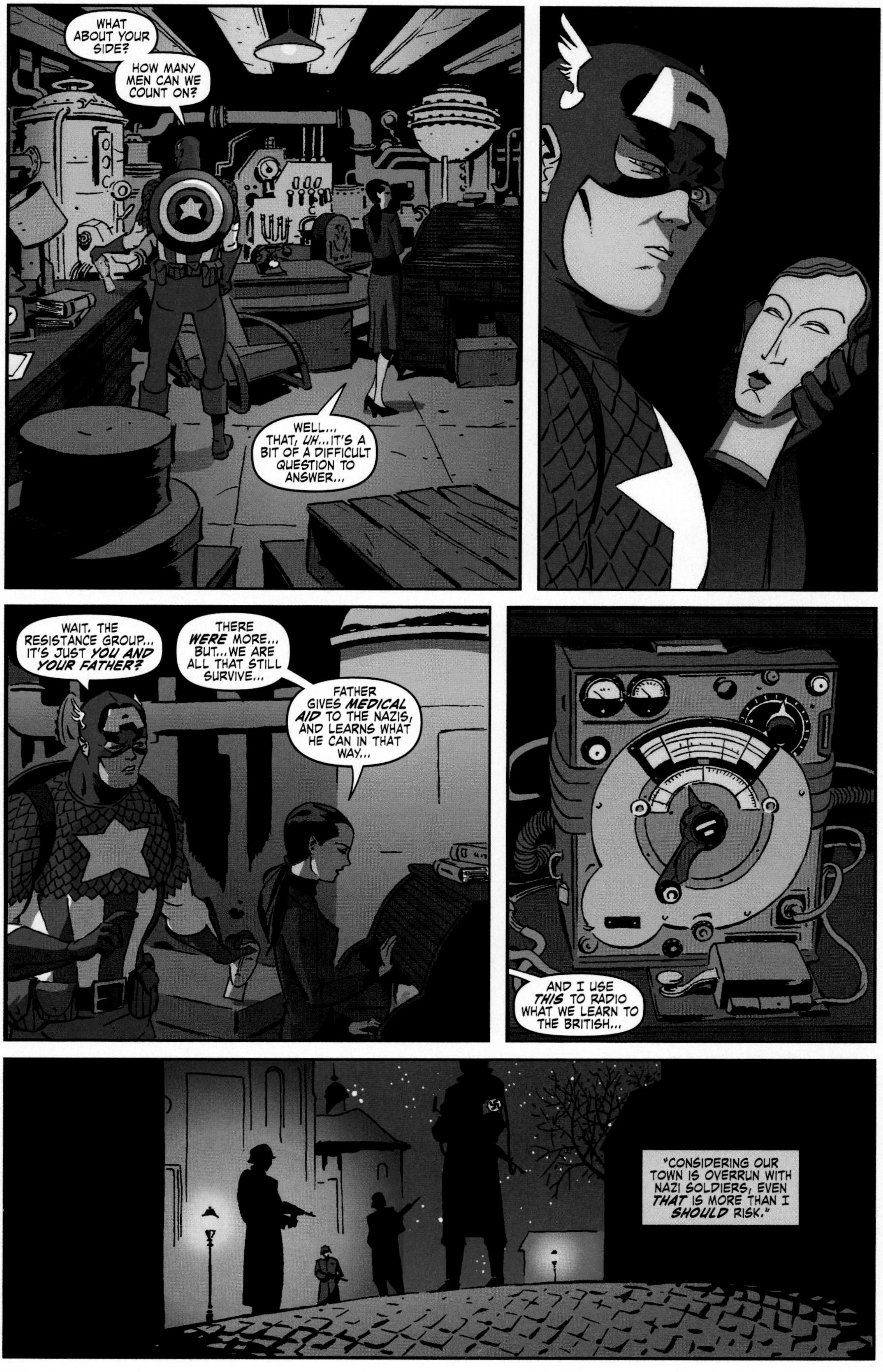
WHAT ABOUT YOUR SIDE?
HOW MANY MEN CAN WE COUNT ON?
WELL... THAT, *UH*...IT'S A BIT OF A DIFFICULT QUESTION TO ANSWER...
WAIT. THE RESISTANCE GROUP... IT'S JUST *YOU AND YOUR FATHER?*
THERE *WERE* MORE... BUT...WE ARE ALL THAT STILL SURVIVE...
FATHER GIVES *MEDICAL AID* TO THE NAZIS, AND LEARNS WHAT HE CAN IN THAT WAY...
AND I USE *THIS* TO RADIO WHAT WE LEARN TO THE BRITISH...
"CONSIDERING OUR TOWN IS OVERRUN WITH NAZI SOLDIERS, EVEN *THAT* IS MORE THAN I *SHOULD* RISK."

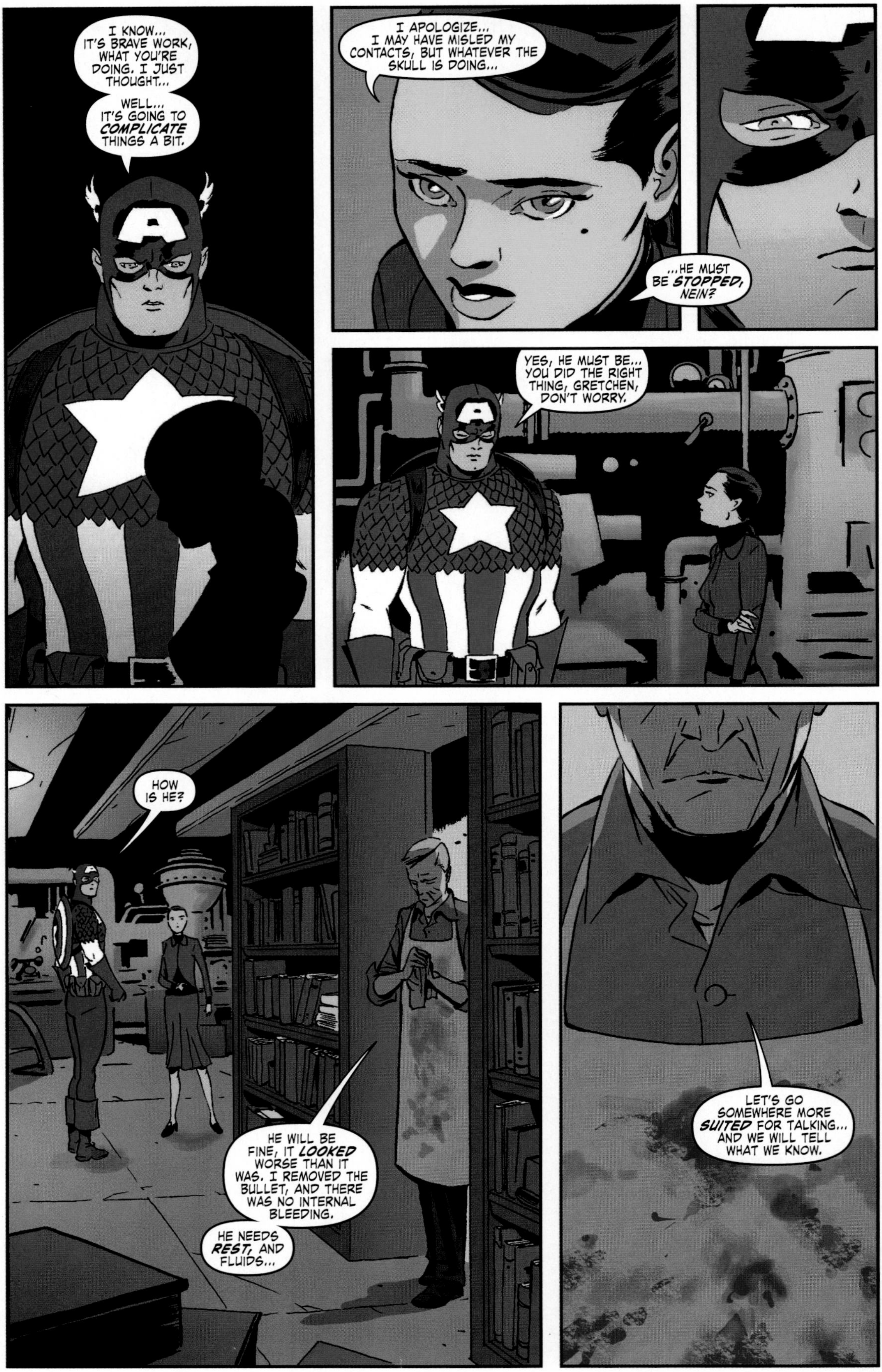
I KNOW... IT'S BRAVE WORK, WHAT YOU'RE DOING. I JUST THOUGHT...
WELL... IT'S GOING TO COMPLICATE THINGS A BIT.
I APOLOGIZE... I MAY HAVE MISLED MY CONTACTS, BUT WHATEVER THE SKULL IS DOING...
...HE MUST BE STOPPED, NEIN?
YES, HE MUST BE... YOU DID THE RIGHT THING, GRETCHEN, DON'T WORRY.
HOW IS HE?
HE WILL BE FINE, IT LOOKED WORSE THAN IT WAS. I REMOVED THE BULLET, AND THERE WAS NO INTERNAL BLEEDING.
HE NEEDS REST, AND FLUIDS...
LET'S GO SOMEWHERE MORE SUITED FOR TALKING... AND WE WILL TELL WHAT WE KNOW.

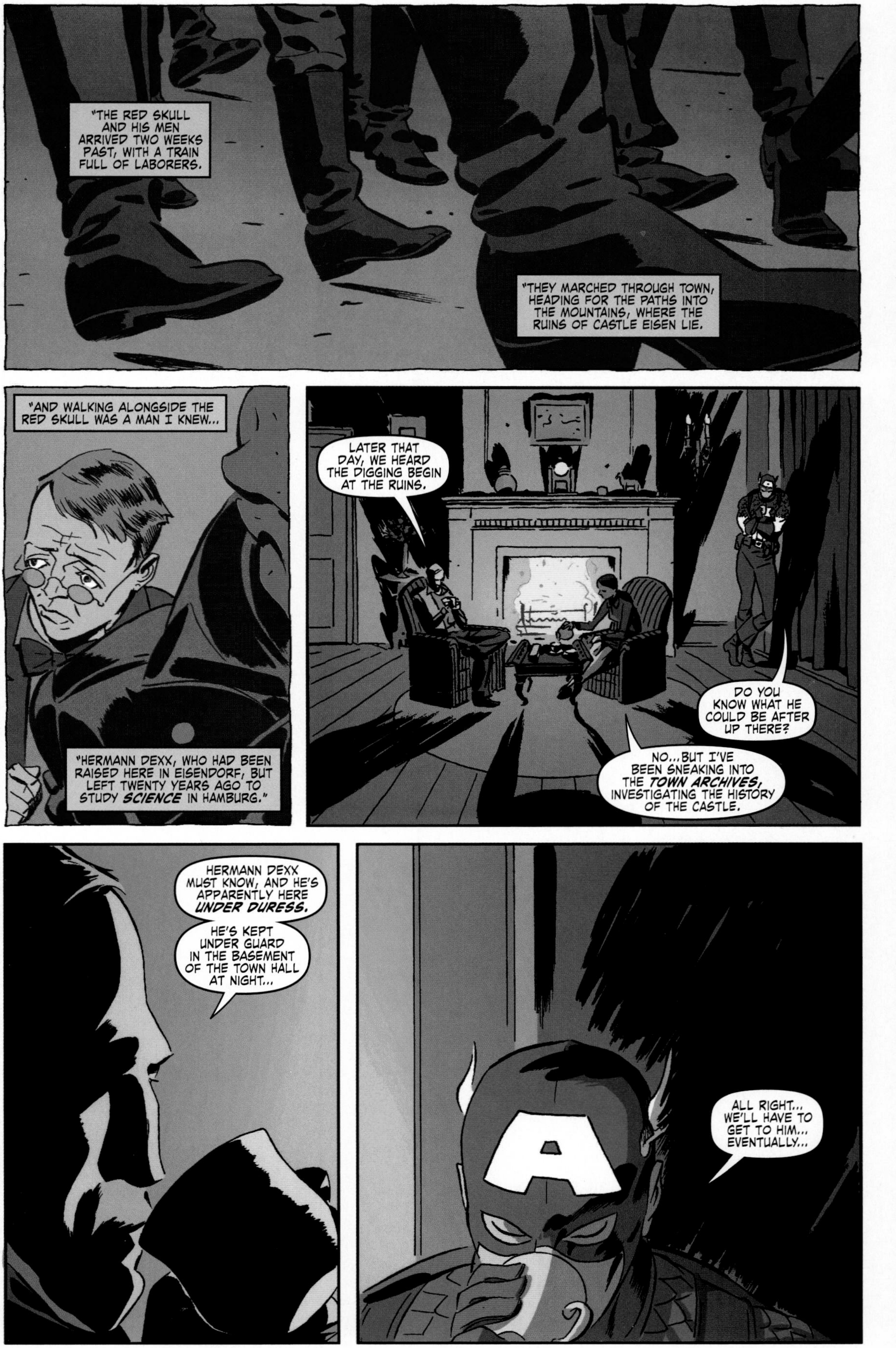
"THE RED SKULL AND HIS MEN ARRIVED TWO WEEKS PAST, WITH A TRAIN FULL OF LABORERS.
"THEY MARCHED THROUGH TOWN, HEADING FOR THE PATHS INTO THE MOUNTAINS, WHERE THE RUINS OF CASTLE EISEN LIE.
"AND WALKING ALONGSIDE THE RED SKULL WAS A MAN I KNEW...
"HERMANN DEXX, WHO HAD BEEN RAISED HERE IN EISENDORF, BUT LEFT TWENTY YEARS AGO TO STUDY SCIENCE IN HAMBURG."
LATER THAT DAY, WE HEARD THE DIGGING BEGIN AT THE RUINS.
DO YOU KNOW WHAT HE COULD BE AFTER UP THERE?
NO...BUT I'VE BEEN SNEAKING INTO THE TOWN ARCHIVES, INVESTIGATING THE HISTORY OF THE CASTLE.
HERMANN DEXX MUST KNOW, AND HE'S APPARENTLY HERE UNDER DURESS.
HE'S KEPT UNDER GUARD IN THE BASEMENT OF THE TOWN HALL AT NIGHT...
ALL RIGHT... WE'LL HAVE TO GET TO HIM... EVENTUALLY...

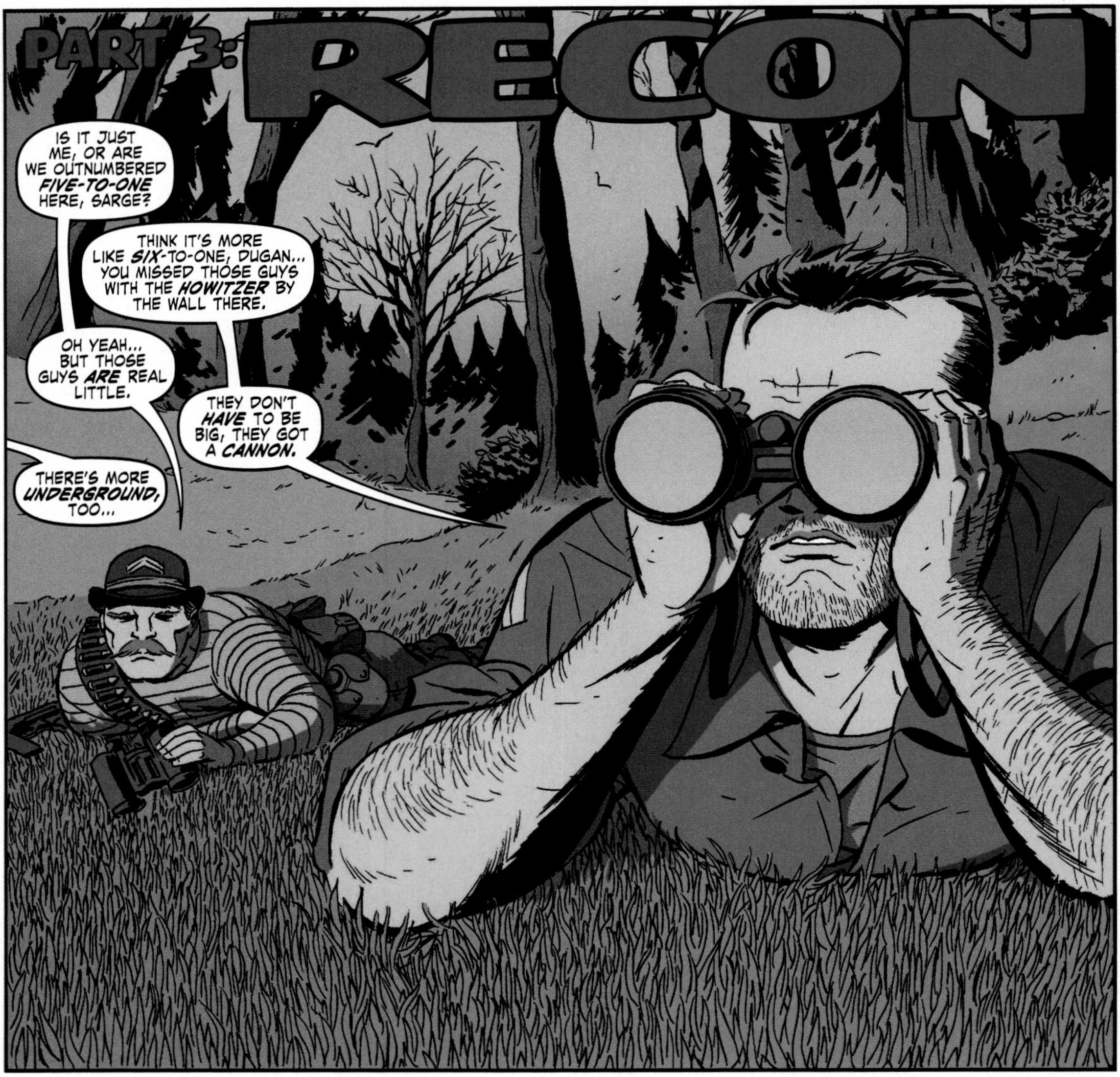
PART 3: RECON
IS IT JUST ME, OR ARE WE OUTNUMBERED FIVE-TO-ONE HERE, SARGE?
THINK IT'S MORE LIKE SIX-TO-ONE, DUGAN... YOU MISSED THOSE GUYS WITH THE HOWITZER BY THE WALL THERE.
OH YEAH... BUT THOSE GUYS ARE REAL LITTLE.
THEY DON'T HAVE TO BE BIG, THEY GOT A CANNON.
THERE'S MORE UNDERGROUND, TOO...

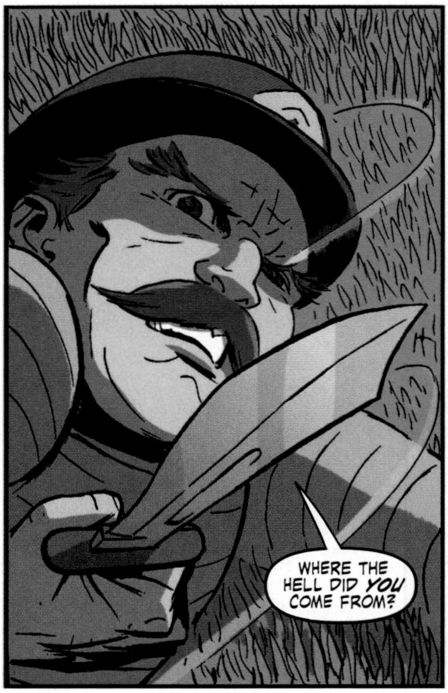
WHERE THE HELL DID YOU COME FROM?

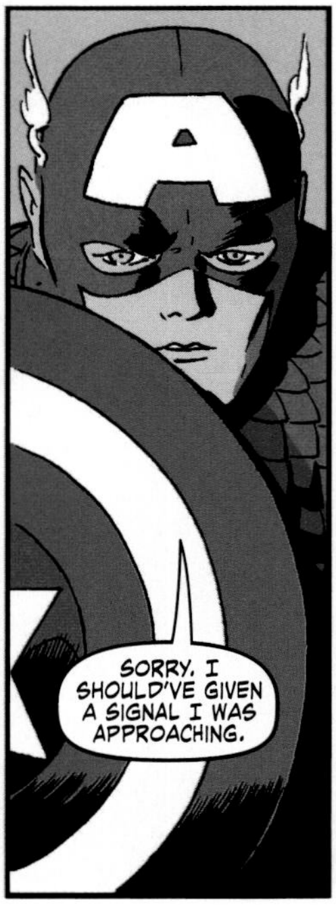
SORRY. I SHOULD'VE GIVEN A SIGNAL I WAS APPROACHING.

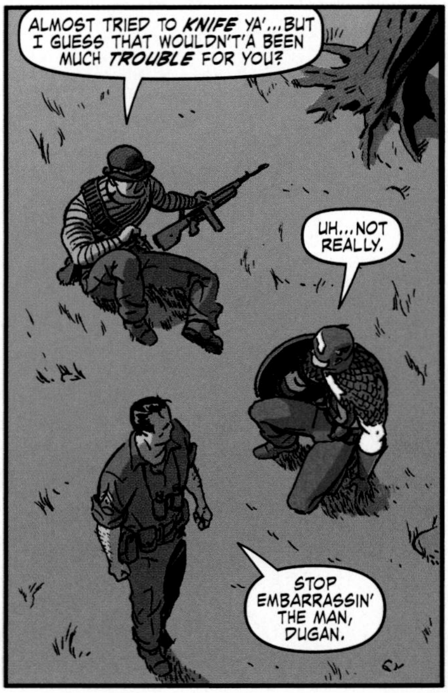
ALMOST TRIED TO KNIFE YA'...BUT I GUESS THAT WOULDN'T'A BEEN MUCH TROUBLE FOR YOU?
UH...NOT REALLY.
STOP EMBARRASSIN' THE MAN, DUGAN.

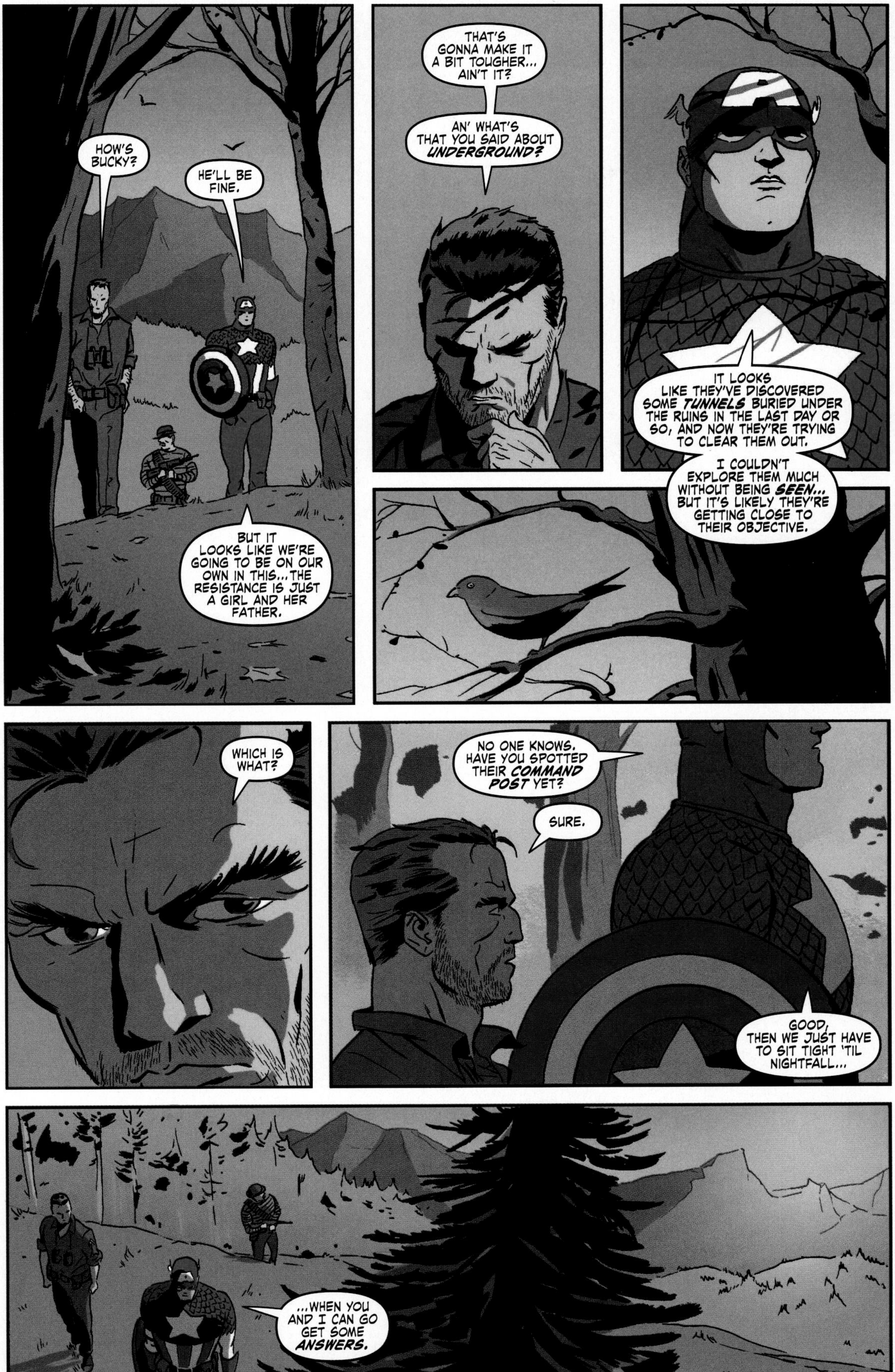
HOW'S BUCKY?
HE'LL BE FINE.
BUT IT LOOKS LIKE WE'RE GOING TO BE ON OUR OWN IN THIS...THE RESISTANCE IS JUST A GIRL AND HER FATHER.
THAT'S GONNA MAKE IT A BIT TOUGHER... AIN'T IT?
AN' WHAT'S THAT YOU SAID ABOUT UNDERGROUND?
IT LOOKS LIKE THEY'VE DISCOVERED SOME TUNNELS BURIED UNDER THE RUINS IN THE LAST DAY OR SO, AND NOW THEY'RE TRYING TO CLEAR THEM OUT.
I COULDN'T EXPLORE THEM MUCH WITHOUT BEING SEEN... BUT IT'S LIKELY THEY'RE GETTING CLOSE TO THEIR OBJECTIVE.
WHICH IS WHAT?
NO ONE KNOWS. HAVE YOU SPOTTED THEIR COMMAND POST YET?
SURE.
GOOD, THEN WE JUST HAVE TO SIT TIGHT 'TIL NIGHTFALL...
...WHEN YOU AND I CAN GO GET SOME ANSWERS.

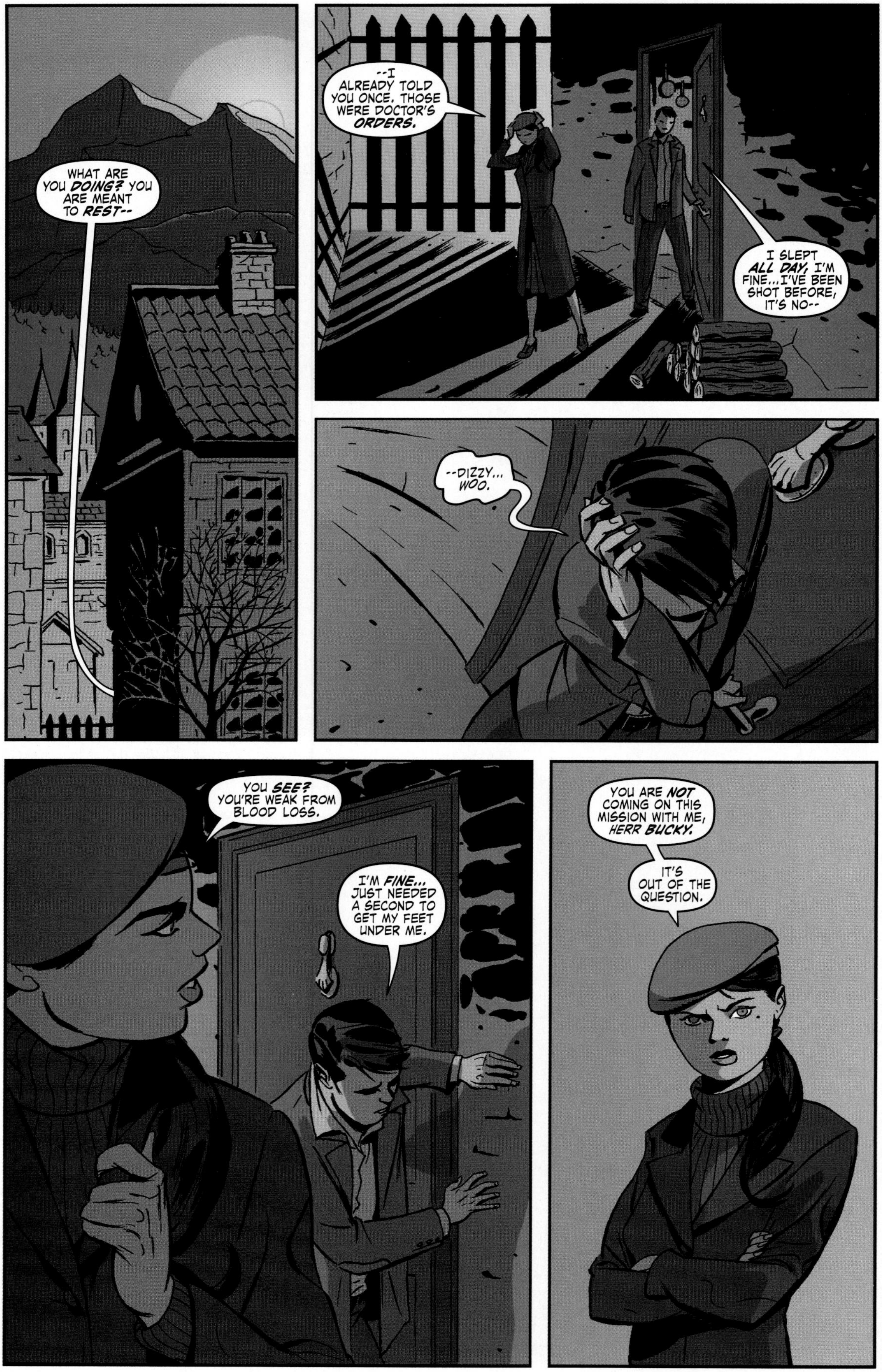
WHAT ARE YOU DOING? YOU ARE MEANT TO REST--
--I ALREADY TOLD YOU ONCE. THOSE WERE DOCTOR'S ORDERS.
I SLEPT ALL DAY, I'M FINE...I'VE BEEN SHOT BEFORE, IT'S NO--
--DIZZY... WOO.
YOU SEE? YOU'RE WEAK FROM BLOOD LOSS.
I'M FINE... JUST NEEDED A SECOND TO GET MY FEET UNDER ME.
YOU ARE NOT COMING ON THIS MISSION WITH ME, HERR BUCKY.
IT'S OUT OF THE QUESTION.

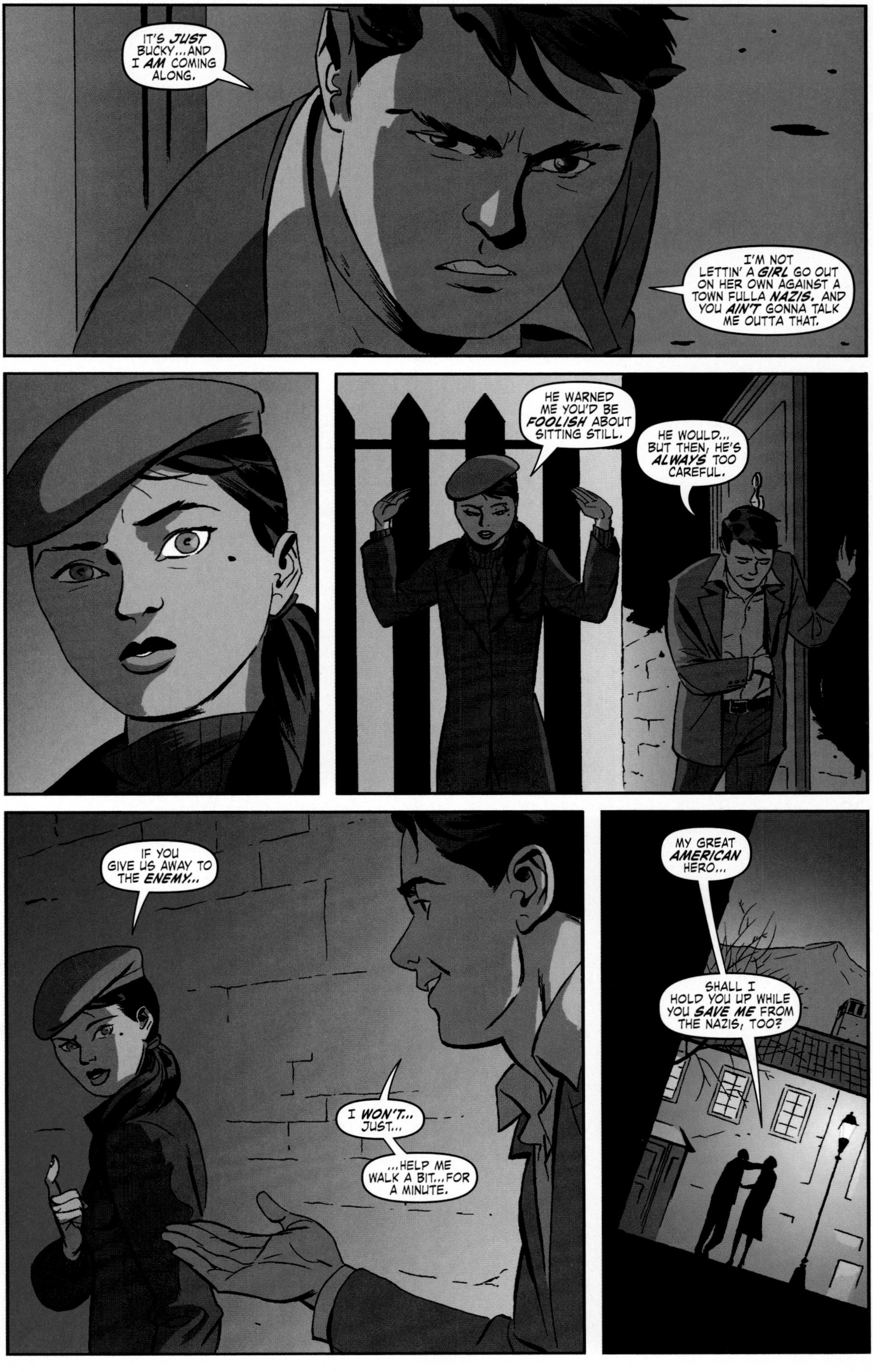
IT'S JUST BUCKY... AND I AM COMING ALONG.
I'M NOT LETTIN' A GIRL GO OUT ON HER OWN AGAINST A TOWN FULLA NAZIS. AND YOU AIN'T GONNA TALK ME OUTTA THAT.
HE WARNED ME YOU'D BE FOOLISH ABOUT SITTING STILL.
HE WOULD... BUT THEN, HE'S ALWAYS TOO CAREFUL.
IF YOU GIVE US AWAY TO THE ENEMY...
I WON'T... JUST...
...HELP ME WALK A BIT... FOR A MINUTE.
MY GREAT AMERICAN HERO...
SHALL I HOLD YOU UP WHILE YOU SAVE ME FROM THE NAZIS, TOO?

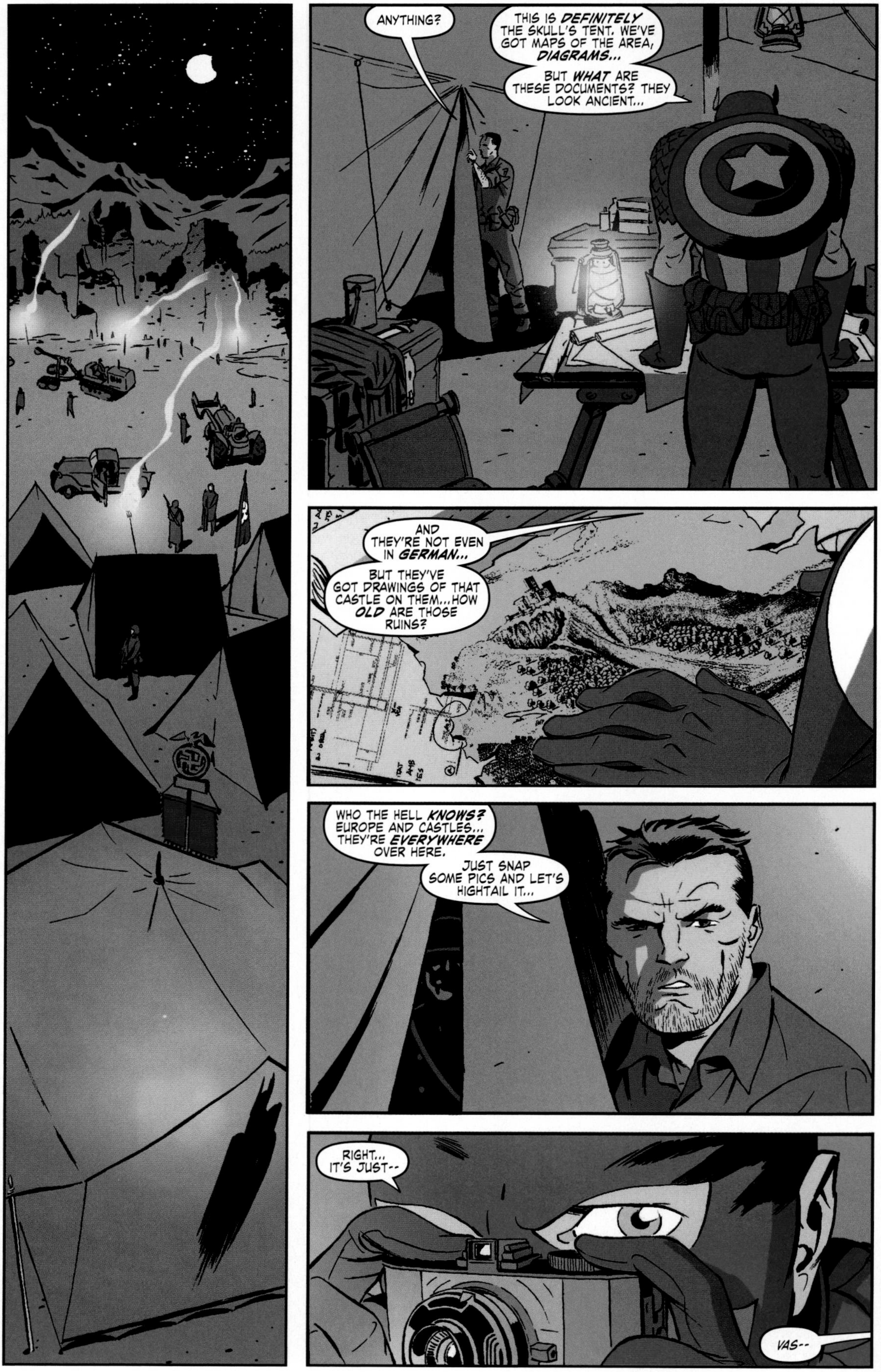
ANYTHING?
THIS IS DEFINITELY THE SKULL'S TENT. WE'VE GOT MAPS OF THE AREA, DIAGRAMS...
BUT WHAT ARE THESE DOCUMENTS? THEY LOOK ANCIENT...
AND THEY'RE NOT EVEN IN GERMAN...
BUT THEY'VE GOT DRAWINGS OF THAT CASTLE ON THEM...HOW OLD ARE THOSE RUINS?
WHO THE HELL KNOWS? EUROPE AND CASTLES... THEY'RE EVERYWHERE OVER HERE.
JUST SNAP SOME PICS AND LET'S HIGHTAIL IT...
RIGHT... IT'S JUST--
VAS--

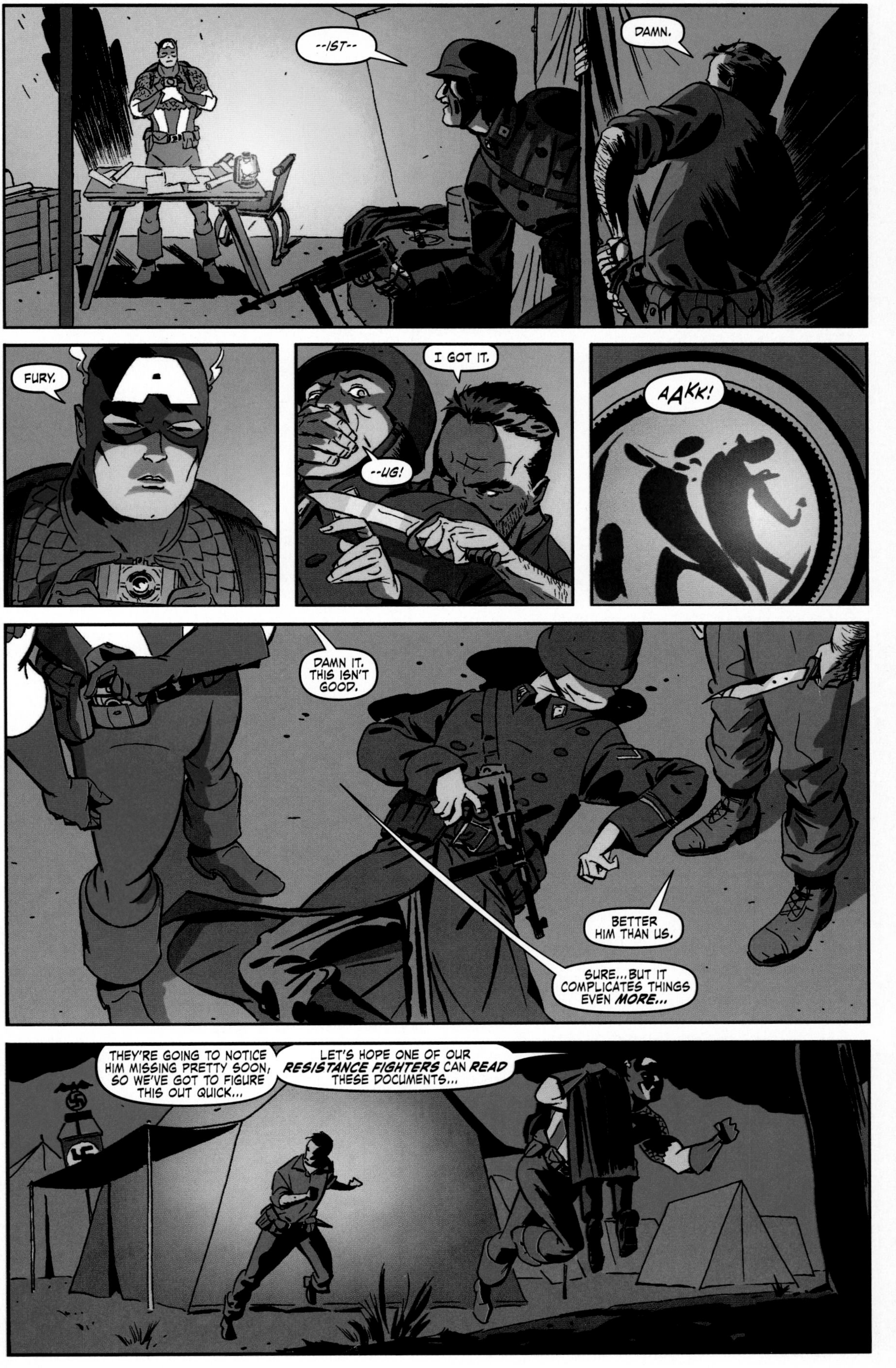
--IST--
DAMN.
FURY.
I GOT IT.
--UG!
AAKK!
DAMN IT. THIS ISN'T GOOD.
BETTER HIM THAN US.
SURE...BUT IT COMPLICATES THINGS EVEN MORE...
THEY'RE GOING TO NOTICE HIM MISSING PRETTY SOON, SO WE'VE GOT TO FIGURE THIS OUT QUICK...
LET'S HOPE ONE OF OUR RESISTANCE FIGHTERS CAN READ THESE DOCUMENTS...

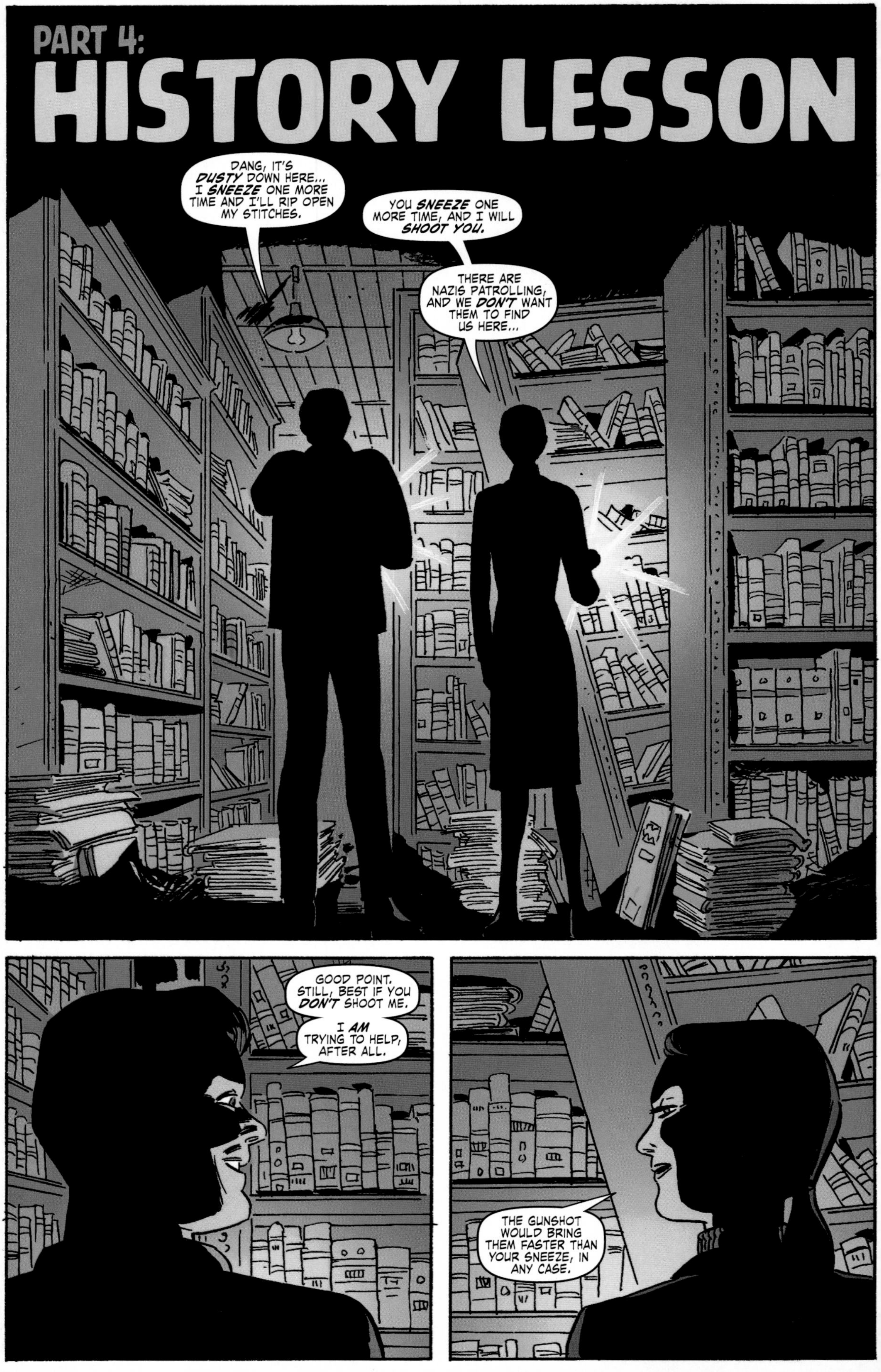
PART 4:
HISTORY LESSON
DANG, IT'S DUSTY DOWN HERE... I SNEEZE ONE MORE TIME AND I'LL RIP OPEN MY STITCHES.
YOU SNEEZE ONE MORE TIME, AND I WILL SHOOT YOU.
THERE ARE NAZIS PATROLLING, AND WE DON'T WANT THEM TO FIND US HERE...
GOOD POINT. STILL, BEST IF YOU DON'T SHOOT ME.
I AM TRYING TO HELP, AFTER ALL.
THE GUNSHOT WOULD BRING THEM FASTER THAN YOUR SNEEZE, IN ANY CASE.

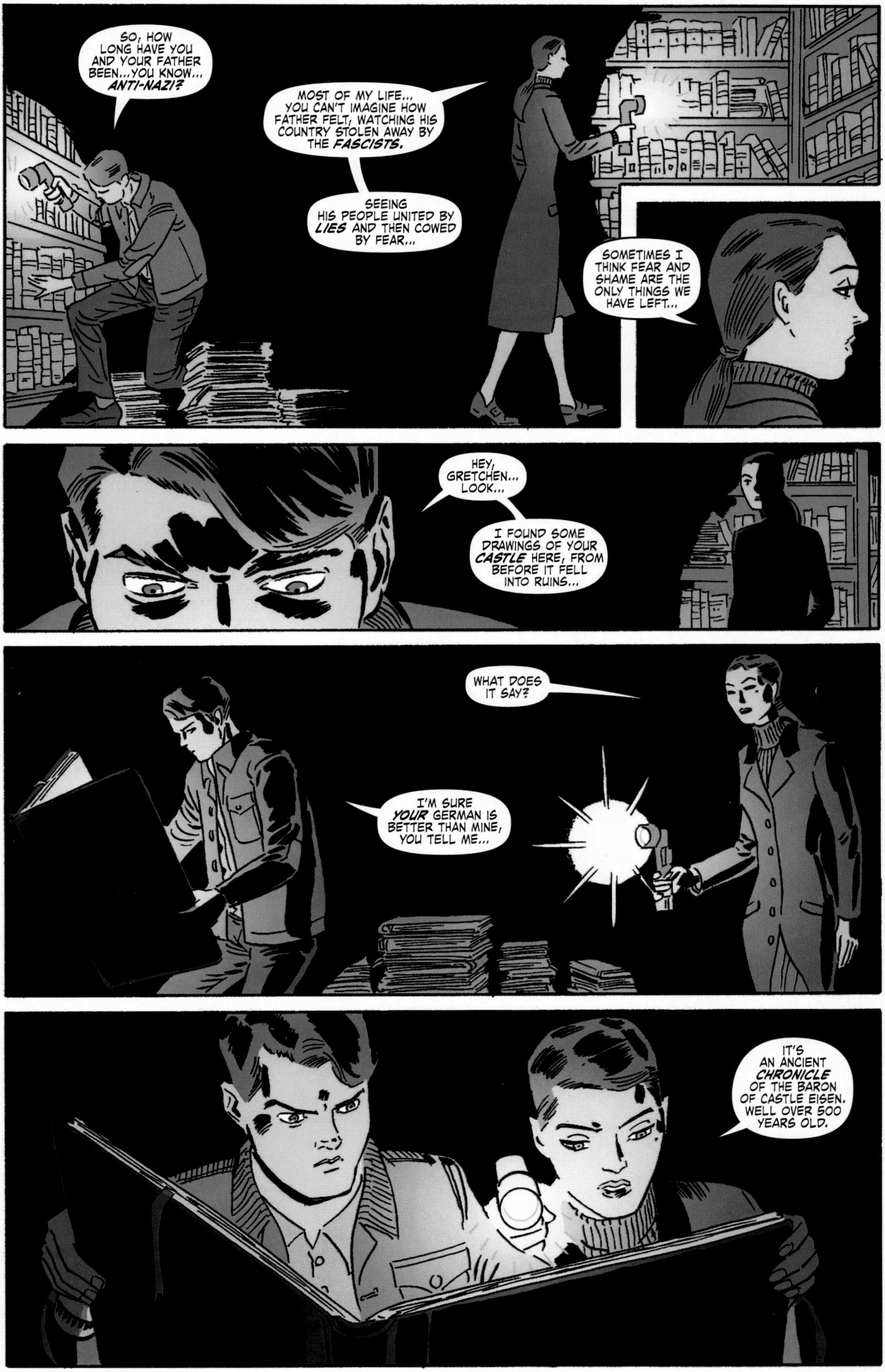
SO, HOW LONG HAVE YOU AND YOUR FATHER BEEN...YOU KNOW... *ANTI-NAZI?*
MOST OF MY LIFE... YOU CAN'T IMAGINE HOW FATHER FELT, WATCHING HIS COUNTRY STOLEN AWAY BY THE *FASCISTS.*
SEEING HIS PEOPLE UNITED BY *LIES* AND THEN COWED BY FEAR...
SOMETIMES I THINK FEAR AND SHAME ARE THE ONLY THINGS WE HAVE LEFT...
HEY, GRETCHEN... LOOK...
I FOUND SOME DRAWINGS OF YOUR *CASTLE* HERE, FROM BEFORE IT FELL INTO RUINS...
WHAT DOES IT SAY?
I'M SURE *YOUR* GERMAN IS BETTER THAN MINE, YOU TELL ME...
IT'S AN ANCIENT *CHRONICLE* OF THE BARON OF CASTLE EISEN. WELL OVER 500 YEARS OLD.

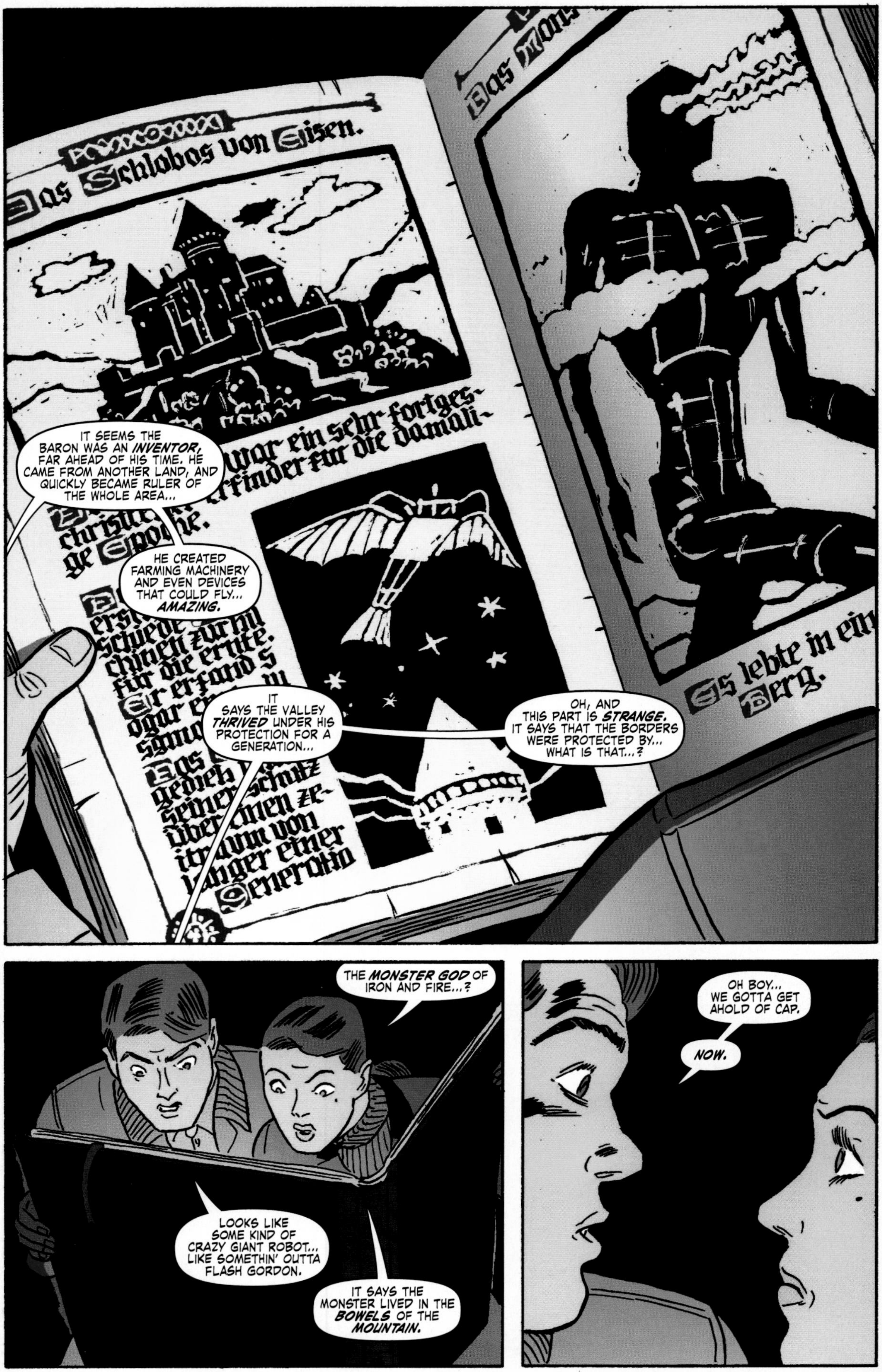
Das Schlobos von Eisen.
IT SEEMS THE BARON WAS AN *INVENTOR,* FAR AHEAD OF HIS TIME. HE CAME FROM ANOTHER LAND, AND QUICKLY BECAME RULER OF THE WHOLE AREA...
HE CREATED FARMING MACHINERY AND EVEN DEVICES THAT COULD FLY... ***AMAZING.***
IT SAYS THE VALLEY ***THRIVED*** UNDER HIS PROTECTION FOR A GENERATION...
OH, AND THIS PART IS ***STRANGE.*** IT SAYS THAT THE BORDERS WERE PROTECTED BY... WHAT IS THAT...?
Es lebte in ein
Berg.
THE ***MONSTER GOD*** OF IRON AND FIRE...?
LOOKS LIKE SOME KIND OF CRAZY GIANT ROBOT... LIKE SOMETHIN' OUTTA FLASH GORDON.
IT SAYS THE MONSTER LIVED IN THE ***BOWELS*** OF THE ***MOUNTAIN.***
OH BOY... WE GOTTA GET AHOLD OF CAP.
NOW.

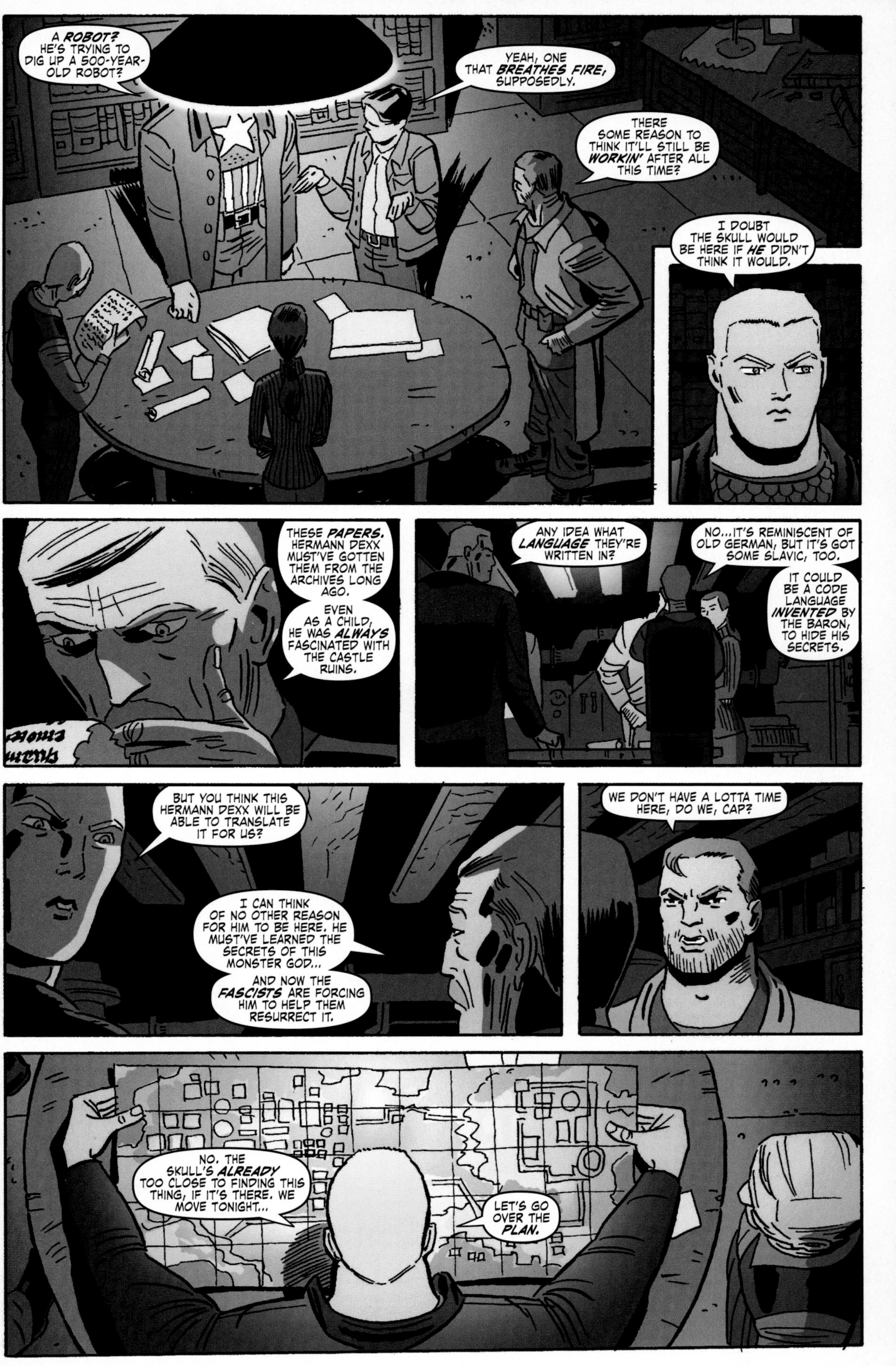
A ROBOT? HE'S TRYING TO DIG UP A 500-YEAR-OLD ROBOT?
YEAH, ONE THAT BREATHES FIRE, SUPPOSEDLY.
THERE SOME REASON TO THINK IT'LL STILL BE WORKIN' AFTER ALL THIS TIME?
I DOUBT THE SKULL WOULD BE HERE IF HE DIDN'T THINK IT WOULD.
THESE PAPERS. HERMANN DEXX MUST'VE GOTTEN THEM FROM THE ARCHIVES LONG AGO.
EVEN AS A CHILD, HE WAS ALWAYS FASCINATED WITH THE CASTLE RUINS.
ANY IDEA WHAT LANGUAGE THEY'RE WRITTEN IN?
NO...IT'S REMINISCENT OF OLD GERMAN, BUT IT'S GOT SOME SLAVIC, TOO.
IT COULD BE A CODE LANGUAGE INVENTED BY THE BARON, TO HIDE HIS SECRETS.
BUT YOU THINK THIS HERMANN DEXX WILL BE ABLE TO TRANSLATE IT FOR US?
I CAN THINK OF NO OTHER REASON FOR HIM TO BE HERE. HE MUST'VE LEARNED THE SECRETS OF THIS MONSTER GOD...
AND NOW THE FASCISTS ARE FORCING HIM TO HELP THEM RESURRECT IT.
WE DON'T HAVE A LOTTA TIME HERE, DO WE, CAP?
NO. THE SKULL'S ALREADY TOO CLOSE TO FINDING THIS THING, IF IT'S THERE. WE MOVE TONIGHT...
LET'S GO OVER THE PLAN.

BECAUSE WE WERE SO BADLY OUTNUMBERED, THE PLAN WAS SIMPLE.

WAIT UNTIL THE MIDDLE OF THE NIGHT, A HALF HOUR BEFORE THE CHANGING OF THE GUARD...

...WHEN THE ENEMY WOULD BE AT ITS LOWEST EBB. AND THEN--

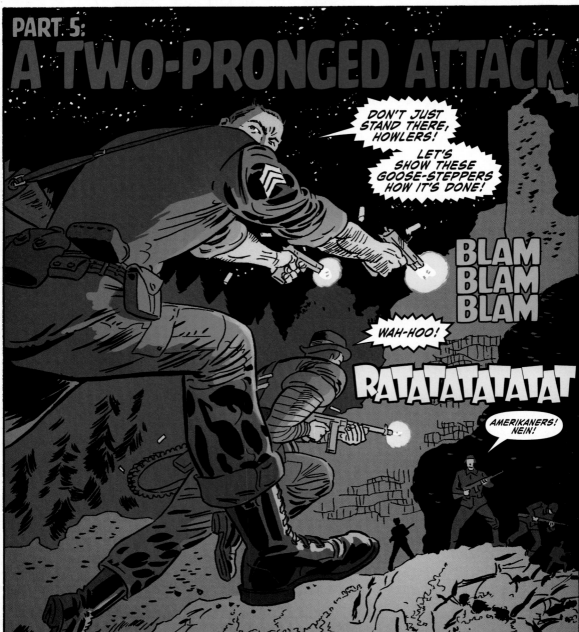

PART 5:
A TWO-PRONGED ATTACK

DON'T JUST STAND THERE, HOWLERS!

LET'S SHOW THESE GOOSE-STEPPERS HOW IT'S DONE!

BLAM
BLAM
BLAM

WAH-HOO!

RATATATATATAT

AMERIKANERS! NEIN!

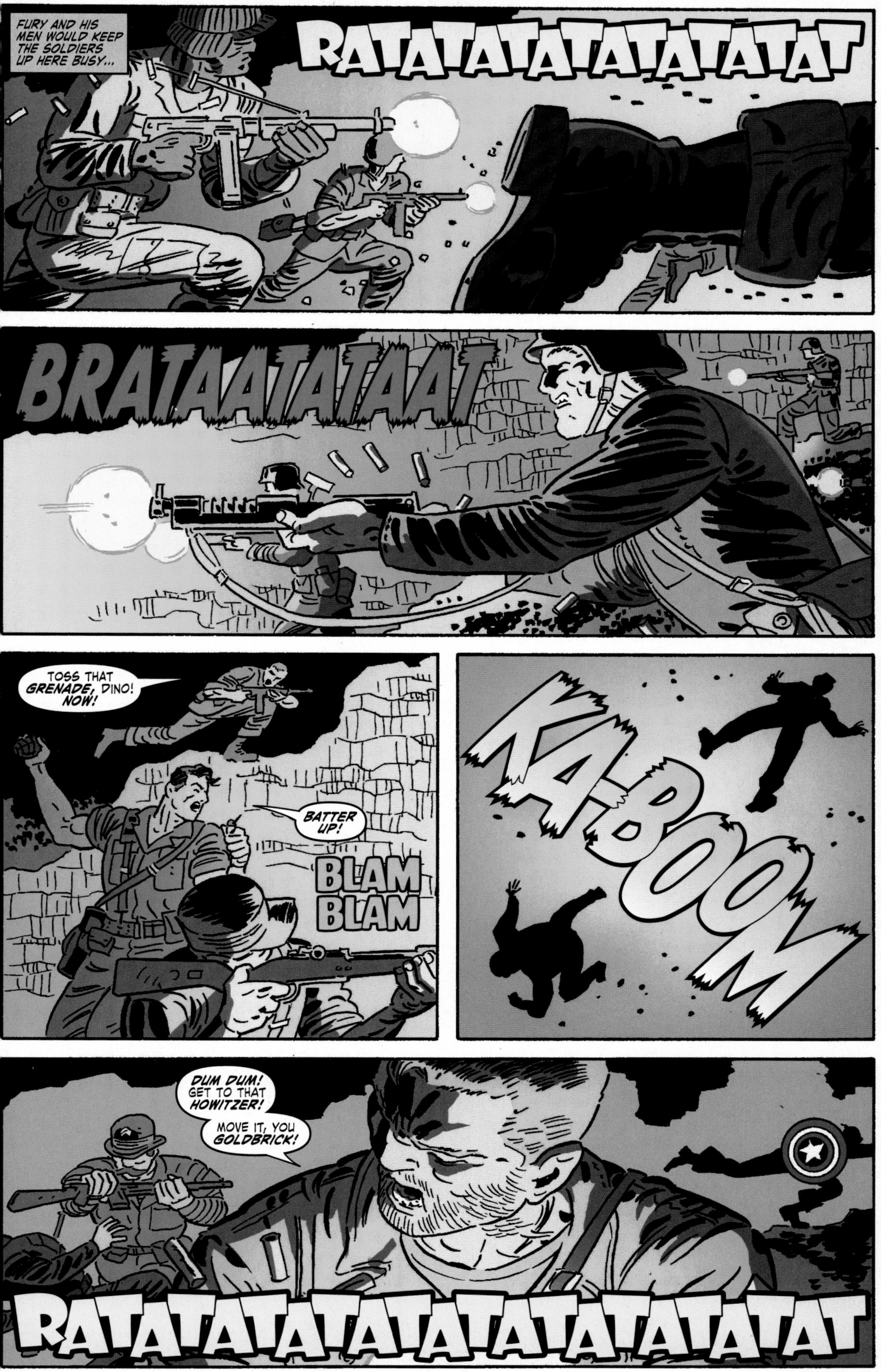
FURY AND HIS MEN WOULD KEEP THE SOLDIERS UP HERE BUSY...
RATATATATATATATATAT
BRATAATATATAAT
TOSS THAT GRENADE, DINO! NOW!
BATTER UP!
BLAM BLAM
KA-BOOM
DUM DUM! GET TO THAT HOWITZER!
MOVE IT, YOU GOLDBRICK!
RATATATATATATATATATATATATAT

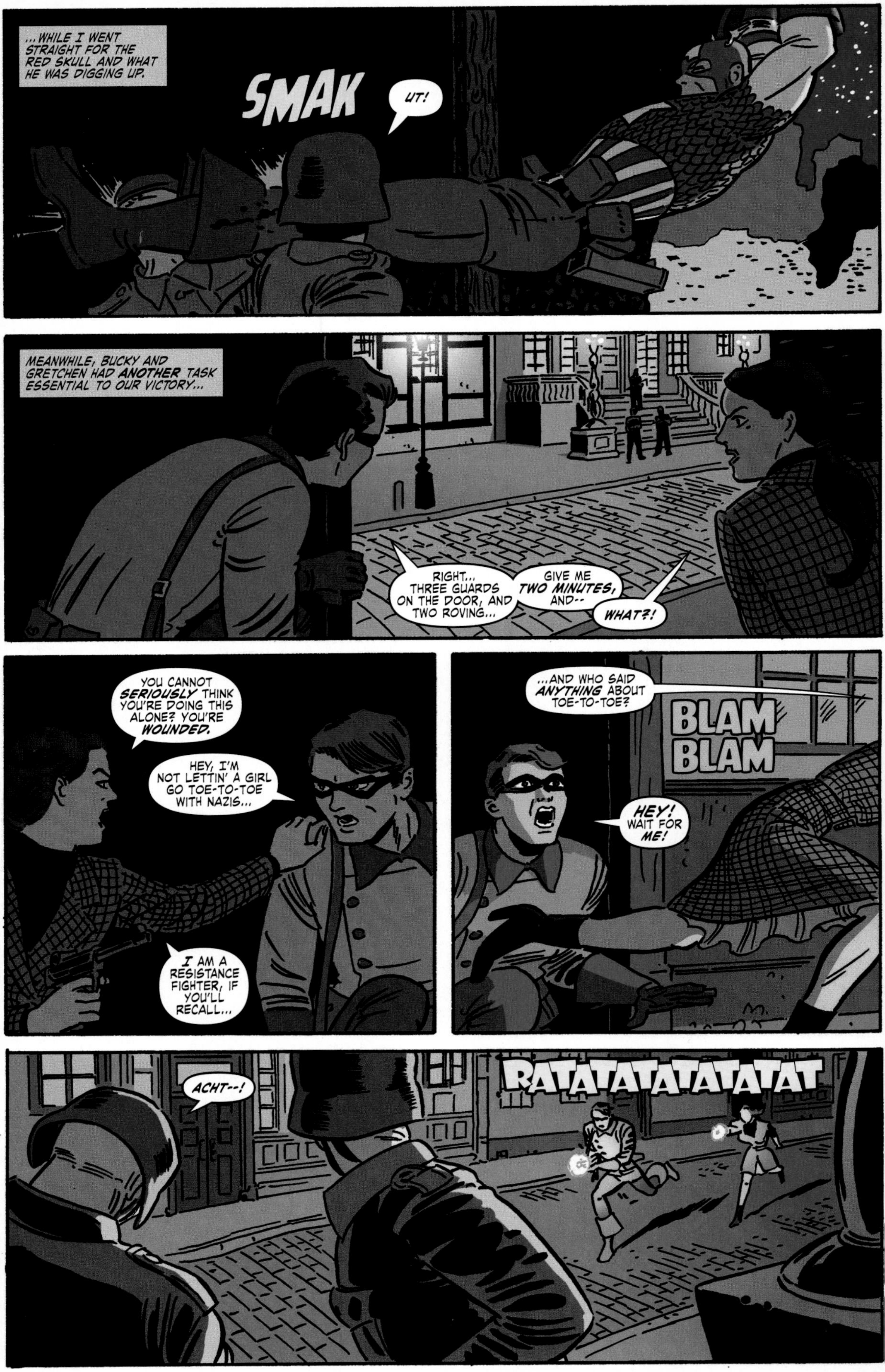
...WHILE I WENT STRAIGHT FOR THE RED SKULL AND WHAT HE WAS DIGGING UP.
SMAK
UT!
MEANWHILE, BUCKY AND GRETCHEN HAD ANOTHER TASK ESSENTIAL TO OUR VICTORY...
RIGHT... THREE GUARDS ON THE DOOR, AND TWO ROVING...
GIVE ME TWO MINUTES, AND--
WHAT?!
YOU CANNOT SERIOUSLY THINK YOU'RE DOING THIS ALONE? YOU'RE WOUNDED.
HEY, I'M NOT LETTIN' A GIRL GO TOE-TO-TOE WITH NAZIS...
I AM A RESISTANCE FIGHTER, IF YOU'LL RECALL...
...AND WHO SAID ANYTHING ABOUT TOE-TO-TOE?
BLAM BLAM
HEY! WAIT FOR ME!
ACHT--!
RATATATATATATATAT

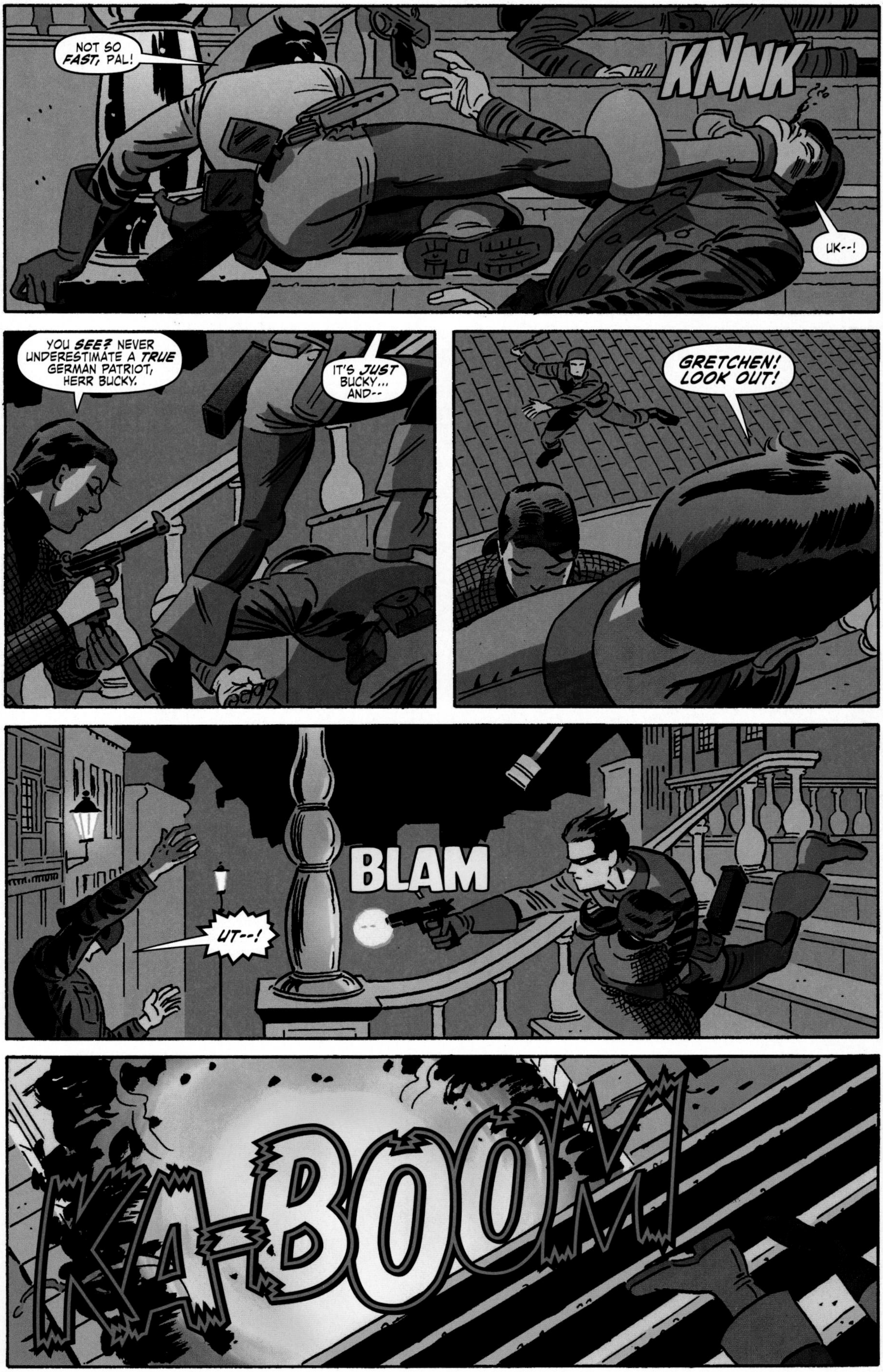
NOT SO FAST, PAL!
KNNK
UK--!
YOU SEE? NEVER UNDERESTIMATE A TRUE GERMAN PATRIOT, HERR BUCKY.
IT'S JUST BUCKY... AND--
GRETCHEN! LOOK OUT!
BLAM
UT--!
KA-BOOM

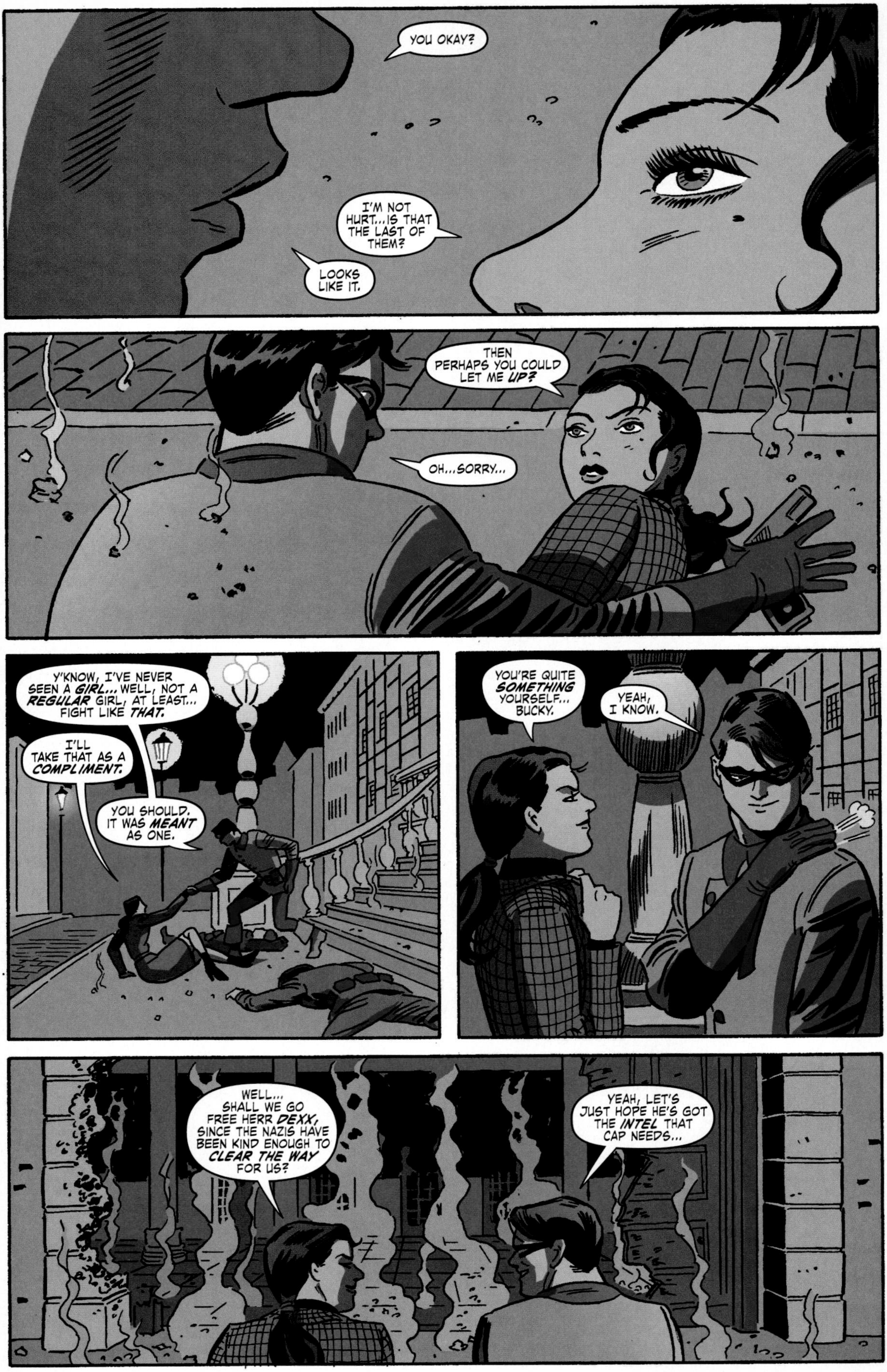
YOU OKAY?
I'M NOT HURT... IS THAT THE LAST OF THEM?
LOOKS LIKE IT.
THEN PERHAPS YOU COULD LET ME UP?
OH... SORRY...
Y'KNOW, I'VE NEVER SEEN A GIRL... WELL, NOT A REGULAR GIRL, AT LEAST... FIGHT LIKE THAT.
I'LL TAKE THAT AS A COMPLIMENT.
YOU SHOULD. IT WAS MEANT AS ONE.
YOU'RE QUITE SOMETHING YOURSELF... BUCKY.
YEAH, I KNOW.
WELL... SHALL WE GO FREE HERR DEXX, SINCE THE NAZIS HAVE BEEN KIND ENOUGH TO CLEAR THE WAY FOR US?
YEAH, LET'S JUST HOPE HE'S GOT THE INTEL THAT CAP NEEDS...

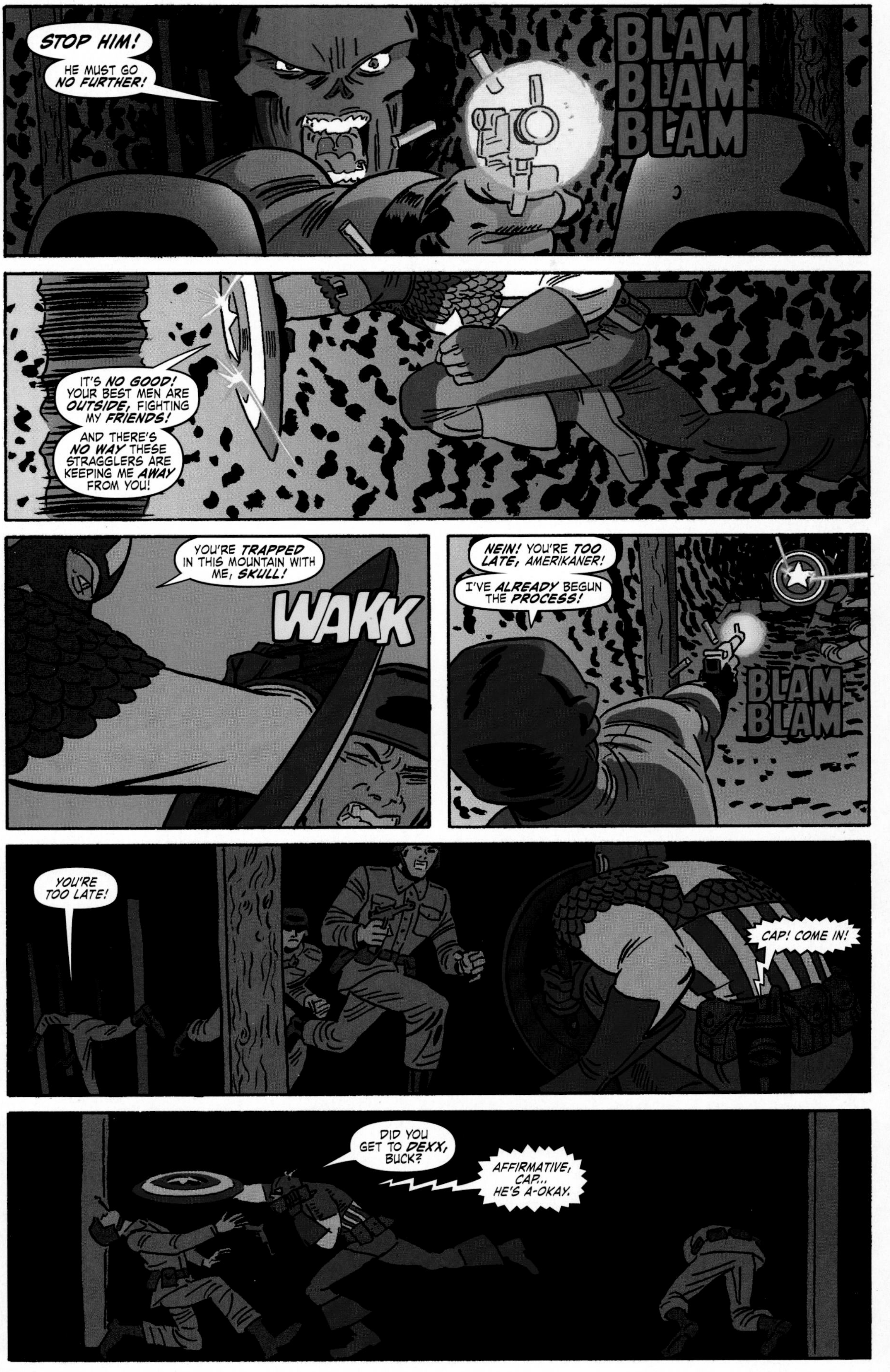
STOP HIM!
HE MUST GO NO FURTHER!
BLAM BLAM BLAM
IT'S NO GOOD! YOUR BEST MEN ARE OUTSIDE, FIGHTING MY FRIENDS!
AND THERE'S NO WAY THESE STRAGGLERS ARE KEEPING ME AWAY FROM YOU!
YOU'RE TRAPPED IN THIS MOUNTAIN WITH ME, SKULL!
WAKK
NEIN! YOU'RE TOO LATE, AMERIKANER!
I'VE ALREADY BEGUN THE PROCESS!
BLAM BLAM
YOU'RE TOO LATE!
CAP! COME IN!
DID YOU GET TO DEXX, BUCK?
AFFIRMATIVE, CAP... HE'S A-OKAY.

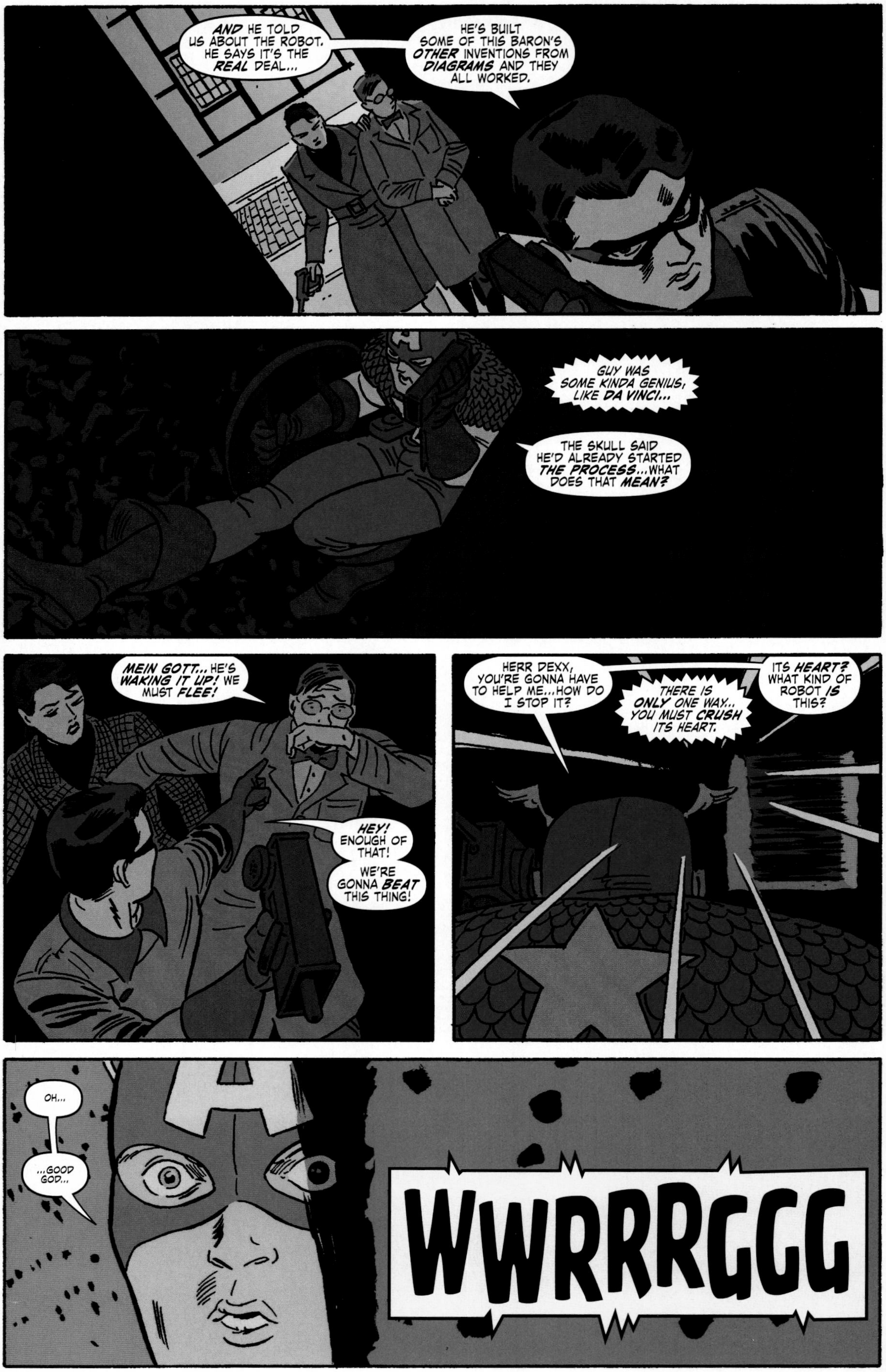
AND HE TOLD US ABOUT THE ROBOT. HE SAYS IT'S THE REAL DEAL...
HE'S BUILT SOME OF THIS BARON'S OTHER INVENTIONS FROM DIAGRAMS AND THEY ALL WORKED.
GUY WAS SOME KINDA GENIUS, LIKE DA VINCI...
THE SKULL SAID HE'D ALREADY STARTED THE PROCESS...WHAT DOES THAT MEAN?
MEIN GOTT... HE'S WAKING IT UP! WE MUST FLEE!
HEY! ENOUGH OF THAT!
WE'RE GONNA BEAT THIS THING!
HERR DEXX, YOU'RE GONNA HAVE TO HELP ME...HOW DO I STOP IT?
THERE IS ONLY ONE WAY... YOU MUST CRUSH ITS HEART.
ITS HEART? WHAT KIND OF ROBOT IS THIS?
OH...
...GOOD GOD...
WWRRRGGG

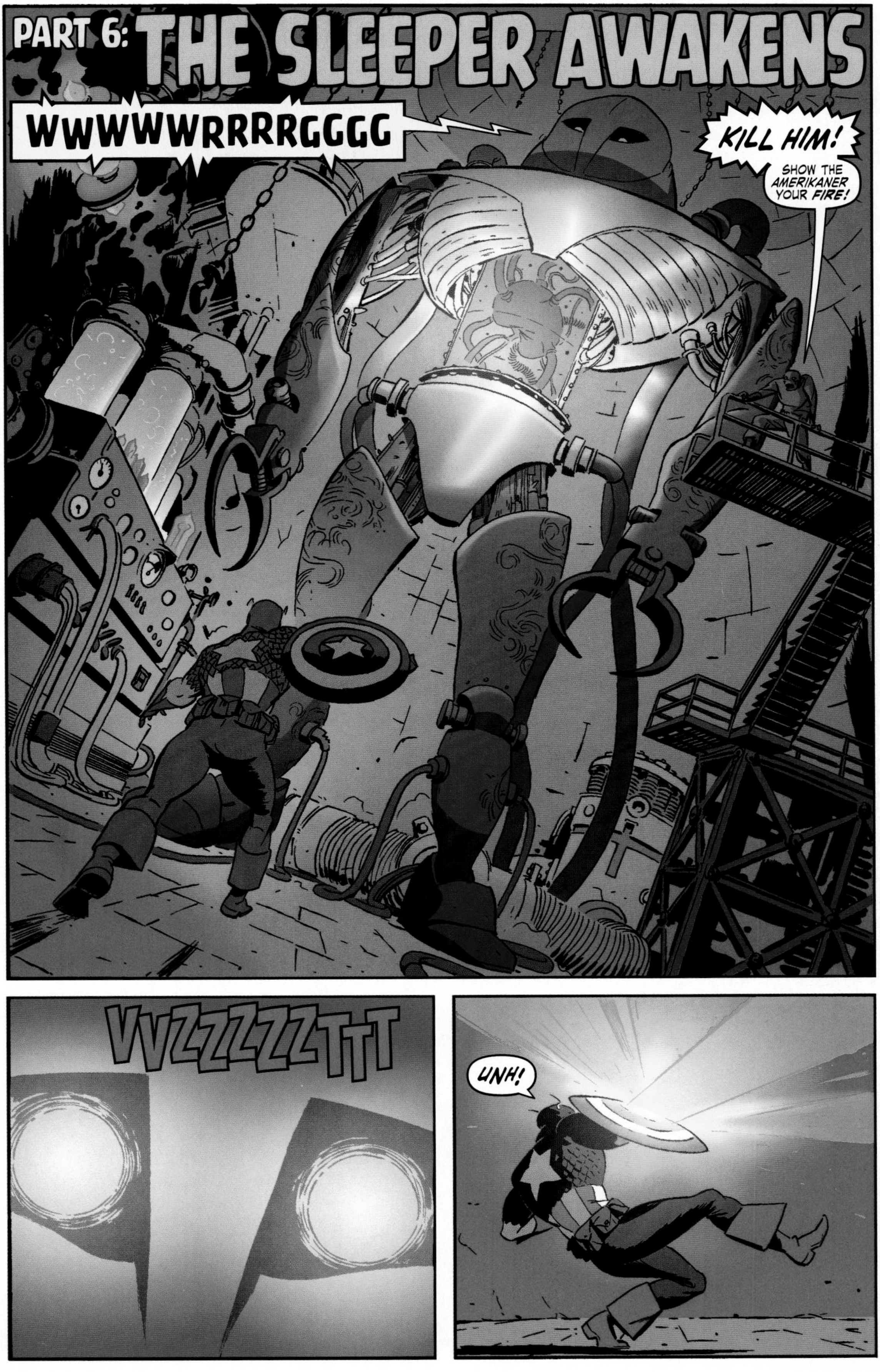
PART 6: THE SLEEPER AWAKENS
WWWWWWRRRRGGGG
KILL HIM!
SHOW THE AMERIKANER YOUR FIRE!
VVZZZZZTTT
UNH!

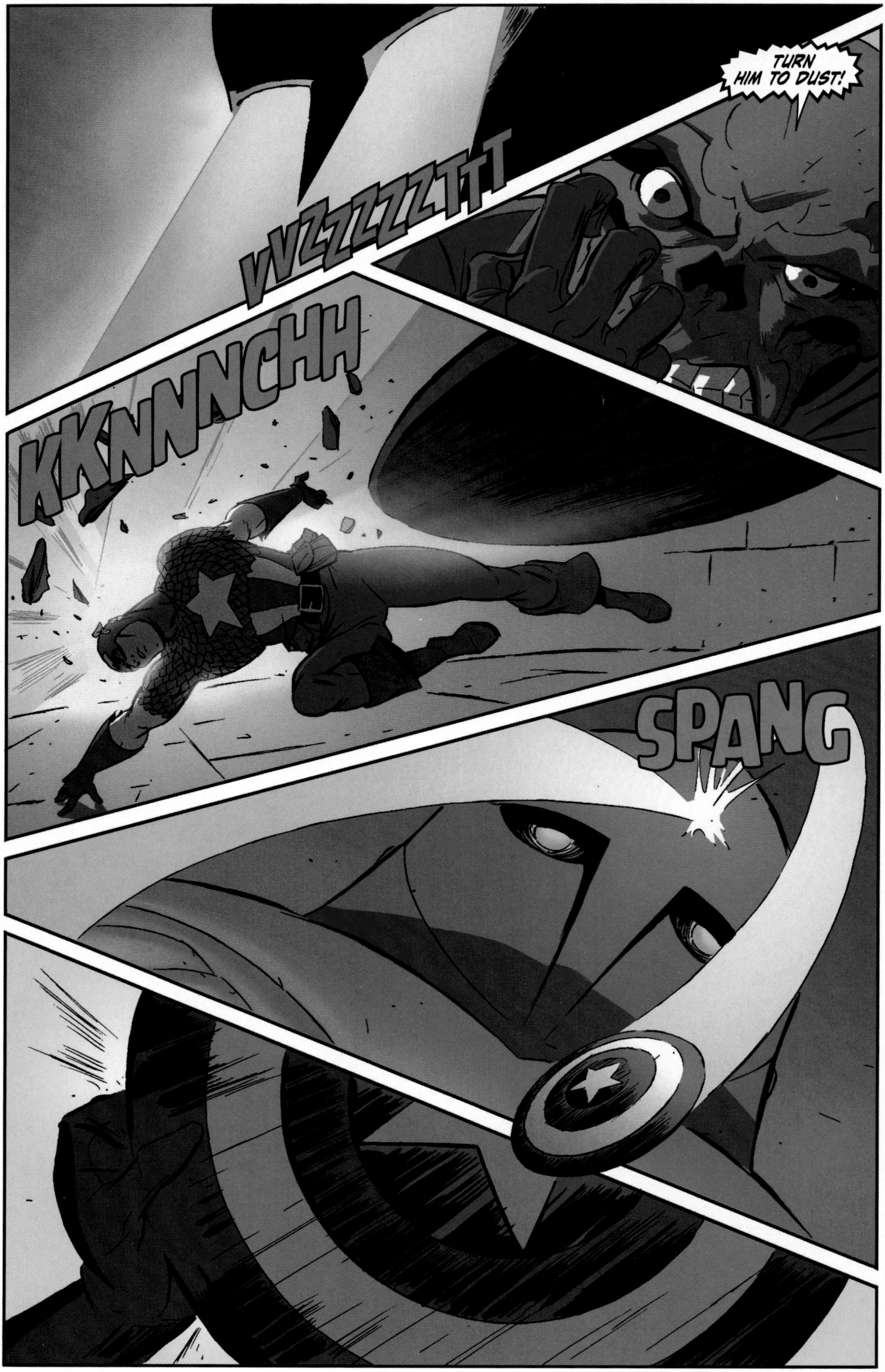
TURN HIM TO DUST!
VVZZZZZTTT
KKNNNNCHH
SPANG

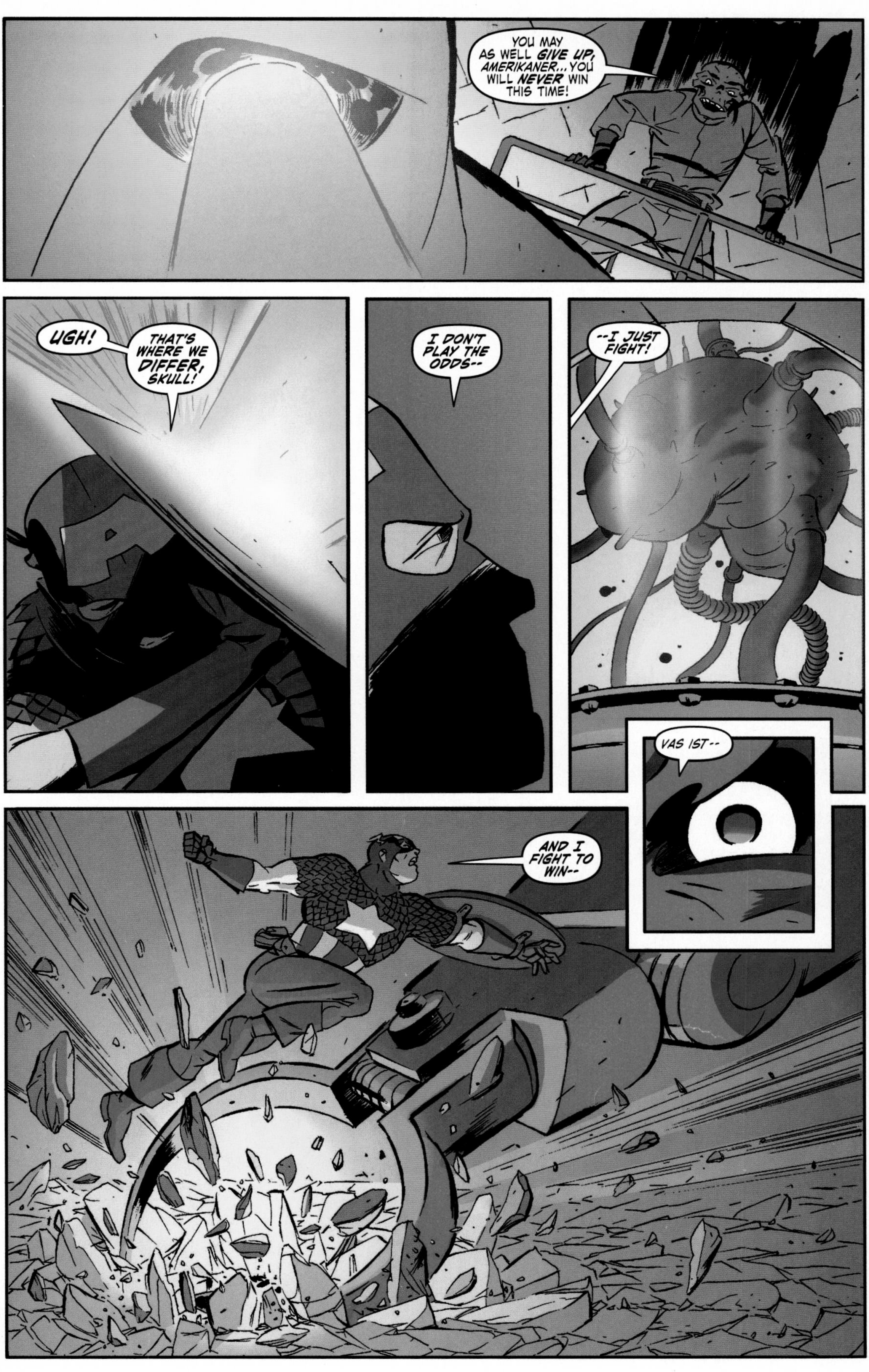
YOU MAY AS WELL GIVE UP, AMERIKANER... YOU WILL NEVER WIN THIS TIME!
UGH!
THAT'S WHERE WE DIFFER, SKULL!
I DON'T PLAY THE ODDS--
--I JUST FIGHT!
VAS IST--
AND I FIGHT TO WIN--

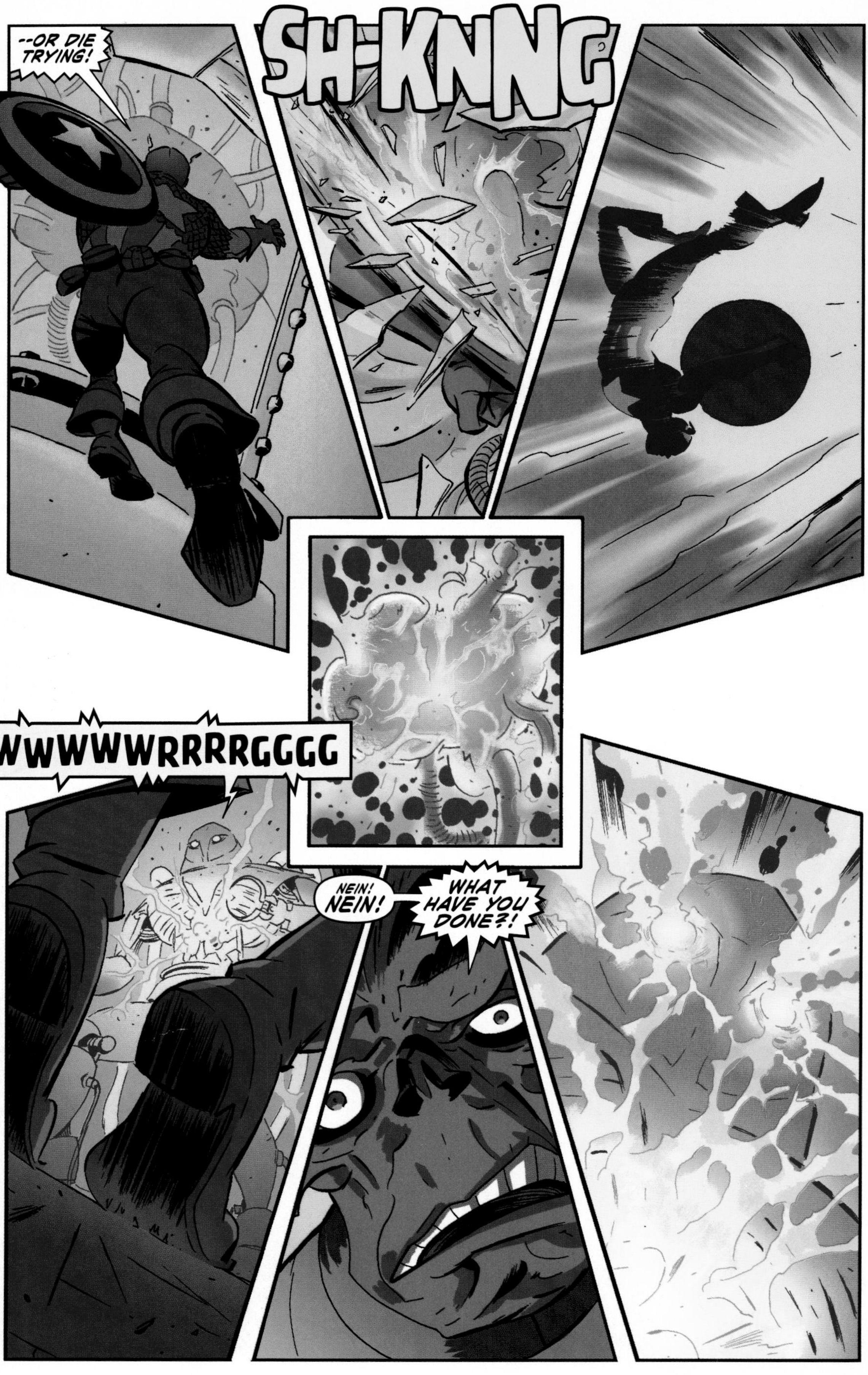
--OR DIE TRYING!
SH-KNNG
WWWWWRRRRGGGG
NEIN! NEIN!
WHAT HAVE YOU DONE?!

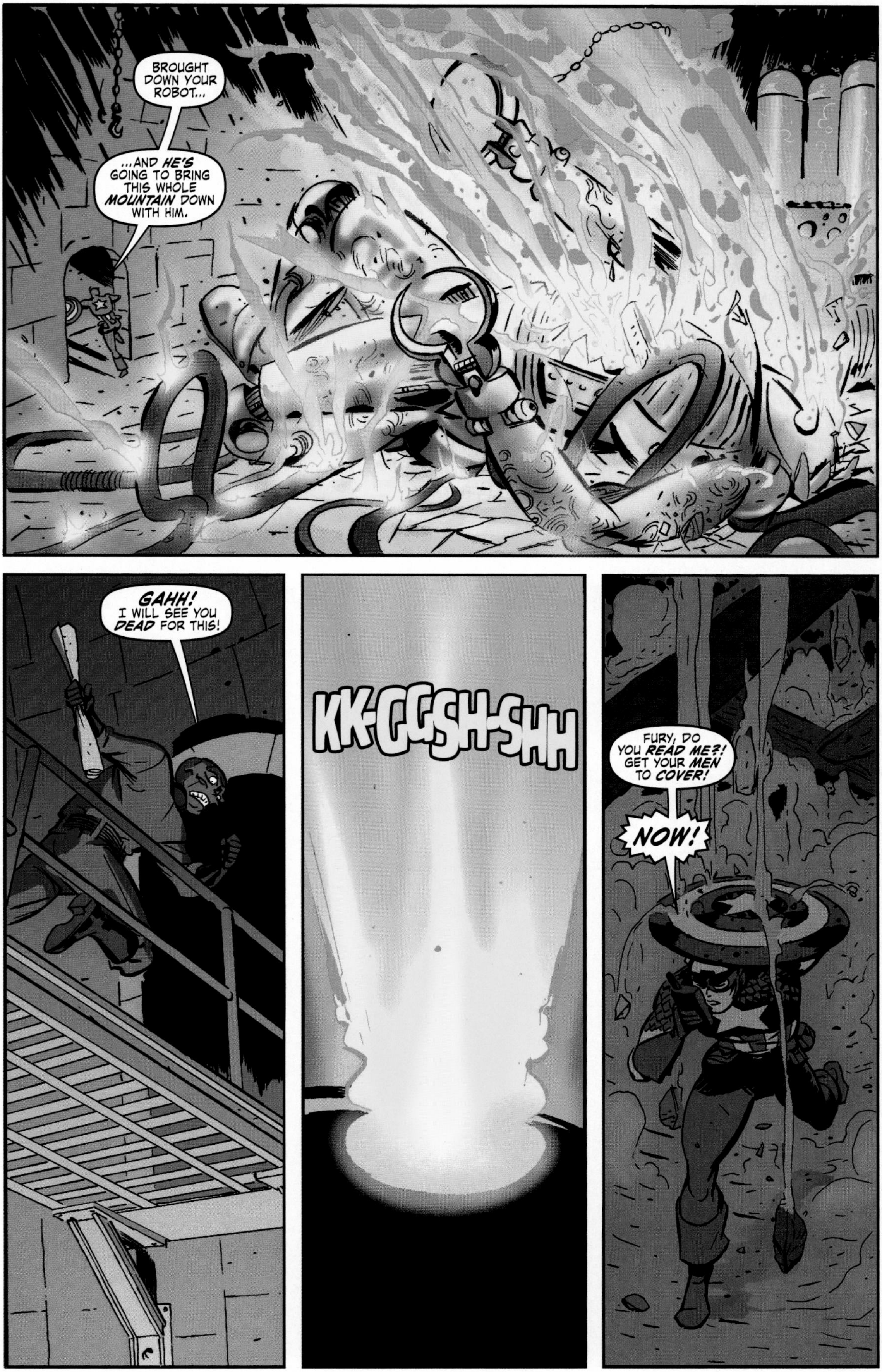
BROUGHT DOWN YOUR ROBOT...
...AND HE'S GOING TO BRING THIS WHOLE MOUNTAIN DOWN WITH HIM.
GAHH! I WILL SEE YOU DEAD FOR THIS!
KK-GGSH-SHH
FURY, DO YOU READ ME?! GET YOUR MEN TO COVER!
NOW!

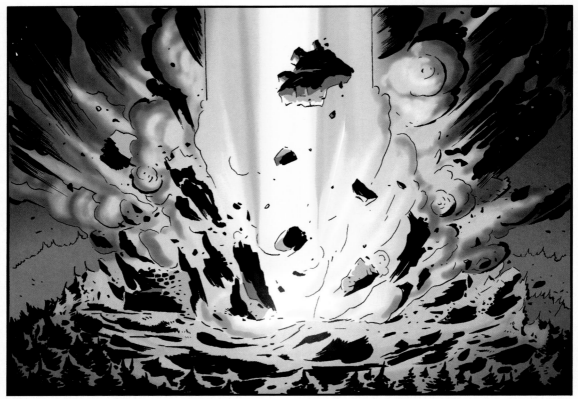

=HKK-HHKK!=
=HKK-HK-HK!=

WONDERED WHEN YOU'D DIG YOURSELF OUT...

SO, I'M GUESSIN' *THIS* IS WHAT *SUCCESS* LOOKS LIKE?

YEAH... SOMETIMES IT *IS*, SERGEANT.

ANY CHANCE THE RED SKULL'S *BURIED* UNDER ALL THAT ROCK AND MORTAR?

MAYBE... I DON'T KNOW.

HE *GRABBED* SOMETHING AND RAN WHEN IT STARTED COMING DOWN.

HOW ABOUT YOUR *MEN*?

THE *HOWLERS*?

AHH, STILL THE *SAME* BUNCHA' USELESS *GOLDBRICKS*...

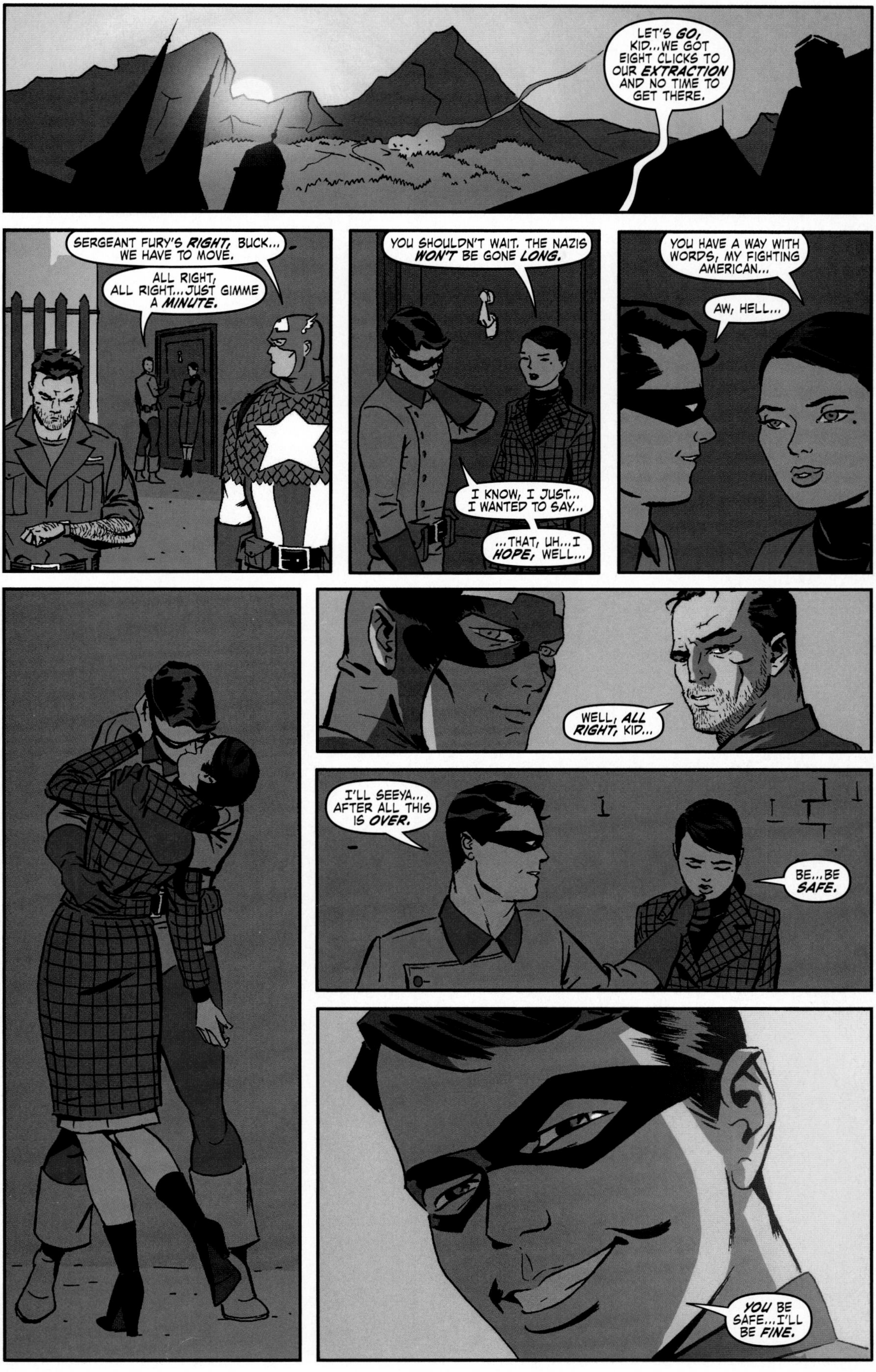
LET'S GO, KID...WE GOT EIGHT CLICKS TO OUR EXTRACTION AND NO TIME TO GET THERE.
SERGEANT FURY'S RIGHT, BUCK... WE HAVE TO MOVE.
ALL RIGHT, ALL RIGHT...JUST GIMME A MINUTE.
YOU SHOULDN'T WAIT. THE NAZIS WON'T BE GONE LONG.
I KNOW, I JUST... I WANTED TO SAY...
...THAT, UH...I HOPE, WELL...
YOU HAVE A WAY WITH WORDS, MY FIGHTING AMERICAN...
AW, HELL...
WELL, ALL RIGHT, KID...
I'LL SEEYA... AFTER ALL THIS IS OVER.
BE...BE SAFE.
YOU BE SAFE...I'LL BE FINE.

EPILOGUE

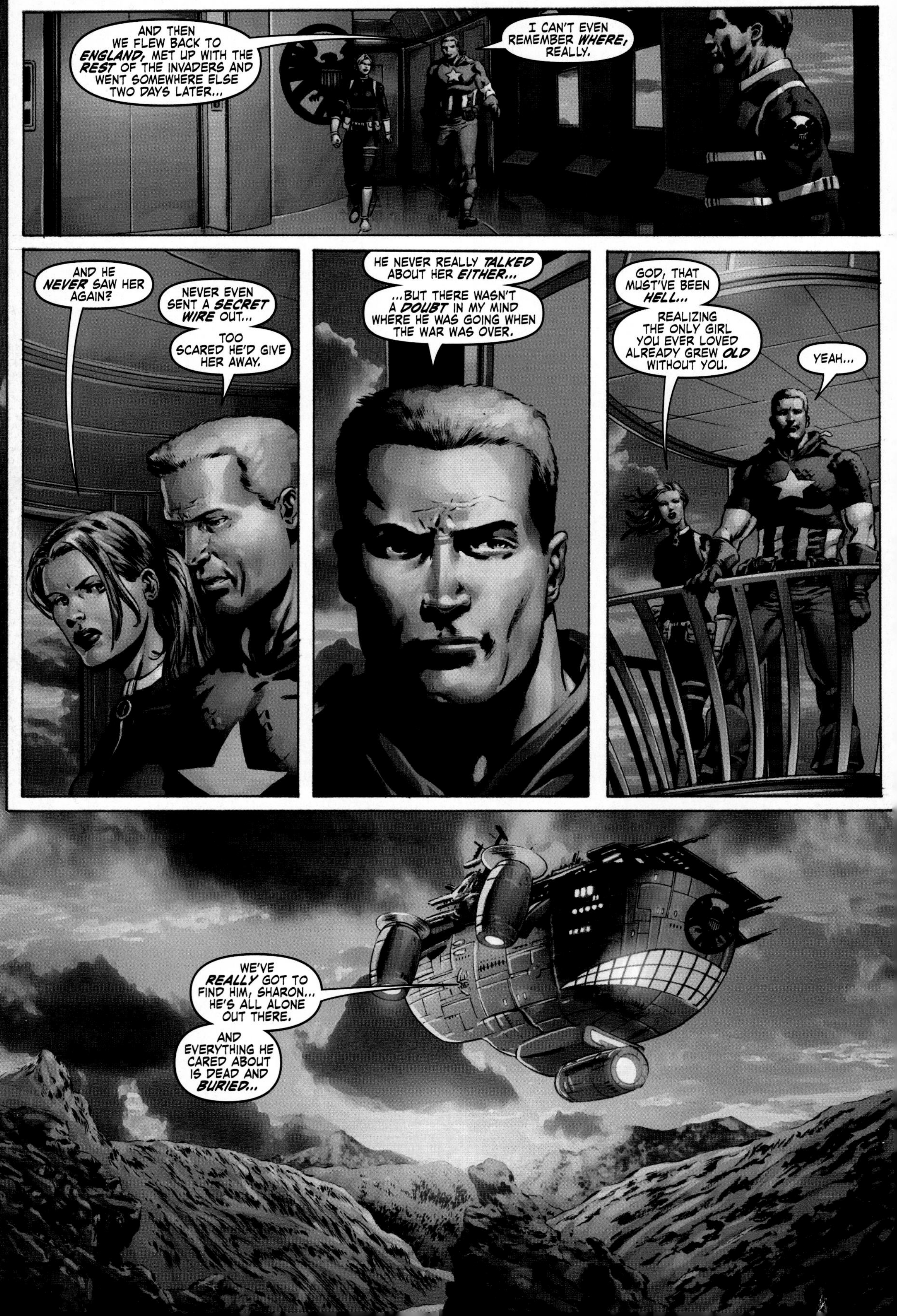
AND THEN WE FLEW BACK TO ENGLAND, MET UP WITH THE REST OF THE INVADERS AND WENT SOMEWHERE ELSE TWO DAYS LATER...
I CAN'T EVEN REMEMBER WHERE, REALLY.
AND HE NEVER SAW HER AGAIN?
NEVER EVEN SENT A SECRET WIRE OUT...
TOO SCARED HE'D GIVE HER AWAY.
HE NEVER REALLY TALKED ABOUT HER EITHER...
...BUT THERE WASN'T A DOUBT IN MY MIND WHERE HE WAS GOING WHEN THE WAR WAS OVER.
GOD, THAT MUST'VE BEEN HELL...
REALIZING THE ONLY GIRL YOU EVER LOVED ALREADY GREW OLD WITHOUT YOU.
YEAH...
WE'VE REALLY GOT TO FIND HIM, SHARON... HE'S ALL ALONE OUT THERE.
AND EVERYTHING HE CARED ABOUT IS DEAD AND BURIED...

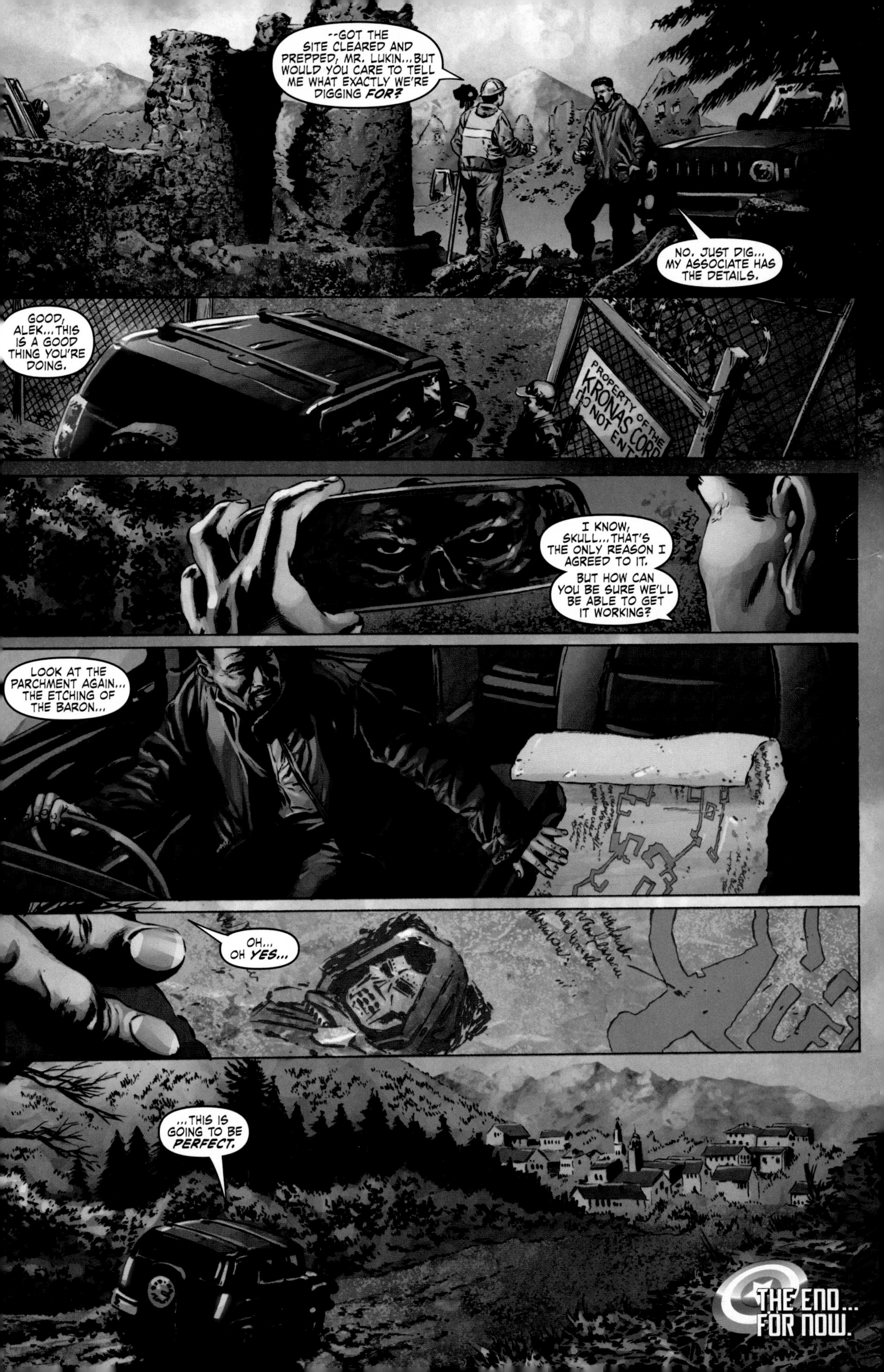
--GOT THE SITE CLEARED AND PREPPED, MR. LUKIN...BUT WOULD YOU CARE TO TELL ME WHAT EXACTLY WE'RE DIGGING FOR?
NO. JUST DIG... MY ASSOCIATE HAS THE DETAILS.
GOOD, ALEK...THIS IS A GOOD THING YOU'RE DOING.
PROPERTY OF THE KRONAS CORP
I KNOW, SKULL...THAT'S THE ONLY REASON I AGREED TO IT.
BUT HOW CAN YOU BE SURE WE'LL BE ABLE TO GET IT WORKING?
LOOK AT THE PARCHMENT AGAIN... THE ETCHING OF THE BARON...
OH... OH YES...
...THIS IS GOING TO BE PERFECT.
THE END... FOR NOW.

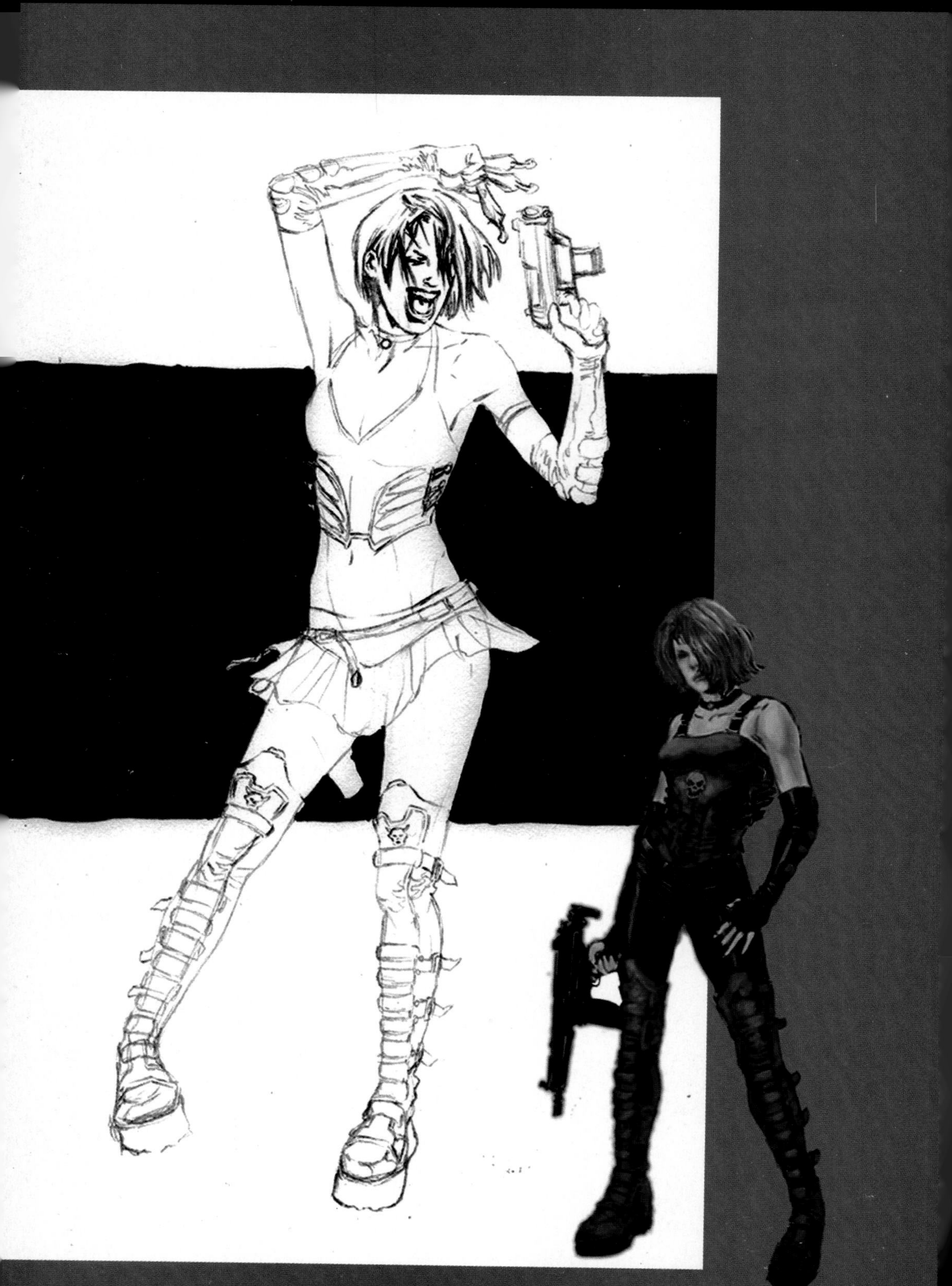